*For my father, Bill Huggens, whose faith
and pride in my work was constant.
Safely home, Dad.*
Kim

*For the one person I strive every day to be more
like, my biggest fan, my most respected and
valued counsel, my greatest mentor and
my most cherished friend: my Mother, Dee Bryan,
who reminds me daily that when walking in the
light all things are possible.
Thank you Mum!*
Erik

TAROT APOKALYPSIS

Texts by Kim Huggens

Based on Tarot Apokalypsis by Erik C. Dunne
Artwork by Erik C. Dunne
Foreword by Donnaleigh de LaRose
Graphic layout by Erik C. Dunne, Lo Scarabeo

© Lo Scarabeo 2016

Lo Scarabeo
Via Cigna 110, 1055 - Torino, Italy
E-mail: info@loscarabeo.com
Internet: http://www.loscarabeo.com
Facebook: LoScarabeoTarot

Printed by Allied Fortune Printing

First Edition: April 2016

All rights reserved.
No part of this book and of this deck may be used or reproduced in any manner whatsoever, including Internet usage, without written permission from Lo Scarabeo s.r.l., except in case of brief quotations embodied in critical articles and reviews.

TAROT APOKALYPSIS

ERIK C. DUNNE ✦ KIM HUGGENS

Acknowledgements

Kim: I would like to thank all those that have given me encouragement and support, especially in the final stages of this project.
To David, Steve and Sophie: thank you for listening to my ravings and enduring my crazy-busy times. Most importantly, I give my deepest thanks to Alex, whose unending love, support and faith made all the difference: as always, shields together.

Erik: Special thanks to Mario Pignatiello, Riccardo Minetti, Matt Suter, Bill Trivett, Giane Portal, Dustin Nispel, Leonardo Chioda and Claudia Ferrari.

Table of Contents

Foreword 6

At the Beginning **9**
Introduction 10
Using Tarot 13
Tarot spreads 19

The Cards **25**
Major Arcana 26
Minor Arcana 171
Court Cards 329

Continued Study **445**
Practice and exercises 446
Further reading 452

About the Authors **453**

Foreword

You are holding before you one of the most powerful tools of transformation known to the psyche: the tarot. The tarot creates an emotional and psychological bonding with the reader, somehow tapping into our subconscious in order to help us find answers to the unknown. The experience of coming to know oneself through something like the tarot is an active journey of seeking and exploring, of finding the best path through an emotional journey, and of bettering oneself through seeking deep awareness and answers. The tarot has been used for centuries for gaming and then for seeking in a more intuitive way. While it has always been powerful, not until now has it been available with such vivid beauty and detail. But this powerful tool you hold is more than just a thing of beauty; it is transformative and can be life-guiding and even life-changing.

The *Tarot Apokalypsis* holds not only the depth and power of a traditional tarot deck, but now the bar has been raised for the level of beauty and rich symbolism. Fiercely bewitching, emotive cards will open themselves before you, filled to the brim with a symbolic level of detail that is unsurpassed in modern or classic tarot card symbolism.

The *Tarot Apokalypsis* is the second deck birthed by the mind and hands of one of tarot's most popular and gifted digital artists, Erik C. Dunne. As the son of parents who were also artists, creativity was always at the forefront of Dunne's childhood experience. His familiarity with tarot symbolism mixed with his passion for beauty was displayed in his first tarot deck creation, the award-winning *Tarot Illuminati*. Immediately upon release, the *Tarot Illuminati* began to win both attention and awards for its detail and uniquely lit beauty. It took the world by storm.

An encore was demanded by his audience, and Dunne strove to uses his gifts toward another venture that would surpass his first artistic victory: the *Tarot Apokalypsis* seed was planted and began to grow.

Once again, author Kim Huggens composes the voice to the cards through her dialogue. With Huggens once again as author and Master of Ceremonies, we are in most excellent hands. This time, however, we are in for an added surprise: Huggens took a very active role with Dunne and collaborated on the artistic and symbolic creation of each and every card, from the details of inception of the first card to the closure and completion of the last. Having studied the tarot since the tender age of nine years, Huggens uses both her lifetime of experience and her undergraduate and postgraduate degrees in philosophy, ancient history and religious studies to tap into the detail and deep metaphors embedded within each card. With their combined knowledge and creativity, this powerful collaboration between Dunne and Huggens has resulted in an outstanding tool that raises every possibility in enjoying both beauty and truth in our readings.

As the book's narrative author, Huggens' practical approach makes esoteric concepts easily revealed and understood. Combined with her unusually vast knowledge of tarot and history, Huggens creates a powerful resource of information so that the reader can understand the finest details of their own life through the metaphors in her descriptions. The pairing of these two minds in symbolism and exceptional art has created a powerful tool of metaphoric exploration.

Now, with the welcoming of the *Tarot Apokalypsis*, the completed second deck, we are treated once again to an opulent world of royal, rich beauty, overflowing with decadence and details that will lead the reader through a new intuitive dance of self-knowledge and learning. Each card appears bejeweled with luxurious color and realism, housed in a world of fantasy and power that is distinctly recognizable as the brainchild of this gifted artist and author. The benefit of the detail in each card is not only in the luxuriant feel that the reader will enjoy when connecting intuitively with these sensuous cards, but also in the generous amount of information that can be gathered through the exquisite amount of symbolism contained in each card's imagery. The copious detail in each card will allow the reader to harvest their intuitive sense with a thoroughness that can dramatically raise the bar in one's readings.

Enter the world of the *Tarot Apokalypsis*, and you'll find that fantasy and reality merge quite easily, where we see mirrors of who we are and where we stand through the crisp images of this deck's active characters. Who are YOU today in the land of *Apokalypsis*? You may be surprised where the cards bring you. Open its jeweled gates and you may be surprised to find yourself within the *Tarot Apokalypsis*, along with sudden clarity to many answers to that which you seek. Enjoy its beauty; behold its wisdom.

Donnaleigh de LaRose

AT THE BEGINNING

Introduction

✎ About Tarot

A tarot pack is a set of 78 cards that is used for divination, fortune-telling, magic, wisdom teaching, problem solving and decision making, among other things. The possibilities for its applications are limited only by the tarot reader's imagination. Each card in the pack has a set of meanings commonly associated with it, which are symbolically represented in the card image. The symbolism on each tarot card works on a number of levels: it can be obvious, revealing a very clear meaning, or it can be more subtle and only reveal its meaning to the reader on a personal level after some time. These meanings will also have a different impact on a reader as they experience changes in their lives, just as a film might strike the viewer in a different way several years after the first viewing.

This book provides a short description of each of the card meanings, as well as explaining some of the symbolism in the images and exploring the ideas that they represent. Every card can be applied on all levels of our lives, from spiritual experiences and important life events to mundane experiences and everyday choices. As such, the meanings provided here are a starting point for a beginner, and a supplement for a more advanced reader. The tarot reader is encouraged to seek more knowledge of the cards through a wide range of sources: other books on tarot, the internet, other readers, life experiences, but most importantly through embarking on a journey to establish and develop a relationship and understanding of the cards. If you are a beginner, this book should be only the first step on a long and meaningful journey; if you are an experienced reader, I hope that this book provides you with a few new insights to add to your tarot toolbox.

ᴥ The Tarot Apokalypsis and revelation

The *Tarot Apokalypsis* is a sister-deck to the *Tarot Illuminati* (Lo Scarabeo, 2013). Whereas the *Tarot Illuminati* was themed around illuminating wisdom, the *Tarot Apokalypsis* shows how the sacred is revealed. The word "*apokalypsis*" is Greek for "revelation". Those who use tarot for divination and magical work will know that it reveals the answers to questions asked, as well as the truth of a matter, the inner self, or the relation of the human soul to the World Soul. Every tarot reading is a process of revelation and it is one of the tasks of the tarot reader to learn how to be open to each revelation and how to deliver it. It is not only the act of tarot reading that offers revelation, however: every card of the tarot pack contains its own mystery that can be revealed on many different levels over time to those who wish to explore it.

In the *Tarot Apokalypsis*, each card reveals a mystery: the Major Arcana through the symbolism and teachings of mystery religions, mystical practices—such as the Eleusinian Mysteries of Greece or Durgā Pūjā of India—, the Minor Arcana through four ancient civilisations and their everyday interactions with the sacred, and the Court Cards through representations of deities worshipped in these civilisations.

Developing an understanding of tarot is a journey made up of many revelations. It is a continual process of sudden realisations and "aha!" moments. These moments make the tarot journey beautiful and life-changing. Yet in order for these revelations to occur and for light to be shed on this vast area of study, we must first become lost: lost in the labyrinth of questioning and uncertainty. We, like the adherents of the mystery cults and religions of the ancient and modern world, must allow ourselves to be immersed in the symbolic darkness of knowing nothing, of being a beginner, a new initiate, undergoing the trials and initiations that will lead to our being brought forth into the light of new understanding, the mysteries having been revealed to us.

A note on the word "cult"
The term "cult" is used throughout this book in the context of mystery cults. In this use it does not refer to strange or sometimes malevolent groups of people who might be viewed as extremists, nor does it refer to a cult of personality. It instead refers to a religious organisation or practice that grows out of a mainstream, often polytheistic, religion, usually (though not always) centred on the worship of one central deity. Most often, these cults were looked upon with favour by the dominant religion of the time, as they involved the worship of accepted deities.

Using Tarot

≈ The tarot toolbox: symbolism

Every card of the tarot is full of symbolism. Symbolism is the language of tarot, the way in which it communicates meaning and the way in which we can engage with a card on a variety of levels. Anything can be a symbol – from an arcane rune to a simple gesture, facial expression or the weather. Symbols also do not have one fixed meaning – they are designed to both evoke and invoke meaning for each reader, so their focus may shift over time or change based on the reading, surrounding cards, inspiration or influence from others. An understanding of symbolism is one tool in your tarot toolbox that will help you give accurate readings.

When a card **invokes** meaning, it draws upon traditional symbolic understanding that is often found in culture, symbolic systems, religion or history.

When a card **evokes** meaning, it pulls out of the individual a personal response to the symbol, based on experience, understanding, aesthetics, feeling and moment.

Example: the symbol of a lion

Invoked meaning	Evoked meaning
Astrological sign of Leo	The lion is your power animal
Alchemical symbol of unrefined matter	The querent's son is named Leo
Alchemical symbol of Sulfur or the masculine	You are a fan of C.S. Lewis and see this as Aslan

Invoked meaning	Evoked meaning
Kabbalistic symbol of the sephira of Geburah	Brings to mind a quote from *The Lion King*: "Remember who you are…"

A tarot reader can discover both the invoked and evoked meanings of a symbol and therefore a tarot card, and recognises both as equally important. Books on tarot and symbolism can often tell you some of the invoked meanings of various symbols that traditionally appear in the cards, but one of your tasks as a reader is to discover new ways in which a symbol presents itself, new dimensions of meaning.

How to read a tarot card

When you are studying a card, ask yourself what symbols are present in it. These can include colours, animals, activity, mood, atmosphere, objects, nature, the age of people, the gender of people, weather and natural occurrences. Allow the symbolism to come alive in your mind so that it might stimulate your knowledge and intuition. A tarot card might say something different to you each time you look at it, so try to remove all preconceptions when you examine the card. Some useful ways of approaching a card include:

- What are your initial feelings about the card?
- What do these symbols mean to you (evoke)?
- Is there a theme in these symbols?
- What are your feelings about the card now you have examined the symbolism?
- What symbols stand out for you?
- How do these symbols relate to each other?
- What do books say about the card meaning?
- How does this card relate to symbolic systems?

⚜ How to read a tarot spread

A tarot spread can be any number of cards. The more cards you have in your spread, the more confusing and daunting it can seem. However, there are some things you can do to get a grip on the spread before you even begin to interpret the cards.

Overcoming the mind blank

Many people experience a "mind blank" when they lay out the cards initially. This is caused by doubt of your knowledge and ability and by fear of getting it wrong. It is important to let go of the fear and doubt, as they can hold you back from giving a great reading. The mind blank at the beginning of a reading can feed doubt, but it is actually a natural part of the tarot experience. As the Fool tells us, the greatest spiritual journey begins with a blank slate, with beginner's mind. Allow yourself to pause and be still in that moment of blankness; allow yourself to let your mind relax, quieten doubts, and let your eyes roam gently over the cards and their images. Breathe. Silence gestates wisdom, as the High Priestess teaches us.

⚜ Finding the keys – approaching a spread

This is a great way to utilise the moment of blankness and it can be done with any spread. It immediately gives you a sense of what the reading is about before you've begun to analyse the cards, their positions and their individual meanings. Scanning the entire spread, take note of any of the following and ask yourself what it means.

Types of cards

Is the majority of the spread Major Arcana or Minor Arcana? If Major Arcana dominate, it might suggest that this is an extremely important issue dealing with the big questions in life, or that the influences upon the situation are out of the control of the questioner. Is there a lot of Court Cards? This might indicate several people being involved in a situation.

Suits

Is there a predominance of a certain suit in the spread? If so, this can indicate the area of life that the spread is focusing on – a majority of Cups, for instance, might indicate a relationship; a majority of Pentacles might suggest issues of work or money. Refer to p. 172 for suggestions of each suit's area of concern.

Is the spread lacking a suit? This might indicate something missing from the questioner's life or the situation, perhaps something that is needed. For instance, a question about a university course that lacks Swords cards might indicate a problem.

Numbers

Do certain numbers repeat, e.g. lots of Fives? If so, they might bring the numerological energies of that number to the spread. A spread with a lot of Fives may indicate a situation of disruption; a lot of Tens might suggest that something is reaching completion.

Remember that the Major Arcana have numbers too: the Magician would be grouped with the Aces, the High Priestess with the Twos, etc. For a Major Arcana numbered 11 and higher, add the two digits of the card together: Justice (11) would be with the Twos, for instance.

Gender

Is there a majority of male figures or female figures in the cards? A large number of male figures might indicate a situation in which the querent needs to be active; a large number of female figures might indicate that they need to wait or turn inward for answers.

Colour

Is there a large swathe of colour in the spread, or an overwhelming colour? Traditional colour symbolism can help you interpret what this might mean. Predominately red? Action, passion, drive. Mostly yellow? Optimistic! Mostly black and greys? Perhaps this is a reading dealing with sadness and grief. Are there patches of colour? Areas of certain colours can indicate groupings of cards or link them to each other.

Examining these aspects of a spread before you begin to interpret the individual cards can give you insight into the focus of the spread, the issues that are being raised and the themes of the cards. It forms a solid foundation upon which to build the more detailed interpretation.

The individual cards
The bulk of the reading will be an examination and interpretation of the individual cards in the reading and how they relate to their position in the spread, the question and the other cards. The way in which you approach them depends on the spread, the question and your intuition. However, it is useful to remember the following:

- Examine the individual cards and their meanings
- Relate these meanings to the card position in the spread and what that position indicates
- Relate the cards to each other.

The Two of Cups, for instance, on its own may mean falling in love or an intimate friendship; what does it mean when it shows up in a reading in the position of "Past"? Its basic meaning will need to be applied slightly differently in this situation in comparison to it appearing in the position of "Outcome" or "Advice". Finally, other cards in the reading might help you apply its meaning even further: maybe it has a Court card either side of it in the spread, perhaps suggesting the two people involved in the relationship.

Just as we lead complex and intricate lives with relationships between many different aspects, so the cards in a reading can have interesting connections.

Tarot spreads

～ Unveiling a situation

Inspired by the threefold mystery that was revealed in the Eleusinian Mysteries (see *High Priestess)*, this spread helps to analyse a situation, how it has arisen and what can be done about it.

1. *Deiknumena*, "things shown": Intention and the underlying reason or cause of the situation.

2. *Dromena*, "things done": Action and what must be done in response to the situation.

3. *Legomena*, "things said": Words and what lessons can be learned from the situation.

◦≈ Mithraic initiation spread

Just as initiates in the cult of Mithras (see *The Sun*) underwent seven initiations assigned to the seven classical planets of antiquity, we can undertake a journey through the planetary grades of the cult's mysteries. This spread can be used to assess our lives, spiritual journeys or a situation, with each of the cards associated with one of the grades of initiation of the cult of Mithras, and therefore one of the seven classical planets.

The Sun – "Pater" (Father). The outcome of the situation. The highest good of the situation. OR the current focus or overarching theme of one's life at this time.

The Moon – "Heliodromos" (Runner of the Sun). The means by which the best outcome can be achieved in the situation. OR one's imaginative world, creativity and generative world.

Saturn – "Perses" (The Persian). The obstacles in the situation. OR obstacles and challenges in one's life at this time.

Jupiter – "Leo" (The Lion). The main players or influences in the situation. OR one's leadership, power and authority at this time. May also show one's money/work situation.

Mars – "Miles" (The Soldier). Your role in the situation or how the situation affects you. OR one's ambitions, goals and drives at this time.

Venus – "Nymphus" (The Bridegroom). The emotional aspects of the situation. OR one's emotional world and relationships at this time.

Mercury – "Corax" (The Raven). The reasons for the situation. OR one's intellectual world and state of mind at this time.

~ Revelations of the four suits

Each of the suits of the Minor Arcana focus on an area of our lives. This spread allows us to take stock of our lives and assess them in each of their aspects.

Separate out the 40 Minor Arcana cards and split them into their suits. Lay out each suit in its own pile, in the order of Pentacles, Cups, Swords and Wands.

Shuffle each pile separately, asking the question "Where am I at this time?" One by one, turn over the top card of each pile.

Pentacles: This is your current situation regarding work, money, family or the everyday world.
Cups: This is your current situation regarding relationships, your social world, emotions and spiritual life.
Swords: This is your current situation regarding intellectual pursuits, your state of mind and communication.
Wands: This is your current situation regarding your goals, ambitions, passions and energy.
Optional: You could add to this spread by shuffling just the Major Arcana at the end and asking "What is the theme of my life at this time?" or "What lesson do I need to learn at this time?" Draw the top card from the pile of Major Arcana cards.

Demeter's four seasons spread

Inspired by the mysteries of Demeter (see *The Wheel*) and the continual process of change in the universe, this spread uses the motif of the four seasons as a way to explore the life cycle of a project, goal, or something being worked on.

1. *The seed*: what has been planted/needs to be planted; the foundations of the project.
2. *Spring*: the first, stimulating stage; how to initiate growth or change.
3. *Summer*: the middle energetic stage; how to nurture the growth of the project or keep it moving forwards.
4. *Autumn*: the penultimate, harvest stage; what will be gained from the project, the results.
5. *Winter*: the final, resting stage; the after-effects and long-term consequences of the project; what lessons can be learned.

~ Hekate Triformis spread for choices and options

This spread is designed for use when there is a choice that must be made or when you are at a juncture on your road, when it is unclear which way is best. It calls upon Hekate Triformis (see *The Moon*) for guidance in her three faces as key-bearer, light-bringer and underworld one.

1. *Hekate Phosphorus*, "light-bringer". The most suitable direction for you to take at this time. Advice on how to approach the choice.

2. *Hekate Chthonia*, "of the underworld". What to avoid. The least suitable direction for you to take at this time.

3. *Hekate Kleidouchos*, "key-bearer". The key to moving forward. What to bear in mind as you make your choice. The important things not to lose sight of.

This spread can be altered slightly if you have a specific choice with clear-cut options. For each option, deal the three cards as above, and read in the following way:

1. *Hekate Phosphorus*, "light-bringer". The positive aspects of this choice; the best that will come from you choosing it.
2. *Hekate Chthonia*, "of the underworld". The negative aspects of this choice; the worst that will come from you choosing it.
3. *Hekate Kleidouchos*, "key-bearer". Advice and anything you have not considered; unknown influences that need to be taken into account.

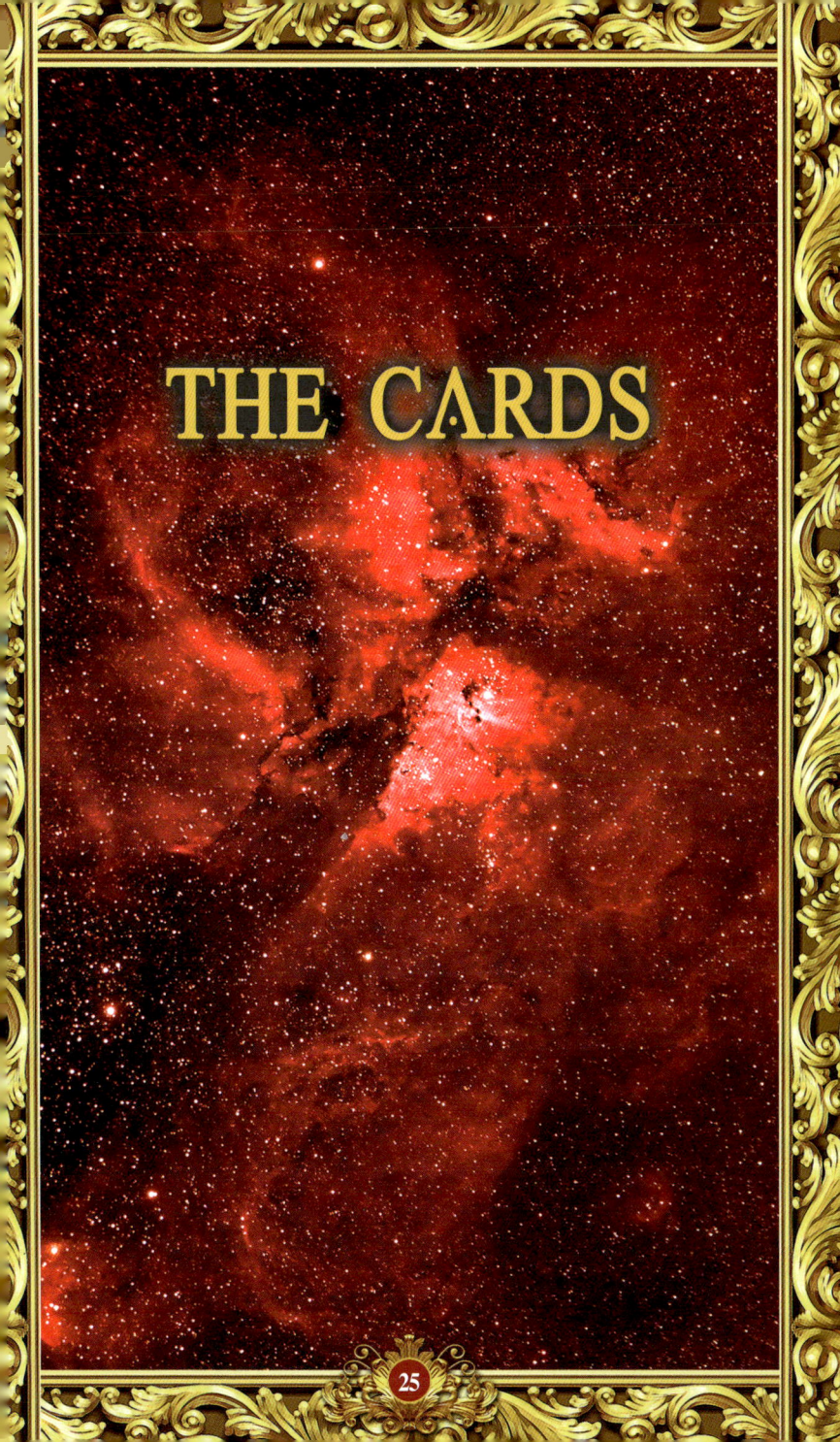
THE CARDS

Major Arcana

In the Major Arcana the mystery of each card is presented as a mystery cult, mystery religion, mystical or magical practice—some from the ancient world that are no longer practiced and some that are still practiced today—for which that particular mystery was/is a prominent focus. The symbolism and imagery of each Major Arcana conveys not only the meanings of the card but also the teachings, beliefs or practices of that mystery religion or practice. The goal of initiates in a mystery religion or cult was to have a mystical experience in which they achieved a union with their deity. Many of the mysteries also offered, through initiation, some kind of salvation or life after death. By presenting the Major Arcana in this way, the reader will be able to participate to some extent in the revelation of mystery that these religions, cults and practices aimed for.

In a reading, the Major Arcana ("Greater Mysteries") often relate abstract concepts, internal processes of change and growing understanding of different aspects of the universe. They are the spiritual truths of the universe and the "big" events of life. However, as the divine is always reflected by the mundane, they can also be applied to the everyday world and our daily experiences. The context of the question and other cards in the reading will suggest when this is the case.

Each of the Major Arcana is traditionally associated with other symbolic systems such as astrology and kabbalah. Although these are not explicitly discussed in this book, it is useful to know the associations so that you can work with them based on your own knowledge or explore them with further reading and study.

Major Arcana	Astrological association	Kabbalistic association
Fool	Uranus	Aleph
Magician	Mercury	Beth
High Priestess	Moon	Gimel
Empress	Venus	Daleth
Emperor	Aries	Heh
Hierophant	Taurus	Vav
Lovers	Gemini	Zayin
Chariot	Cancer	Cheth
Strength	Leo	Teth
Hermit	Virgo	Yod
Wheel	Jupiter	Kaph
Justice	Libra	Lamed
Hanged Man	Neptune	Mem
Death	Scorpio	Nun
Temperance	Sagittarius	Samekh
Devil	Capricorn	Ayin
Tower	Mars	Peh
Star	Aquarius	Tzaddi
Moon	Pisces	Qoph
Sun	Sun	Resh
Judgement	Pluto	Shin
World	Saturn	Tav

Recommendations for books to help you study this aspect of the Major Arcana can be found in the Further Reading section, p. 452

The All-Gifted

Pandora

My name has been whispered throughout the ages as a byword for guile, for curiosity and for weakness; yet these tongues know not the true power of the secret gifts hidden within, taken up from the earth and granted as boons to humankind. They know not of the strength of my heart, nor that it was only through me that life could come into being. For I am All-Gifted and All-Giving, the great opener, the gateway through which all seekers must pass to become self-aware. I am the mother of Hope and of Despair, the bride of Beginnings and the descendant of the Gods. There is no mystery in this world except that which I give to you. Heed my words and let them take root in your heart, for then you will come to know that I am not only the first woman, but all of humankind: my origin is yours, my purpose is yours, my divine nature is yours. Be not afraid to give of yourself to the universe and others. It is in giving that you receive, in blessing that you are blessed. You will not be diminished by the act but filled with All Things, and thus you shall come to stand before me as my child, All-Gifted and All-Blessed.

~ Mystery

The All-Gifted is an additional, optional card for use with *Tarot Apokalypsis*. It is inspired in part by the Lenormand tradition, in which there are two cards – the Man and the Woman – that may signify the reader or querent in a reading, but it can also be used with further meanings to represent the self on many levels.

The card portrays Pandora, whose name means "All-Gifted" and "All-Giving", and gifts are a significant theme in her story.

Hesiod tells us that, as a punishment for Prometheus' theft of fire from the gods and his gifting it to humans, Zeus commanded the smith-god Hephaestus to fashion a maiden from clay and give her a voice and strength. Athena taught her needlework and weaving, Aphrodite gave her grace and longing, Hermes gave her cunning, and the Graces, Peitho and the Horae clothed her in fine jewels and garlands of flowers. [1] Hesiod suggests that the reason for her name is that she received a gift from all the gods of Olympus.

Pandora was the first woman, from whom all other women came. [2] She shares this in common with Eve, the biblical first woman, also created by a divine force. Like Eve, Pandora was gifted to a man to be his wife, in this case Epimetheus, the younger brother of Prometheus. The tale continues that she was gifted a jar (which was later interpreted as a box in the Middle Ages, giving rise to the famous term "Pandora's Box") by Zeus, which contained a great number of evils (in some versions), blessings (in other versions) or both. This box became irresistible to either Pandora or Epimetheus, who opened it and released its contents to the world. Different versions of the myth and commentators disagree about what was released and what remained, as well as whether the act of releasing caused that which had been released to be lost or given to the world. The common thread is that this act, like the act of Eve in sharing the apple with Adam, had a profound impact on the world and changed it forever into the world in which we live today.

Another name given to Pandora in inscriptions is Anesidora, "she who sends up gifts". [3] This may relate to ancient imagery

---

1   Hesiod, trans. Hugh G. Evelyn White, **Works and Days**, 54ff. Loeb Classical Library, 1914.

2   Pausanius, trans. W. H. S. Jones, **Description of Greece** 1.24.7. Loeb Classical Library, 1918.

3   Jane Ellen Harrison, **Prolegomena to the Study of Greek Religion**, p. 281. Princeton University Press, 1992.

that abounds of her rising up out of the earth, like many chthonic or earth goddesses. [4] Although there is very little mention of any cult associated with her, a scholium to a line in Aristophanes' *The Birds* makes reference to a cult "to Pandora, the earth, because she bestows all things necessary for life". [5] This suggests that Pandora gifted to humankind, through her act, everything that makes life sustainable and makes it what it is.

Called All-Gifted, gifted to Epimetheus by the gods as a bride, her only mentioned act in myth being to gift that which is required for life (and in some versions, hope, as well as the evils that plague us) to humankind, Pandora asks us what we can give to the world and to others, what strengths and blessings we have that we can use to make the world a better place and improve the lot of others.

≈ Revelation

Giving of oneself to others; bestowing goodness and blessings; identifying one's strengths so they can be used for the benefit of others or the wider community; acknowledging oneself as divinely created and gifted; hope for the future; the self.

Negatively aspected…
Fear of the self; fear of negatively affecting others and a situation; withholding one's gifts and oneself.

---

4   Ellen D. Reeder ed., **Pandora: Women in Classical Greece**, p. 70. Princeton University Press, 1995.

5   Jeffrey M. Hurwit, **"Beautiful Evil: Pandora and the Athena Parthenos"** in **American Journal of Archaeology**, vol. 99, no. 2, (April, 1995), pp. 171–186.

The Fool

The Mevlevi Sufi sama ceremony

At the beginning it is the end; at the end it is the beginning. The highest point is the lowest, but from the lowest the highest might be attained. This is the path of the holy fool, the madman filled with the ecstasy of union: what wisdom is concealed in his insane words, what love hidden in the chaos of his whirling cloth and mind? Truly God comes to us as the madman crying aloud in the streets, as the unutterable truth that spills from the tongue in ululations and wild cries for its ineffability. You see me dance, you see the wildness in my step and only the whites of my eyes in my drunkenness, but you do not see the union in my heart nor the indescribable peace in my soul. For I am not I: I is the trap that will hold you in this grave-world, knowing your self is knowing only your tomb. Join my dance, let your head grow dizzy from the maddening spinning, drink deeply of the wine of the Beloved, inhale the opiate of the divine breath that is All, and you shall be as the sacred fool. You shall know the ecstasy of union and liberation from the chains of I; you shall be crazy and holy, knocking as a madman at the door of the Beloved. Only when you cannot think of I without thinking of God, when you turn your head in all directions and there is always God, will the door be opened to Not-You. And then there shall only be One and All and Nothing, and your days will be an eternity and a moment, all in the divine bliss of union.

⇜ Mystery

The Fool is as abstract and seemingly paradoxical as the final card of the Major Arcana, the World. Together they each are a beginning as well as an end, an instigation as well as a conclusion. As its name suggests, it is associated with foolish action, yet its presence in the lofty Major Arcana and its im-

agery says otherwise. This "foolishness" manifests as a divine foolishness, a sacred drunkenness, a mad ecstasy. This unity with godhead is also a form of self-annihilation, in which the boundaries between I and Not I are destroyed, leaving only the divine. This, in itself, becomes its own form of spiritual madness, as the mystic acts contrary to social convention, seeming crazy to those who do not understand.

The Islamic Mevlevi order of Sufi mysticism performs a practice that is aimed at achieving this state: the *sama* ceremony. Initiation into the Sufi path means "the surrender of will, the transformation of desire from self-centredness to God-centredness, a seeking not so much to escape from self as to transcend or transmute self, and thus enter into timeless experience". [6] The whirling dance of *sama* has caused followers of this order to be known as Whirling Dervishes (a dervish is another term for an initiate of the Sufi path, though they are properly called *Tasawwuf*). The whirling is a form of *dhikr* (remembrance of Allah) which can bring about an altered state and ecstasy. Like the Fool, although the dance may look chaotic and physically exciting, it is actually a symptom of an ascent of the soul towards unity with the divine. The outward chaos conceals the inner peace.

An important part of the *sama* ceremony that accompanies the whirling dance is listening – to music, poetry and readings from the Qur'an. This listening can bring about an altered state of consciousness. [7] This reminds us that one of the associations of the Fool, as the first card of the Major Arcana, is beginner's mind, the totally receptive state in which all preconceptions

---

6   J. Spencer Trimingham, ***The Sufi Orders in Islam***, p. 199. Clarendon Press, 1971.

7   Kenneth S. Avery, ***A Psychology of Early Sufi Sama: Listening and Altered States,*** p. 16. Routledge, 2004.

and assumptions are removed to enable a greater understanding to grow. It is as a reminder of this that the sky in the card image is the fiery orange and red of a new dawn. It should be noted that "at the more advanced stages of Sufi practice, the need for external stimuli to heighten consciousness, such as that provided by *sama*, is not required at all". [8] Therefore, the Whirling Dervish in the card image, despite his lofty position and the ascent of his soul towards Allah through the practice of *sama*, is a beginner on the mystical path.

The purpose of *sama* is to reach *wajd*, a state of spiritual ecstasy that leads to annihilation of the self in union with Allah. A state called *khamra*, "spiritual drunkenness", is also attained. During these states there may be excitation of the body resulting in strange, unexpected and chaotic movement. However, the *sama* ceremony is also ordered into several stages, each representing a different aspect of the practice. The first stage affirms the unity of Allah by the crossing of the arms over the chest. In the second part, drumming represents Allah's command to all of creation: "Be". The wind instrument of the third part represents the first divine breath that gave life to the world. In the fourth part, the *sama*, the dancers greet each other in acknowledgement of soul meeting soul. The fifth part is perhaps the most interesting, as it is here that the whirling creates spiritual ecstasy. It consists of four *selams*, salutes: first to the mystic's awakening to truth, second to the rapture of witnessing the splendour of creation, third to the transformation of rapture into love and submission to the divine, and fourth to the return to earth as a servant of Allah. In the third salute, the mystic reaches the highest state of ecstasy called Fenafillah. [9] The movement of the body during the *sama* is also symbolic:

---

8   ***Ibid.**, p. 21*.

9   *Dr. Celaleddin Çelebi, **Whirling Dervishes, Sema**. Online at http://mevlana. net/sema.html [Accessed 24 January 2016].*

the dancing is the "circling of the spirit round the cycle of existing things on account of receiving the effects of the unveilings and revelations; and this is the state of the gnostic. The whirling is a reference to the spirit's standing with Allah in its inner nature (*sirr*) and being (*wujūd*) […]. And his leaping up is a reference to his being drawn from the human station to the unitive station". [10]

Although the result of *sama* outwardly appears to be full of life, the clothing of the dervishes is symbolic of death: the white gown is a death shroud, a black cloak thrown off at the start of the ceremony represents the concerns of the world and the grave, and the tall hat represents the tombstone that will stand at the head of all one day. [11] This death symbolism acts as a reminder of the final purpose of *sama* and the highest meaning of the Fool: self-annihilation, the removal of all conceptions of self, I and boundaries. The state of mind and heart of the Mevlevi Sufi who has achieved its highest goal "remains the same before, during and after the *sama* session" [12] – there are no longer any boundaries between the mystic and Allah, divine unity. It is for this reason that the Sufi masters write:

*"Rose and mirror and sun and moon—where are they?
Wherever we looked, there was always Thy face."* [13]

The annihilation of the self in the Sufi *sama* and in the Fool does not come from a belief that the self is worthless: it is only the notion of the self as separate and removed from the divine

---

10 *The Sufi Orders in Islam*, p. 195.

11 Niki Gamm, **Symbolism and dervish clothing**. Online at http://www.hurriyetdailynews.com/symbolism-and-dervish-clothing.aspx?pageID=238&nID=49220&NewsCatID=438 [Accessed 22 January 2016].

12 Kenneth S. Avery, **A Psychology of Early Sufi Sama**, p. 21.

13 Mîr, quoted in **Travelling the Path of Love: Sayings of the Sufi Masters**, ed. Llewellyn Vaughan-Lee, p. 171. The Golden Sufi Center, 1995.

that is destroyed, as it is an impediment to unity with God. Rûmî writes of this in a poem in which the "Friend" (Allah) welcomes a guest (the mystic) to his door:

"A certain person came to the Friend's door and knocked.
"Who's there?"
"It's me."
The Friend answered, "Go away. There's no place for raw meat at this table."
The individual went wandering for a year. Nothing but the fire of separation can change hypocrisy and ego. The person returned completely cooked, walked up and down in front of the Friend's house, gently knocked.
"Who is it?"
"You."
"Please come in, my Self, there's no place in this house for two." [14]

~ Revelation

The death of the ego, boundaries and self; removing that which holds one back; spiritual ecstasy and drunkenness; unity; a feeling of oneness; divine inspiration ad revelation; what appears foolish to others is a mark of spiritual awareness; new beginnings; the start of a new path or journey; new awakenings and realisations; beginner's mind.

Negatively aspected…
Foolish behaviour; being unprepared to begin something new; naivety; reckless abandon; dangerous spiritual practices; losing sight of the self and the goal; destroying the self for the sake of destruction; feeling worthless.

---

*14 Rûmî, quoted in **Ibid.**, p. 193.*

The Magician
Jewish Merkabah mysticism

From the divine chaos came light and a word of power that created the universe; the smallest and the greatest parts of this world alike were pulled from nothingness into blazing life, manifested and given form. This was the path of magic, of will and energy directed into creation; this is the path you also can tread with words of power and the invocation of divine names. Follow my mysteries, and I will show you how to draw down the very angels and manifest their wisdom within your self; I will show you how to control the heavens and the earth, the sun and the sea; I will give you dominion over all the things before you. When I ascend towards the Divine it descends towards me: at the point of meeting the universe is recreated. In me divine fire is transformed into the waters that nourish the earth; in my actions, my will and energy are directed towards a goal. My mysteries are those of focus and will, active creation and manifestation; walk my roads and I shall show you your nature as a conduit of the divine, that you may project your will into the world and make it anew with each word you speak.

~ Mystery

This card, the first of the Major Arcana to be given a proper number, helps us move from the chaotic ecstasy and divine bliss of unity found in the Fool to forceful action and manifestation. The title of this card does not refer to stage magicians or sleight of hand, however: this magician is creating change to occur in conformity with his will, through the manipulation and control of the universe. His word creates reality, he binds supernatural beings to his will and controls the divine forces he summons. The Magician of the tarot is a figure utterly in control of his resources, takes an active role in all things, has a strong influence

on results and manifests the changes he desires through his single-minded focus, will and direction of his energy. He acts as a conduit between heaven and earth, drawing down divine energy and channelling it into the mundane world: he performs magic. This is not only "results magic" (to gain mundane results), however: it is also mysticism and magical practices that lead to an ascent towards the Divine.

There are many traditions throughout the ages that have used magical techniques to gain results and become closer to the Divine. In the *Tarot Apokalypsis* the tradition depicted is Jewish Merkabah mysticism, also called *Ma'aseh Merkabah* – the Work of the Divine Chariot. That it is identified as "work" reminds us that the Magician is an active participant in every aspect of his life and that effort is required to gain results. The body of literature that gives the earliest full-scale presentation of Merkabah is called Hekhalot literature, [15] written in Hebrew and Aramaic with several borrowings from Greek [16] between ca. 200–700 CE. [17] Although disparate, the texts are characterised by lists of divine and angelic names, hymns of praise, words of power, conjurations and descriptions of the visions the practitioner will have. [18] Most of the texts emphasise the knowledge and use of various seals, described as magical names of angels or God, which are used as passports to gain passage on the ascent through seven heavens. [19] They focus on the ascent to heaven,

---

15 Translations in English of a large number of these texts can be found in James Davila trans. **Hekhalot Literature in Translation**. Brill, 2013.

16 Vita Daphna Arbel, **Beholders of Divine Secrets: Mysticism and Myth in the Hekhalot and Merkavah Literature**, p. 8. State University of New York Press, 2003.

17 Ithamar Gruenwold, **Apocalyptic and Merkavah Mysticism**, p. 3. Brill, 2014.

18 Gideon Bohak, **Ancient Jewish Magic**, p. 330. Cambridge University Press, 2008.

19 Gershom G. Scholem, **Jewish Gnosticism, Merkabah Mysticism, and Talmudic Tradition**, p. 32. The Jewish Theological Seminary of American, 1965.

paradoxically called a "descent", to view the throne of God, also called the Chariot (Merkabah) of God. This vision is based on Ezekiel's vision of the Chariot of God, attended by four beings that each had four faces: one face of a lion, one of a man, one of an ox and one of an eagle. [20] Tarot traditionally uses the lion, man, ox and eagle as symbols of the four elements on the Wheel of Fortune and the World cards. The Magician in the *Tarot Apokalypsis* sees the living creatures in a streamlined format: four wings surround the Chariot of God. This gives the Magician the role of a commander of the four elements, the four suits of the tarot, and therefore all the resources of the world.

The practice of Merkabah mysticism was primarily intended to "cause the practitioner to ascend to the throne room of God, see a vision of it and sometimes participate in the events there, then return safely". [21] Similarly, the Magician of the tarot seeks gnosis and divine ascent, acting like an arrow shot towards the heavens in his single-minded focus on the highest goal. Another of the aims of Merkabah practice is to gain supernatural knowledge of the universe and the Torah. In the *Ma'aseh Merkavah*, the completion of the practice is marked by the Prince of the Presence and angels of mercy descending from heaven and placing wisdom in the heart of the practitioner. [22] In the *Book of Enoch*, a mystic reports that Metatron commanded him to "[c]ome and behold the letters by which the heavens and the earth were created, the letters by which the mountains and hills were created, the letters by which the seas and rivers were created, the letters by which the trees and herbs were created, the letters by which the planets and zodiacal signs were created, the letters by which the throne

---

20   *Ezekiel 1: 5–11.*

21   *James R. Davila, "Ritual in the Hekhalot Literature" in **Practicing Gnosis: Ritual Magic, Theurgy and Liturgy in Nag Hammadi, Manichaean and Other Ancient Literature**, eds. April D. DeConick et al., p. 450. Brill, 2013.*

22   ***Ibid.**, p. 453.*

of glory and the wheels of the Merkabah were created, the letters by which the necessities of the world were created, the letters by which wisdom, understanding, knowledge, prudence, meekness, and righteousness were created, by which the whole world is sustained". [23] Through this knowledge the mystic, like the Magician of the tarot, understands the workings of the universe. The great knowledge that is granted to practitioners reminds us that the Magician is associated with the planet Mercury, and therefore the Roman god of intellect, messages and insight.

Just as the Magician can draw up great reserves of energy and control the resources at hand, so Merkabah practice was also used to give the mystic theurgic powers to adjure, control and bind angels to do his bidding. [24] Texts such as the *Merkavah Rabbah* give instructions for doing this and explain how to bind angels by oath. [25] The *Hekhalot Zutarti* claims that it was through its wisdom that Moses was able to perform the "wonders and the miracles in Egypt". [26] The miracles and powers granted to the Merkabah mystic include being enabled to "ascend on high, to descend below […] to behold what is on high, and to behold what is below, to know the meaning of the living, and to see the vision of the dead, to walk in rivers of fire, and to know the lightning". [27] He is also given a seal to use "by which the Earth is bound, and by which the Heavens are bound and the Earth flees before it and the Universe trembles before it", [28] giving him unearthly power and control over both the heavens and the earth.

---

23   Gershom G. Scholem, *Jewish Gnosticism, Merkabah Mysticism, and Talmudic Tradition*, p. 79.

24   *Ibid*, p. 456.

25   Ithamar Gruenwold **Apocalyptic and Merkavah Mysticism**, p. 235.

26   *Ibid.*, p. 178.

27   Gershom G. Scholem, *Jewish Gnosticism, Merkabah Mysticism, and Talmudic Tradition*, p. 78.

28   *Ibid.*, pp. 82–83.

The Magician's role as a channelling force to manifest higher energy on an earthly plane is reflected in the practice of Merkabah mystics of bringing an angel down to earth in order to gain mystical insight from them. Part of this practice was the invocation of divine and angelic names, itself a process by which divine power is drawn down and manifested in results. This is represented in the card image by the heavenly fire being drawn down in the mystic's left hand and becoming desert-quenching water from his right hand; in the same hand he holds the rosary by which he counts the 112 repetitions of the holy names he invokes.

Many of the Hekhalot texts prescribe a strict regime of fasting, bathing and rules for a number of days prior to the practice, reminding us of the single-minded focus of the Magician of the tarot. Like the Aces, he carries the energy of the number One: undivided focus and effort, will and the projection of self. He is the card that kickstarts the creation process and shows us how to use the resources of the tarot to gain control and manifestation in our lives.

∽ Revelation

The initial burst of energy at the beginning of a process; manifestation; cause change to occur in conformity with the will; drawing energy from somewhere and channelling it into something; bringing the sacred to the mundane; magic; theurgy; ritual; having power and control over one's resources; knowledge; an active role; single-minded purpose; direction towards a goal.

Negatively aspected…
Lack of control and power; being acted upon; lack of urgency and agency; weak will; lack of energy; a charlatan; no driving force; power being used in the wrong direction.

The High Priestess

Persephone and the Eleusinian Mysteries of Ancient Greece

The mysteries are for all; initiation is oath-bound to be given if you tread this path. Therefore, I urge you: close your ears if you do not wish to hear; close your eyes if you do not wish to see, but know that even now you cannot close your soul to initiation, to that stair leading down, to that underworld road. You have come so far, seeker, and all that is left is to part the veil and see. Know that man is destined to forget, to pass as a shadow in this world, but you have the secret of memory before you. You need only drink deeply of the river that passes through Hades to know again. Would you turn your eyes from the visions that come so easily in the vapours of the earth? Would you close your heart to the mystery I can show you? In the depths of midnight, kissed by the moon in her fullness, you will see the sun glittering with a splendid light and know the ineffable silence. You will be virgin, veiled and voiceless, in this trinity full of potential, a channel for vision and revelation. You will know yourself, and the beyond-truths, and the ever-present darkness of the chasm will bring the oracle's tongue. I am the veil and the road; I am the stair leading down and the cavern; I am the cosmos painted on the ceiling of the temple and I am the seed that is planted. I am Virgin, Veiled and Voiceless, yet it is my womb into which you pass, my voice that will whisper and hiss in your ear. Oh, my beloved initiate: things have been done, things have been shown and things have been said. Know how to walk the path that leads to the splendid light and to memory. Do not be afraid: the seeds are sweet.

☙ Mystery

Many of the Major Arcana in the *Tarot Apokalypsis* depict a mystery religion, yet it is the High Priestess that most embodies mystery. In many tarot decks she is seated before the veil that covers the door to the Holy of Holies in the Temple of Solomon. She is not only the veil that guards the mystery of the Holy of Holies, but also the initiation that must take place to make the seeker worthy to enter that most sacred temple and the secrecy that by necessity surrounds its contents.

The oaths of secrecy placed upon initiates of the Eleusinian Mysteries (often referred to as "the Mysteries") were strong, so we know little of the rites and revelations that were performed and imparted. The penalty for speaking of the secrets of initiation or the features of the rites was death. Cicero and Athenagoras of Athens both attested that this was the penalty given to Diagoras of Melos for speaking of the Mysteries, and the tragic playwright Aeschylus is said to have been tried in court for revealing the sacred secrets in his plays. [29] This same secrecy makes the High Priestess so entrancing: like the Mysteries, she contains great wisdom that can be revealed once we enter the temple and undergo initiation; until we have passed through that veil we remain ignorant.

The Mysteries were split into the Lesser Mysteries, occurring annually, and the Greater Mysteries, occurring every five years. Few rules governed eligibility: all were allowed admission providing they had not committed murder and were not "barbarian" (i.e., could speak Greek). Even slaves were eligible – the Mysteries were for everyone. Upon completion of the Lesser Mysteries, participants were deemed *mystai* ("initiates") worthy of witnessing the Greater Mysteries. The Ele-

---

29   Aristotle. **Nichomachean Ethics**, *1111a 8–10*.

usinian Mysteries were based on the myth of Demeter and her daughter Persephone, in which the maiden Persephone (also called Kore, "the maiden") was abducted by her uncle Hades, the ruler of the underworld, and taken as his wife. When Demeter discovered this she grieved, wandering the earth looking for Kore, blighting the land and disguising herself as a mortal. She eventually came to Eleusis, where she was given hospitality and brought out of her depression by bawdy joking; there she founded the rites by which she and her daughter could be worshipped and the event of her wandering and searching remembered annually. [30] Although the focus of the myth is on Demeter's search, only the first part of the rites were concerned with it; the mysteries that were revealed in initiation are likely to have concerned the maiden Kore in the underworld.

The first part of the initiation and celebration of the Mysteries was a reenactment of Demeter's search for Persephone. In one ancient depiction, initiates are led by Iakhos and the goddess Hekate, both bearing torches. The initiates are dressed as wanderers and follow the path Demeter took while searching. The female initiates carry *kykeon* vessels on their heads and the men carry small pitchers. [31] The *kykeon* drink was instituted by Demeter when she drank it after coming out of her grieving. Entheogenic theories suggest that this *kykeon* was psycho-active, inducing hallucinations.

We know little of what followed this reenactment, held within the Telesterion ("initiation hall", from Greek τελείω, to fulfil, consecrate, or initiate). We may know much about the journey that leads to the High Priestess' feet, but we know little of what

---

30 The myth is found in the **Homeric Hymn to Demeter**, written c. 7th century BCE, the most common version translated by Hugh G. Evelyn-White, Loeb Classical Library, 1914. It is believed that this text served as the main sacred text for the Eleusinian Mysteries.

31 Carl Kerényi. **Eleusis: Archetypal Image of Mother and Daughter**, p. 62. Princeton University Press, 1991.

lies beyond her veil. Our High Priestess is Persephone herself, or Kore as she once was, now the Queen of the Underworld, mistress of the dead and keeper of mysteries. Our torch-lit search for her has been successful, but now she is the doorway through which we must pass to gain initiation. Initiates into the Mysteries were taught after death to drink from the river Mnemosyne ("memory") rather than Lethe ("forgetfulness") as the dead usually do; thus, they were promised a better afterlife. It is Mnemosyne that runs through the cave in the card image. This was a promise of the soul's liberation from matter and return to its divine source. It is in the descent of Kore into Hades that we find a powerful image of the soul: this virginal maiden descending into the darkness of the earth can be seen as a symbol of the soul entering matter. Then, because the soul is mired and hidden in the earth, just as Kore is hidden in Hades, there is a quest to find it again. We search for our soul and our divine origin as Demeter searches for her lost daughter, finally finding it trapped in matter, disconnected from its source; yet even in the darkness the soul's divine light shines, as Apuleius' account of his initiation into the Mysteries suggests:

"I approached the confines of death: and having trodden on the threshold of Proserpina returned, having been carried through all the elements. In the depths of midnight I saw the sun glittering with a splendid light, together with the infernal and supernal gods." [32]

The myth continues when Demeter discovers her daughter and demands that Hades return her. Hades feeds Persephone a single seed of a pomegranate. It is because of this seed that she must return yearly to reside with Hades in the Underworld, hinting perhaps at a return to life after death for the soul that undertakes

---

32   Thomas Taylor, ***The Eleusinian and Bacchic Mysteries***, p.102. J. W. Bouton, 1891.

initiation. The pomegranate is believed to be the fruit shared by Adam and Eve in the Garden of Eden, and therefore it signifies knowledge. In many cultures it represents fertility due to its womb-like shape and abundance of seeds. One author comments:

"[T]he red color evokes associations, not only of mortal wounds, but also menstrual blood, the blood of defloration, and the blood of parturition: blood of life, as well as death; sexual blood; women's blood. Again, the prodigious number of seeds within a pomegranate has always made it a symbol of exuberant female fertility." [33]

It may seem odd that fertility should be ascribed to a virginal maiden, yet this mystery, like the High Priestess, represents the potential to be found in secret silence. Just as the womb is silent so it also contains the potential for all life. The blood-like juice from the pomegranate in the image refers to the first menses, reminding us of fertility yet to come; after all, the Empress follows the High Priestess in the tarot. This silence is so powerful and all-engendering that Proclus said of it in reference to the Mysteries that "initiation and *epopteia* [the veiling and the revealing] are symbols of ineffable silence, and of union with mystical natures, through intelligible visions". [34] The Church Father Hippolytus wrote that "...the Athenians [...] display to those who are being admitted to the highest grade at these mysteries, the mighty, and marvellous, and most perfect secret suitable for one initiated into the highest mystic truths: *an ear of corn in silence reaped*". [35]

---

33 Bruce Lincoln, *"The Rape of Persephone: A Greek Scenario of Women's Initiation"* in *The Harvard Theological Review*, vol. 72, no. 3/4 (Jul. – Oct., 1979), p. 234.

34 Thomas Taylor, *The Eleusinian and Bacchic Mysteries*, p. 104. J. W. Bouton, 1891.

35 Hippolytus, *Refutation of All Heresies*, 5.5.3.

The *epopteia* referred to by Proclus means "revealing", related to the term *epopt,* seer or visionary, one who knows interior wisdom. This reminds us that the knowledge gained from the High Priestess is not factual or learned wisdom, but instead understanding and experience. Aristotle wrote that the initiates of the Mysteries did not learn (*mathein*) but experienced (*pathein*), and through this were brought to an appropriate state of mind. [36] It is the role of the Hierophant to impart received wisdom and factual knowledge, but the role of the High Priestess to plant the seeds of understanding within us, just as Hades gave Persephone a single pomegranate seed.

It is believed that the rites within the Telesterion were composed of three elements: *dromena* ("things done"), a dramatic reenactment of the Demeter/Persephone myth; *deiknumena* ("things shown"), displayed sacred objects; and *legomena* ("things said"), commentaries that accompanied the *deiknumena*. Combined, these three elements were known as the *apporheta* ("unrepeatables"). We are thus reminded that mystery is manifold and may be experienced and received in a variety of ways, but the silence in which it gestates is always the same.

Inspiration for the image of the *Tarot Apokalypsis'* High Priestess was also found in the oracles of the Greek and Roman world, in particular the Oracle of Apollo at Delphi in the classical period. This oracle was consulted by seekers from all over the Mediterranean. The Pythia (oracular priestess) was seated upon a three-legged stool over cracks in the temple's floor. It is believed that these cracks went deep into the earth, with excavations in recent decades suggesting that vapours rose from these cracks and put the Pythia into an ecstatic trance-state. Her prophecies were uttered in an ecstatic form of speech, which was then translated by the priests. The snake in the card im-

---

36 Walter Burkert, **Greek Religion,** *p. 286. Wiley-Blackwell, 1987.*

age refers to the origin myth of the Oracle of Delphi, in which Apollo slew the monstrous Python and threw his body into the chasm, where it gave off the fumes that the Pythia would inhale.

The cup held by Persephone contains the *kykeon* for initiates to drink before they enter the Telesterion. The small white flowers adorning the card are the flowers that Kore picked before she was taken by Hades to the Underworld; they trail downwards into the earth upon the stairs that all initiates must tread. Beyond that is the cavern of the Mysteries, the hall of initiation, the great pillars of polarity guarding it, and the glittering light of the sun glimpsed in the depths of midnight.

∽ Revelation

Silence and its generative power; mystery; gestating within mystery; initiation; potential within the untouched and untried; needing to see beyond the veil; something hidden; the occult; secrets and secrecy; unspoken understanding; oracles, seers and intuition; listening to inner wisdom instead of received wisdom; channelling the divine; a powerful person representing non-traditional spiritual authority; a call to spirituality; knowing that the answer lies within.

Negatively aspected...
Talking too much; ignoring signs; not trusting one's intuition; relying too much on facts; choosing to remain ignorant; being kept in the dark; revealing truths; speaking about what one knows; refusal to see; difficulty remaining silent; breaking vows and promises of secrecy.

The Empress

The Sumerian cult of Inanna

Before words were given form and the world's cycles charted, mankind sought after me. When the first temples were built and the first rhythms danced, I was there. In the quickening of every womb and the sprouting of every seed I rejoiced and I gave my blessing to the gap between bodies filled by lovers in their ecstasy. I was called Queen of Heaven, warrior, queen who rides beasts, and bride, and it was given to me to love and desire and give fullness. The woman cried out in labour and I steered that boat into the safe harbour. The fields lay bare and the man lacked desire: I walked among them and planted within them the need to create and grow. I crept into the belly of every nervous bride and coiled within there honey-sweet love. I have been called Bride a thousand times, yet I am unmarried and belong to no man; I have been called Mother in the hearts and on the tongues of millions, yet no swelling belly has loosened my girdle nor a babe broken from me in blood. I am the ties that bind you by blood and by love. I am both Mother and Lover, nurture and desire, for it is impossible that one exists without the other, and both are Love. It is my love that draws the king into my arms and my loins that bestow sovereignty upon him; he cannot rule without my blessing, for only from our union can the fields become fertile, women birth their young and households prepare the marriage beds of eager brides. All that once was, is now and ever shall be has come from and through me, for I am the House of Life. I am Venus – the Morning Star and the Evening Star. Set for us a marriage bed, sweet one. Take the part of the king desiring sovereignty, and come to be enthroned within me – I will steer that boat into the safe harbour, and I will decree a sweet fate for you.

~ Mystery

As one of the more archetypal cards of the tarot, the Empress is one of the biggest. She represents parts of human existence so fundamental to us all that the road she walks on is long and wide; thus, the interpretations and imaginings of her are as vast as she is. To some she is a nymph-like maiden, desirable and sensual. To others she is the pregnant mother-to-be, bearing within her all of creation, and the mother with a babe at her breast, or a wife, or a female ruler of her kingdom. All of these presentations have in common her relation to other beings: to a lover, a husband, a child or her subjects; they rely on the union between them and the emotions that create it. She is also deeply tied to femininity, which is not used in the tarot to signify women but instead to signify the conception, gestation, creation and nurturing of life. The powers of the Empress are found in the lives of people of all genders and sexualities, for she is in all acts of conception, gestation, creation and nurture. *Tarot Apokalypsis* reimagining of the Empress presents her as Inanna, the ancient Sumerian goddess of love, fertility, sensuality, art, civilisation and midwifery.

As a goddess whose worship spanned millennia, Inanna had many areas of concern. Like Isis of the ancient Egyptians, her worship was conflated with that of other goddesses, particularly the later Akkadian, Assyrian and Babylonian Ishtar, with whom she became synonymous. The two share a number of themes: both ruled over love and sex; both took the king as a lover to bestow sovereignty upon him; both had a lover who died and was taken to the underworld; both were seen as the planet Venus. However, Ishtar seems to have had a more martial nature than Inanna.

Inanna's earliest manifestation is in the late 4th millennium BCE as the patron deity of Uruk, representing the spirit of the city's central storehouse. Her earliest epithets were *nun*, "princely", *UD/hud*, "morning", *sig*, "evening" and *kur*, "mountain land". [37] Her cuneiform ideogram was a twisted knot of reeds, which represented the doorpost of the storehouse that she watched over (and thus, fertility and plenty). [38] She was portrayed as young, maiden-like and beautiful, wearing elaborate headdresses.

The traditional Empress of the tarot is associated astrologically with the planet Venus, which bears the name of the Roman goddess of love. Venus's Greek counterpart was Aphrodite, and Inanna was often called Aphrodite by the Greeks and was seen as Venus on its journey through the sky. Most of the texts concerning her that have survived are "sacred marriage texts"; scholars believe that the king would have to ritually marry Inanna in order to legitimize his rule. This ritual took place every year on the tenth day of the new year festival of Akitu. In one text, the *Blessing of Shulgi*, the second king of the Third Dynasty of Ur learned from Inanna that he would acquire the powers of kingship as a result of their love-making. Inanna sang to the people before the new king that when he had made love with her she would decree a "sweet fate" for him and give him the shepherdship of the lands. [39]

In another text, the fertility of the land is a direct result of the king's marriage to Inanna; she even describes her genitalia as a high field, wet ground, asking who will "plow it" for her, directly linking her sexual nature to the fertility of the land. Once her marriage to the king is consummated, the text describes the

---

37 Lucy Goodison and Christine Morris, ed. ***Ancient Goddesses***, *p.73*. *University of Wisconsin Press, 1998.*

38 *Thorkild Jacobsen*, ***The Treasures of Darkness: a history of Mesopotamian religion***. *Yale University Press, 1976.*

39 *Samuel Noah Kramer*, ***Sacred Marriage Rite: Aspects of Faith, Myth and Ritual in Ancient Sumer.*** *Indiana University Press, 1970.*

land growing lush with crops around the happy couple. [40] In this way, a mundane human biological function is made sacred: just as the goddess Inanna is fruitful, so is the land; just as she and the king make love and create a prosperous kingdom through their union, so a married couple create a prosperous household.

In these sacred marriage rites, the king takes on the mythical role of Inanna's chosen lover, Dumuzi, a shepherd (note that the king in *The Blessing of Shulgi* is given the "shepherdship" of his lands). It is in these texts that the sensual and loving nature of Inanna shows itself: she is presented as a young, eager lover desirous of uniting with her chosen. Dumuzi is called a "wild bull" and she a "wild cow", the analogy calling upon the rampant nature of the bull and the fertility of the cow. The relationship between the two is not only sexual but deeply loving:

"He will put his hand by my hand,
He will put his heart by my heart,
His putting of hand to hand—its sleep is so refreshing,
His pressing of heart to heart—its pleasure is so sweet." [41]

Inanna also ruled over human love and marriage, and it was believed that her worship brought harmony to a household, joy to life, and industriousness and creativity. [42] Conversely, she was able to prevent fertility, love and tenderness from blessing a home or city that did not pay her the proper respect. [43]

---

40   *"Prosperity in the Palace"*, translated in **Ancient Near Eastern Texts Relating to the Old Testament**, pp. 642–644.

41   *"Love in the Gipar"*, translated in **Ancient Near Eastern Texts Relating to the Old Testament**, p. 638.

42   Hans G. Guterbock, **"A Hurro-Hittite Hymn to Ishtar"** in **Journal of the American Oriental Society**, vol. 103, no. 1 (Jan–Mar., 1983), pp. 155–64.

43   *"The Hymnal Prayer of Enheduanna: The Adoration of Inanna in Ur"*, 51–59, translated in **Ancient Near Eastern Texts Relating to the Old Testament**, p. 580.

Inanna's worship and the performance of her yearly rites tied love, pleasure and sensuality to fecundity, fertility and growth. It is easy to forget that these concepts are inextricably linked: we have a tendency to segregate our image of motherhood from an idea of sensuousness. But for the worshippers of Inanna, and for the Empress of the tarot, there is nothing more attractive than somebody in their creative prime. For this reason, Inanna often sings hymns in which she anoints her genitalia with honey – symbolic of sweetness and enjoyment as well as fertility. [44]

Although Inanna undertakes a sacred marriage to the king, she is not referred to as a wife or spouse as other goddesses of ancient Sumer were. Like the Empress, she is desirable and unattainable, yet all might know her. She is not described as having any children, despite giving fertility to the wombs of women and animals. Inanna's fertility was not seen as literal but as metaphorical: she was given the role of *nu-gig* (midwife) to assist women in childbirth [45] and the role of bringing culture and civilisation to the lands she ruled over. One myth tells how she tricked her father, Enki, into giving her the sacred *me*, aspects of culture, so that she may take them back to Uruk, her home city. These *me* included all aspects of cultural creativity, law, the arts and everything created by the expression of emotion. [46] As *nu-gig*, Inanna "steered the *Gi*-boat through the water" (symbolic of the child being steered through the amniotic fluid of the womb by the

---

44 *"Love in the Gipar"*, 21, translated in **Ancient Near Eastern Texts Relating to the Old Testament**, p. 638.

45 Joan Goodnick-Westenholtz, **"Tamar, Qĕdēšā, Qadištu,, and Sacred Prostitution in Mesopotamia"**, *The Harvard Theological Review*, vol. 82, no. 3 (Jul., 1989), pp. 245–65.

46 *"Inanna and the God of Wisdom"* in **Inanna: Queen of Heaven and Earth, Her Stories and Hymns from Sumer**, by Diane Wolkstein and Samuel Noah Kramer. Harper & Row, 1983, pp. 12–27.

midwife) [47] and as the bringer of the sacred *me* she steered a more literal boat from her father's home to her city to deliver the stolen *me*.

Although she embodies love, sweetness, desire and fertility, the Empress – and Inanna – is not a passive feminine force but an active one. She is a ruler in her own right as well as through her relationship with the Emperor (or king); however, it is she that grants him his power, for she also represents the earth and kingdom that he governs. It is this active creative force of the Empress that is represented by Inanna as a great queen of heaven who is also a goddess of battle: she will fight to protect what she loves. The "Self-laudatory Hymn of Inanna" expresses this power, queenship and creativity, in which Inanna lists the things her father has given her, including lordship, queenship, battle, heaven and earth; she proclaims herself as a queen, a life-giving wild cow and a warrior, [48] reminding us of the Empress' active feminine role in the creation, preservation and perpetuation of the world.

∽ Revelation

Love, sensuality, beauty, sexuality; a lover; active creation; the "Great Goddess"; femininity; the waiting womb; motherhood in the literal and metaphorical sense; nurture and care for others and the self; growth and fertility; seeing projects grow; the creative process; artistry; giving everything to a creative goal; birthing something; uniting creativity and beauty; giving life to something; sweetness; joy in love and relationships; bounty; fecundity; embodying love and compassion.

---

47 Gertrud Farber, **"Another Old Babylonian Childbirth Incantation"** in ***Journal of Near Eastern Studies***, *vol. 43, no. 4 (Oct., 1984), p. 314.*

48 *"Self-Laudatory Hymn of Inanna and Her Omnipotence"*, translated in ***Ancient Near Eastern Texts Relating to the Old Testament***, *pp. 578–9.*

Negatively aspected...
The smothering mother; neglecting to care for the self; being a martyr to the needs of others; creative projects that are blocked or progressing too slowly; lack of creativity; difficulty finding beauty in self or others; infertility in a literal or metaphorical sense.

The Emperor

The Romano-Celtic cult of Taranis

Power is the language of the gods, shown to man in the lightning and thunder, the sun and the rain; this world is the sign of their dominion, the living soul of their active creation and continued preservation. He that rules it with firm hand and strong will stands at the feet of the highest gods and makes a vow of protection to them: not of himself but of all others. This is the mystery of the king, the god on an earthen throne: that by serving he rules. If you wish to walk the mountainous roads of ambition and power, you must face me and know me. I am the Thunderer, the Turning Heavens, the One Who Sees All, the Sun Warrior. Mine is to destroy in the name of that which I serve, to protect and to preserve; the earth that I rule shall not be diminished for my rulership, but increased. I am the great eagle of the heights and the ram of the earth; my arms are the strength of my people and my throne only the authority they give me. To learn my mysteries you must take up the spear and shield of the warrior and make war, for it is in your war cry that you will discover the seat of your power, the drive of your ambition, and the true understanding of what you are. I am the Master of War and my song is the clash of blades upon shield; to those I rule I would give my blood as sacrifice to make the world anew again.

∽ Mystery

Just as the mother goddess of love appears in the tarot among the first cards of the Major Arcana to remind us of her primacy in the world, so too the god of war comes, following his queen, the prime image not only of a warrior but of a father and king. He is dominion, power, authority and rulership; with his strength he both protects that which he rules and destroys that

which would bring harm. As a king he is ambition and the will to power and he represents in each of us our aggressive, active nature that might be directed towards our goals. Without the Emperor, we have no structure or drive.

Most cultures had a father god who ruled the sky and the sun, both of which could nourish the earth or blight it. The father god of Gaul, the Iron Age region of a large swathe of Western Europe inhabited by Celtic tribes, was Taranis, whose cult reaches us through the Roman enemies of the tribes. Julius Caesar wrote that the Celtic Jupiter "possesses the sovereignty of the heavenly powers". [49] In *interpretatio romana* – interpretation of the Gallic religion in terms of Roman religion – the gods of the Gauls were referred to by what the Roman writers saw as their Roman equivalents. We are, however, given the name of a god, Taranis, by Lucan, who states that his altars were "cruel as were those loved by Diana, goddess of the north", a reference to the practice of human sacrifice at shrines of Diana. [50] Given that the name Taranis derives from the Celtic (or Indo-European) root "*taran*", meaning "thunderer" or "thunder", [51] the "Celtic Jupiter" that Caesar wrote of is likely to have been Taranis. As the thunderer, this god may have been a representation of overwhelming force and loud demonstrations of power, just like the Emperor of the tarot.

There is more evidence of this in the Rhineland that in Britain, and there are just seven inscriptions to the god that survive. [52] However, in the later *Berne Scholia*, he is called "master of

---

49 Julius Caesar, **Gallic War** 6.17, trans. W. A. McDevitte and W. S. Bohn, 1869. Online at Perseus Digital Library: http://www.perseus.tufts.edu/hopper/

50 Lucan, **The Pharsalia**, 1.444–6, trans. Sir Edward Ridley, 1905. Online at Perseus Digital Library.

51 J. A. MacCullough, **The Religion of the Ancient Celts**, p. 30. T&T Clark, 1911.

52 Ronald Hutton, **The Pagan Religions of the Ancient British Isles: Their Nature and Legacy**, p. 156; 209–10. Blackwell Publishers, 1998.

war"; [53] as such, Taranis would have played a significant role in the power and position of a society at war with Rome, reminding us that the Emperor of the tarot is concerned with the gaining and maintaining of positions of power, not for their own sake but in order to better perform his duties.

Several examples of a bearded god accompanied by a six- or eight-spoked wheel have been identified as Taranis. In some of these images he holds a thunderbolt. The thunderbolt is associated with fire, giving Taranis a fiery nature. The wheel was a symbol of the sky throughout the Romano-Celtic world, representing the sun [54] or the turning of the heavens. [55] When a wheel brooch was dug up in Suffolk with a statuette of an eagle, the symbol of Jupiter, it was clear that this was Jupiter-Taranis. [56] Further, an army officer dedicated an altar to Taranis in which he paired him with Jupiter, and several similar altars dedicated to Jupiter and featuring wheels come from forts on Hadrian's Wall. [57] The apparent prevalence of Taranis-Jupiter among military men demonstrates that he was a forceful and powerful deity of dominion and rulership. His wheel even appears as a frequent design on Gallic army helmets, further associating him with warriors. [58] There is also suggestion that Taranis was the same personality as the Anglo-Saxon Thunor (Norse Thor), [59] another god of thunder and war, who was also known for hallowing oaths and protecting humans.

---

53 *The Berne Scholia*, online at http://www.chronarchy.com/esus/lucan-commentaries.html

54 M. J. Green, *Sun Gods of Ancient Europe*, pp. 86–106. Batsford, 1991.

55 Ronald Hutton, *The Pagan Religions of the Ancient British Isles*, p. 210.

56 *Ibid*, p. 211.

57 Malcolm Todd, ed. *A Companion to Roman Britain*, p. 214. Blackwell Publishing, 2004.

58 Peter Wilcox and Angus McBride, *Rome's Enemies: Gallic and British Celts*, p. 11. Osprey, 1995.

59 Ronald Hutton, *The Pagan Religions of the Ancient British Isles*, p. 269.

The practice of dedicating altars to a deity is a distinctly Roman one, so we might assume that Taranis was worshipped in a similar fashion to Jupiter. We are left with an image of a strong, powerful warrior with dominion over the life-giving and sometimes earth-parching sun and the lofty heavens and all their movements; like the Emperor of the tarot, he is a father and a king, representing the active, masculine qualities that complement the passive, feminine essence of the Empress. In the card image he holds his spear aloft and rests his hand on the sun wheel by his side; behind him, a ram represents his masculine qualities and above him an eagle symbolises his rulership. He wears the winged helmet that the Gauls were famed for and the warrior's woad. He is ready for war.

⁓ Revelation

Authority and power; being in a respected position; being in a position to have influence over others; dominion and rulership; owning one's power; typically masculine traits; aggression as a means to an end; an active approach to a situation; ambition and goals; parenthood, specifically fatherhood; a declaration of ownership, rulership or power; responsibility.

Negatively aspected…
Conflict for conflict's sake or to undermine the power, authority or dominion of another; refusing to take responsibility; feeling uncomfortable in a position of influence; hiding from one's duties; power used for unscrupulous ends; a destructive influence.

The Hierophant
Tibetan Buddhism and the Dalai Lama

The sacred is given to man as an open book to be read, but a teacher is required to teach the art of reading. No student learns alone: even the rocks, the rivers and trees may impart their wisdom to those with ears and an eager heart. Man is gifted with a desire to know and build for himself a fort of wisdom, yet he must first learn that there is nothing new on this earth and that all revelations and invention rest on the foundations of history. That which I teach has been spoken by countless guides across the ages; it has reached the ears and touched the hearts of those who have long-since passed on. Though the teachers and students have gone, the song still remains. I am the singer of that song and you are the listener: follow my mysteries and you will find the foundation upon which you may build your journey. Pay heed to my words and you will come to know the strictures and rituals by which you are bound in order to be set free. Watch the gestures of my lesson and you will come to understand the discipline required so that the sacred may be revealed to you. For these are mysteries and secrets, though they are dressed in the appearance of the mundane: do not think that they will be given to you without devotion and faith. I am your Teacher and your Test; I am the Revealer of Wisdom and the Concealment in plain sight. The fickle may hear my words without listening to the lesson, may see my rituals without seeing their meaning. But come to know me as the channel through which the divine speaks, understand the establishment of wisdom as truth, and you shall truly be a seeker in the mysteries of the sacred.

☙ Mystery

All seekers need a teacher. It is through a teacher that the mysteries are revealed, guidance given, and the established wisdom of the ages passed on to the newest person to walk that path. The teacher does not always take the form of a person – it may also be private research, nature or a sacred text, for instance. Through the established wisdom given to us, we learn what does and does not work, what is beneficial and harmful, hopefully avoiding the mistakes of history. As such, the Hierophant not only represents a teacher or a guide, somebody to whom we listen as a source of wisdom, but all forms of established wisdom – books, sacred texts, conventions, societal mores and values, traditions and history. It represents the body of knowledge available to us. To some, established knowledge and tradition are restrictive; however, even the newest ideas cannot be born without a foundation of what has gone before. The Hierophant also represents the process by which the sacred is revealed – the act of teaching and guiding.

Although there are a great many teachers of traditional wisdom and the sacred throughout the ages and across the world, here we see a child Dalai Lama conversing with two monks; behind him are two of his previous incarnations. The auras around each signify a chakra, with the yellow of the solar plexus chakra around the living Dalai Lama and the green of the heart chakra and the white of the crown chakra around each previous incarnation respectively.

The Dalai Lama signifies a title and office given to one senior monk in the Tibetan Buddhist tradition; it is not a personal name given to an individual. The Dalai Lama is also a *tulku*, a custodian of a lineage of teachings who is trained in that lineage from a young age. The title comes from the Mongolian word for "ocean", *dalai*, and the Tibetan word for "wisdom", *lama*, so the Dalai Lama is the Ocean of Wisdom. He is the reincarnation of all the previous Dalai Lamas before him, back to the first – Gendun Drüppa – from the 14th century. [60] The first Dalai Lama was, in turn, the reincarnation of Avalokiteshvara, or Chenrezig, the bodhisattva of compassion; [61] thus, every Dalai Lama is an earthly manifestation of this bodhisattva. This repeated reincarnation of a spiritual being serves as a reminder of the revelation of the sacred: the soul of the Dalai Lama is repeatedly reborn and revealed so that he may continue his work and teaching. This reincarnation also ensures an unbroken lineage and tradition of teaching and reminds us of the spiritual connection we create between ourselves and past teachers and seekers when we dedicate ourselves to a path. The fourteenth Dalai Lama, Tenzin Gyatso, reflects on his feelings about the credibility of his reincarnations:

"I am often asked whether I truly believe this. The answer is not simple to give. But […] when I consider my experiences during this present life, and given my Buddhist beliefs, I have no difficulty accepting that I am spiritually connected both to the thirteen previous Dalai Lamas, to Chenrezig and to the Buddha himself." [62]

Although it is not only the Dalai Lama that is a reincarnation of a previous lama (there are many other "lineages" of reincarnation in Tibetan Buddhism, the first of which began in the 12th century), [63] it is that of the Dalai Lama that is most well known. The process by which the next reincarnation of the Dalai Lama

---

60   *Geoffrey Samuel,* **Introducing Tibetan Buddhism**, *p. 146. Routledge, 2012.*

61   *His Holiness the Dalai Lama,* **Freedom in Exile: The Autobiography of the Dalai Lama**, *p. xiii. HarperCollins Publishers, 1990.*

62   *His Holiness the Dalai Lama,* **Freedom in Exile: The Autobiography of the Dalai Lama** *p. 11.*

63   *Geoffrey Samuel,* **Introducing Tibetan Buddhism**, *p. 145.*

is found is a form of revelation of the sacred and undertaken in stages. At death, the Dalai Lama will often give some indication as to where he will be reborn; this may be through a letter, through speaking, or through the direction in which his head falls after death. Senior lamas may visit Lhamo La-tso, a lake that, according to tradition, will often give an indication through a vision or sign as to the direction in which they should search. The guardian spirit of this lake was said to have promised the first Dalai Lama in a vision that she would protect his reincarnation lineage. [64] Other lamas may also receive visions and delegations of lamas and government officials will be sent out to the area that has been indicated. When they have a shortlist of candidates, they may visit them to ascertain their character and look for any further signs – such as the child recognising somebody known to the previous Dalai Lama – and present a series of tests. Once the reincarnation is revealed, the child begins his re-learning of the lineage's teachings. In the same way, there are many ways and stages by which wisdom and the sacred may be revealed to us.

The role of the lama in Tibetan Buddhism – as with clergy from all religions – is also one of mediation between mankind and the sacred. Some have suggested that the baseline of the development of Tibetan Buddhism was the ability of its clergy to offer mediation with the spirit world. Further, the role of the Dalai Lama is a governmental, political one: the clergy of many religions usually have an influence on everyday life despite their links with the sacred. [65]

In Tibetan Buddhism, the teaching of yogic practices and the sutras is vitally important to all monks and nuns; even lay prac-

---

64 Thomas **Laird, The Story of Tibet: Conversations with the Dalai Lama**, p. 265. Grove Press, 2006

65 Geoffrey Samuel, **Introducing Tibetan Buddhism**, p. 14.

titioners learn some of the practices and engage with the wisdom of the tradition beyond simple religious observance. The practice of Tantra, a system of esoteric or secret teachings in which the teacher plays a crucial role, is a staple of Tibetan Buddhism. The term means "thread", emphasising the lineage of teaching that passes down from teacher to student. In this case, the lama not only teaches but also ensures that the teaching is passed on correctly and that the lineage is protected. This importance of a good teacher is emphasised by the *Candavyuha Sutra* when it states "Please realize that the method for all bodhisattvas to attain omniscient wisdom unquestionably results from following a true spiritual teacher." [66]

∼ Revelation

Spiritual dedication; religious service; dedication to a monastic life or spiritual practice; discipline; regimenting one's spiritual life to encourage discipline; a teacher or guide; seeking a teacher; learning from somebody with experience; mediation; traditional and established spiritual practices or religions; ritual; faith; manifesting the sacred in one's everyday life; learning from established wisdom.

Negatively aspected...
Being held back by tradition and custom; devotion through fear; being trapped in a material mind-set; needing advice but finding nobody willing to help; a lack of faith or loyalty; a teacher or figure of authority using their power poorly.

---

[66] Erik Pema Kunsan, ***A Tibetan Buddhist Companion***, p. 31. Shambhala, 2003.

The Lovers

The Hieros Gamos – 'sacred marriage'

In the beginning we were One, unified and everything, undifferentiated and containing all. The stars were our bodies and souls, and our love was boundless. Yet love became yearning and gave way to reflection and desire to know; the heavens burst and let forth the rain from the firmament, and this was our love and our pain, our separation and our joy. We became One and Not One, dark and light, moon and sun, matter and spirit, man and the divine. There we found the sweetest bliss, for our yearning found manifestation: we have journeyed through the aeons and the stars to return to each other. I am that which is above, and you are below. I am the calling you hear pulling you towards the heights, and you are that which draws me near. Oh, beloved one, know that you are born from the highest starfire, unified and one; know that to reunite with me is your only quest. The mysteries of the bridal chamber are the only truth. Yet a little of the fire that you seek – my fire – can be found in other seekers of the mystical marriage: in them I am found. Love is all, and yearning, for they guide you on the path to reunion. Open yourself to love – of others, of the universe, of life – and you shall come to die in my arms at the last.

≈ Mystery

The mystical and magical universe functions on the basis of duality, yet it does not require that the universe or the divine be dual in nature. Instead, the duality of our world – creation and destruction, masculine and feminine, active and passive, mundane and divine – is created from unity. The Lovers card tells us that, once, all was One, but in order for manifestation to occur it must become two – equal but opposite. One was divided for the sake of creation and that creation now yearns pas-

sionately for reunion with its origins. As the name of the card suggests, this is a card of love, but it does not explore only the relationship between people; rather, it shows the relationship between the divine and the mundane, man and god, the "masculine" and "feminine" within each person, between opposite parts of the self, as they strive for union with their complement. This relationship has had a profound expression in many different religious and spiritual traditions, so it is fitting that the card image encompasses all of them.

Primarily, the symbolism of the card is that of masculine and feminine, red and white, mundane and divine. Although here a male figure is used to represent typically masculine traits and a female figure typically feminine traits, this too is only a symbol: it does not reflect a notion of gender roles. We are all both the male and female figure. This becomes even clearer when we examine the alchemical symbolism in the card image.

The goal of the alchemist (see *Temperance* for further discussion) is to perform a chemical process of physical transmutation that reflects a spiritual transformation through which the different aspects of the self – symbolised as male and female – are united and through their unity produce the philosopher's stone – wisdom and spiritual enlightenment (or, immortality). These two sides of the self are seen as the Red King / Sun King – the active, aggressive self – and the White Queen / Moon Queen – the passive, creative self. The union is represented as a sacred marriage between these figures, after which they will undergo further transformation until they are, finally, not just two separate figures united in marriage but one figure possessing all the parts of both. [67] Their union is known as *hieros gamos* – sacred marriage. Greek and Roman mythology might also

---

67 Alexander Roob ed. *The Hermetic Museum: Alchemy and Mysticism*, pp. 438-55. Köln: Taschen, 2001.

be recognised in this sacred marriage of opposites, in that the god of war – Ares/Mars – and the goddess of love – Aphrodite/Venus – were lovers. It is interesting to note that the Empress is astrologically associated with Venus and the Emperor with Aries, which is ruled by Mars, making the *hieros gamos* of the Lovers card their wedding.

This sacred marriage is also found in Buddhism, in the form of the *yab-yum* ("father-mother"), an image of the masculine – wisdom – in sexual congress with the feminine – compassion. In Hinduism this same image is seen as Shiva and Shakti, particularly in Panchamakara Tantra, in which sexual union between man and woman is symbolic of the union of spirit and matter. Here, the couple become Shiva and Shakti, thus transforming their physical union into a spiritual one. [68] In Taoism, the forces represented in the *yab-yum* figure by the masculine Shiva and the feminine Shakti are illustrated by the yin yang symbol, in which the active and the passive complement each other. Thus, it can be said that "[t]he esoteric function of sexual love is the resolution of the complementary intelligences of Heaven and Earth". [69] The union between masculine and feminine can also be found in the sacred marriage of the king to the goddess Inanna/Ishtar in ancient Mesopotamia (see *The Empress*). This union represented the blessings of the gods on the rulership of the king, as well as the union of the divine and the human. In ancient Greece, a priestess annually "married" Dionysus in the form of a ceremonial king during the Anthesteria. [70]

---

68 Georg Feuerstein, **Tantra: The Path of Ecstasy**, p. 80. Massachusetts: Shambhala Publications, Inc., 1998.

69 Nik Douglas and Penny Slinger, **Sexual Secrets: the Alchemy of Ecstasy**, p. 46. Vermont: Destiny Books, 2000.

70 Rosemarie Taylor-Perry, **The God Who Comes: Dionysian Mysteries Revisited**, p. 71. New York: Algora, 2003.

Seeing the divine as one's loving spouse is well known in many traditions. The Valentinian Gnostics (see *The World*) described the union between a believer and their heavenly counterpart, the light, in terms of a wedding [71] and it is also suggested that initiation into the Valentinian mysteries involved the preparation of a bridal chamber. [72] In Vodou, a devotee may choose to marry a *lwa* – spirit – in a ceremony very similar to the Catholic rite. The *lwa* will appear in possession in one of the priest/esses, and another priest/ess will perform the wedding ceremony. The couple will both give vows, a marriage contract will be signed and the guests will enjoy a wedding feast. Typically, a Vodou practitioner who marries a spirit will vow a certain number of nights each month to that spirit, during which they will sleep in a specially prepared bed, make special offerings, and eschew the company of human lovers or spouses. In return, the practitioner will be given special blessings and particularly insightful dreams from that spirit. [73]

Similarly, a great number of mystics over the centuries have written about their mystical experiences of union with God using sexual or bridal symbolism and language. In his mystical poem, *Dark Night of the Soul*, St John of the Cross describes himself and God as "lover and loved one", using imagery such as the caressing of lovers and post-coital bliss to describe union with God. [74]

The motif of marrying a divine power is so prevalent throughout human history that it must be acknowledged as one of the

---

71   Irenaeus, **Against Heresies** *1:13:3*.

72   Gerhard Wehr, **The Mystical Marriage: Symbol and Meaning of the Human Experience**, trans. Jill Sutcliffe, p. 51. Northamptonshire: Aquarian Press, 1990.

73   Maya Deren, **Divine Horsemen: Living Gods of Haiti**, pp. 263–70. New York: McPhersom & Company, 2004.

74   St John of the Cross, **The Poems of St John of the Cross,** trans. John Frederik Nims, pp. 19–21. New York: Grove Press Inc., 1968.

driving forces behind all mystical endeavours. Our union with our chosen god(s) is actually a *re*union, for we once were part of the Oneness that we now seek. It can also be seen that our union with other human beings is another manifestation of this yearning for reunion, for in each of us there is a spark of that Oneness, the divine, from whence we came.

～ Revelation

Love; positive relationships of all kinds; partnership; duality; opposites coming together to one end; uniting two different aspects of something; drawing things together; union and reunion; marriage; spiritual oneness; spiritual marriage; the acknowledgement of the divine in another; complementary forces.

Negatively aspected…
Absence makes the heart grow fonder; separation as an excuse for sweet reunion; a relationship in difficulty; a need for separation; unrequited love; difficulty reconciling two different parts of one's life.

The Chariot

The Roman Triumph, Imperial cult and apotheosis of heroes

Call my name in triumph, sing my praises in victory, give sacrifice only unto me, and I shall show you the mysteries of the triumphant road. I am winged apotheosis, pulling your soul from dirt into the shining heavens, there to place you as an immortal star, unconquered and unrivalled. I am the song of your name that lives long after the singer has gone, the rhyme of your deeds to last through the ages. I am the overcoming and the rising, the procession of the soul to greatness and the achievement of your greatest ambitions. Know this: that the heavens were not created for the humble and mediocre and only greatness can ensure your immortality. What man is mortal whose name is remembered? What woman is not a goddess whose deeds are still spoken of? Yet do not mistake me: this is not the aggrandisement of the self alone, for this is the only service of the ego to the world. In your triumph you shall show to others the possibility of greatness, bringing into their reach the highest of goals; your virtue shall be enshrined in the holy words of the poets and inspire the journey to godhood of those who come long after you are gone. Victory, Imperator, and the mantle of the gods!

❧ Mystery

The Imperial cult, in which a ruler became deified and offerings given to his *genius* (spirit), is a reminder of the ability of human beings to become divine. It is this quest for divinity and immortality through godhood that is represented by the Chariot, for it is the ultimate quest. It found manifestation not only in the Imperial cult of Rome but also in the hero cult of ancient Greece. Through these cults, the rulers of empires and men and women who performed great deeds were immortalised by their people and those who came after, given cult and petitioned as gods. The Chariot

represents a journey and quest, but is also concerned with our triumphs, achievements and reputation. Thus, while the quest of this card can be a spiritual one, it can also be the quest for remembrance long after we have gone, a quest for greatness.

The card image shows a great Triumph, a parade during which the achievements of a general or war leader were showcased. The Triumph displayed the details of the general's successful war or campaign in painted panels, [75] as well as by displaying the spoils of war and high-ranking captive enemies. A great number of rulers and generals had Triumphs, with some celebrating several (Julius Caesar had five). These Triumphs were so grandiose and influential that they "provided a model for the celebration of military success for centuries. Through the last two millennia, there has been hardly a monarch, dynast, or autocrat in the West who has not looked back to Rome for a lesson in how to mark victory in war and to assert his own personal power". [76] The motif of the Roman Triumph acts as a reminder of the capacity for our achievements to allow us to be remembered beyond death; it is also a symbol of the investiture of value in the ego and the concept of self, as well as its glorification, all of which can be found in the meaning of the Chariot.

The figure of Victory stands behind the lauded general in the Triumph, holding aloft the laurel wreath of victory and divinity. It was Victoria, the Roman goddess of victory, who bequeathed success in war. She was particularly favoured in Rome and had several temples, appearing frequently on Roman coins, often on those commemorating successful war leaders. [77]

---

75   *Clifford Ando*, **Imperial Ideology and Provincial Loyalty**, *pp. 253–9. University of California Press, 2000.*

76   *Mary Beard*, **The Roman Triumph**, *p. 2. The Belknap Press of Harvard University Press, 2007.*

77   **Ibid**., *pp. 19–20.*

The achievements of a Roman ruler might lead to him becoming deified as a state god, in an example of an almost immediate journey to the divine. The first ruler to be given this honour was Julius Caesar, whose apotheosis (elevation to divine status) took place in three phases. After the battle of Thapsus in 46 BCE, the Senate decreed him a chariot and statue – on which an inscription stated that he was a demigod – on the Capitol. After the battle of Munda in 45 BCE, a statue of him was placed in the temple of Quirinus bearing an inscription declaring him an "unconquered god". Finally, he was decreed as a state divinity, given the cult name Divus Julius, and given a state priest, temple and sacred couch upon which his sacred image would be placed. [78] Caesar's apotheosis possibly helped perpetuate the nascent Imperial cult in Rome. In 30 BCE, the Senate decreed that the *genius* of Octavian, Caesar's heir, would be given libation at every banquet. Later, the household offerings to the Lares became linked with libations to the Emperor, with household altars being dedicated to the Lares Augusti (Augustus was Octavian's name as Emperor). [79] The Imperial cult continued, with a number of inscriptions attesting to the placing of an image of the current Emperor in a temple alongside images of the gods [80] and an explicit command by Augustus that temples should be built to him and sacrifices offered to him as a god. [81] This deification, while living, of the Emperor also served to incarnate deified virtues – previously manifested in a deity – in the ruler. [82] This reminds us that the Chariot gives heightened expression to ideals and ambitions, as well as suggest-

---

78   Ittai Gradel, ***Emperor Worship and Roman Religion***, p. 55. Oxford University Press, 2002.

79   Allen Brent, ***The Imperial Cult and the Development of Church Order***, p. 62. Brill, 1999.

80   Duncan Fishwick, ***The Imperial Cult in the Latin West***, vol. II, p. 540. E. J. Brill, 1991.

81   ***Ibid.***, p. 502.

82   Allen Brent, ***The Imperial Cult and the Development of Church Order***, p. 64.

ing that human beings can become expressions of that which is considered sacred.

The goal of immortality through achievement and the striving for godhead can also be seen in the Greek cult of heroes. Men and women who performed great deeds in life might be heroised, in most cases after death, and given cult, which included a site of worship and sacrifice. While war dead were often given a hero cult, individuals could be given cult, such as Tlepolemos on Rhodes, who received an athletic contest "like a god", Alkmaion on Aegina, who had a sanctuary of prophecy, and Pelops at Olympia, who received blood sacrifices and had an altar and athletic contests. [83] Athletes could also be heroised and given cult, both before and after death. [84] For such heroes, immortality could also be gained through renown and reputation, so the composition of tales and songs about their deeds could be a stairway to the gods. Thus we are reminded that in the Chariot card it is the showing of our achievements and the cultivation of the concept of the self as great in the eyes of others that leads to progress, victory and a continual journey of improvement.

∽ Revelation

Victory and success; achievement; ambition; a journey or quest; the road to discovery or greatness; swift movement; progress towards a goal; everything is part of the plan towards achievement; achieving greatness; astounding deeds; reputation and renown; a spiritual journey towards the divine.

Negatively aspected…
Slow progress or blocked progress; a journey without a goal; an uncertain path; failure; not achieving something desired.

---

83 Bruno Currie, ***Pindar and the Cult of Heroes***, pp. 47–48. Oxford University Press, 2010.
84 ***Ibid.***, pp.120–23.

Strength
Durgā Pūjā

There are those that will tell you the world is love and beauty: these are fools and liars. The world is a great battlefield, filled with struggle and the spilling of blood: this is the nourishment of the earth. Yet in this vast arena of conflict, you forget that the final battlefield is yourself. I am the Bringer of Victory over demons, the Rider of Lions, Mistress of Power and the Invincible Warrior. Make offerings of flowers and blood to me and I shall open my arms bedecked with weaponry to take you into my bosom as my child. Dance not for me, but show me your battles; give me your fighting in all your strength of will. Listen to my war cry, and you shall understand the light of the fires within that blaze higher at the sound of the clashing of swords: it is bloodlust, lifelust and a lust to overcome. This overcoming is the greatest mystery and the longest journey: it is the road that never ends. There is no highest, no completion, only greater challenges. I, Power Awakened, demand your knowing of your raw power, your embodiment of that dynamic force that creates the world, your acceptance of the warrior's austere road of self-will and inner strength. Sing banner songs for me and raise to me spears: cry out my name in the midst of battle, and I shall cry out within you as the fire that burns in your soul.

∼ Mystery

Following on from the victorious, fast-moving Chariot, Strength continues the theme of power and overcoming. However, where the charioteer drove the beasts that pulled his chariot here the beast is the chariot, demonstrating a more intimate connection between the rider and her raw, ferocious power. Strength seeks a way to become one with the wild, primal force, channelling it to a purpose. Here is the card of warriors

and the empowered, of the overcoming of the baser instincts and that which holds us back.

In India, it is the goddess Durgā who represents the strength of will, power and energy that is required to overcome. She is given a large and widespread festival, Durgā Pūjā, every autumn during the first nine days of the waxing moon of the month of Asvin. For this festival, devotees purchase or donate to the creation of beautiful, brightly coloured clay images of Durgā, recreating her most famous myth, attended by a variety of other deities. Into these statues Durgā will be called to reside for the duration of the Durgā Puja, and once installed she will be given offerings, worshipped with song and praises, and petitioned. At the end of the festival, these statues will be deposited into a sacred body of water such as the Ganges, there to return to their primal state as unformed clay. The scene depicted by these clay images is of Durgā slaying the buffalo demon Mahiṣa in battle, a story that is told in several versions but most famously in the *Devī Māhātmya* of the *Markaṇḍeya Purāṇa*, composed in Sanskrit around 400–500 CE. In this myth, Durgā comes forth from the light created by the anger of the gods upon being threatened by a great demonic army led by Mahiṣa, who could not be killed by any man. Durgā thus represents the ferocity of the need to fight and be triumphant over evil and the action required to do so. When she had come into being, the gods armed her with various weapons sacred to them. [85] That she is given her weapons by the gods demonstrates her divine strength and power: the gods "assumed a subordinate position and she became a supreme powerhouse". [86] As she was created by the active energy of the gods, Durgā is an embodiment of śakti,

---

85 Thomas B. Coburn trans., **Devi Mahatmya** 2.19-2.30, p. 41, **Encountering the Goddess: A Translation of the Devī Māhātmya and a Study of its Interpretation.** State University of New York Press, 1991.

86 Sudha Chandola, **Entranced by the Goddess: Folklore in North Indian Religion,** p. 18. Heart of Albion Press, 2007.

the primordial cosmic energy of dynamic force that moves the universe. [87] As the śakti force sent out and surrendered by the gods in her creation, Durgā is also the force that recreates the cosmos. Thus, in Durgā Pūjā, devotees "awaken the Devi from her latent presence within the constituent elements (e.g., earth, water, and life) of Nature into active and expansive, yet accessible, manifestations". [88] She is power awakened and made manifest. One of the functions of the Durgā Pūjā is empowerment on a personal and communal level and the orchestration of the movement of feminine power and energy to a creative pursuit.

Durgā is clearly defined as a warrioress from the moment of her creation. One tale of her origin says that she emerged from Parvati when she shed her outer skin, which took on an identity of its own as a warrior goddess. [89] In many of the myths, Durgā's male opponents discounted her prowess in battle, saying that, as a woman, she was too fragile for anything but marriage; they made her offers of marriage in order to subdue her. In one instance, she replied by saying that she would not marry anybody that could not defeat her in battle; in another, she replied by telling her opponent the ways in which she would defeat him on the battlefield. The would-be suitors attempted to defeat her in battle and were destroyed. In the context of the ancient Hindu world, in which the gender roles afforded to men and women put women in the domestic, private realm and men in the political, public realm, this represents the refusal to be subdued or have one's power removed by others.

---

87   Reema Datta and Lisa Lowitz, **Sacred Sanskrit Words**, *p. 111. Stonebridge Press, 2005.*

88   *Hilary Rodrigues,* **Ritual Worship of the Great Goddess: The Liturgy of the Durgā Pūjā with Interpretations**, *p. 12. State University of New York Press, 2003.*

89   *David R. Kinsley,* **Hindu Goddesses: Visions of the Divine Feminine in the Hindu Religious Tradition**, *p. 96. University of California Press, 1998.*

Durgā's destruction of the demon Mahiṣa as the focal image for Durgā Pūjā tells us that the most obvious function of this festival is to worship a deity of empowerment. Her lion mount, given to her by the gods at her creation, is a symbol of her *śakti* power, the active principles of creation and ferocity. She does not seek to tame it or control it but instead rides it, both her and the beast battling together. Devotees see in Durgā a "pure (*sattva*) and awesome power (*śakti*) that crushes unrighteousness (*adharma*), ignorance, and egotism, symbolised by the dark (*tamas*) buffalo form of the demon Mahiṣa". [90] The demon is also symbolic of other enemies, such as those created by political issues and the demands of the modern world. In modern India, she is "a natural icon for emerging Indian feminism". [91] During the time of the British Raj in Bengal, she also became identified with the Indian independence movement, becoming a symbol of India overcoming its oppressors. [92] This is a powerful, fierce, protective goddess who is called upon to grant victory, destroy evil and bless those who would rise up in triumph over adversity.

In the liturgy of Durgā Pūjā, Durgā is given many praises and epithets. She is called "giver of victory and killer of enemies", "suppressor of the arrogance of demons", "dread incarnate" and "the remover of fears arising from all quarters". [93] The ritual praises her as having "enormous strength/might born of the divine energy of the gods". [94] Even her name reminds us of the inner strength and active power that she embodies, coming

---

90 Hilary Rodrigues, ***Ritual Worship of the Great Goddess: The Liturgy of the Durgā Pūjā with Interpretations,*** *p. 265.*

91 June McDaniel, ***Offering Flowers, Feeding Skulls: Popular Goddess Worship in West Bengal***, *p. 222. Oxford University Press, 2004.*

92 ***Ibid.***, *p. 181.*

93 Hilary Rodrigues, ***Ritual Worship of the Great Goddess: The Liturgy of the Durgā Pūjā with Interpretations,*** *p. 164–6; 192.*

94 ***Ibid.***, *p. 167.*

from the Sanskrit for "fort", [95] giving rise to epithets such as "invincible". In the card image her hair is long and wild, a reference to East Javanese period statues (10th–15th century) that show Durgā in this manner (a feature not often found in depictions of Indian goddesses). [96] The wild hair is associated with power and wildness, an inner strength that can intimidate and protect. During Durgā Pūjā, the inner power of every devotee is called up and given strength: the battles of the world are to be found around every corner, and Durgā blesses her warriors with an understanding of how to channel their ferocity and raw energy towards victory.

∼ Revelation

Strength and inner strength; inner resources; power and its manifestation towards a goal; wildness and ferocity; fighting for something; striving and overcoming; learning to channel one's raw power and energy; identifying one's strengths; a process of gaining mastery over the self; taming the dangerous aspects of one's self.

Negatively aspected…
Weakness and fear; not being able to understand or identify one's power and strengths; giving in and giving up; being controlled by one's weaknesses and fears; allowing one's inner demons to take over.

---

95 Pushpenda Kumari, **Sakti Cult in Ancient India,** *p. 120*. Bharatiya Publishing House, 1974.

96 Santiko Hariani, "**The Goddess Durga in the East-Javanese Period**", *p. 211*, in **AFS**, *vol. 56, 209–226*.

The Hermit

Inuit shamanism: the angakkoq

I see your eyes, and see that you are called to the roads beyond this world, to the night roads. You carry the flame of yearning, but you desire darkness. This is the answer your soul has been looking for, but you did not discover it: it was already seeded in your heart. In the realm of the Other you might plant the seeds of wisdom; in the realms of the ancestors and the spirits you might battle with Fear and Self, thereby to gain the hard-won prize of illumination. O seeker, I know you: you hear the call of the pieces of your soul torn away, pulling you to them. This is the only path that can be taken, for all are journeys to the enlightenment of self. Some say, Seeker, travel only the light roads of the heavens; some say, Seeker, take the road of the underworld. But these roads take you in the same direction: within. Listen to my song: know that I say this because I have travelled these roads; I have descended and ascended, have faced the fears in the darkness and defeated them, have been destroyed and reborn. I carry the fires of hell and the blazing stars in one place, and it is by virtue of the darkness that they shine so brightly, so others may know their way by them. I am the mystery of the Pole Star, the guiding light, the drumbeat of the initiation leading your way in the darkness; I am wisdom won through battle and strife; I am the journey within.

❦ Mystery

Beneath the heavenly lightshow of the Northern Lights, surrounded by the stark beauty of the Arctic, an *angakkoq* – Inuit shaman – drums to call forth the spirits of the land and her helping spirits. She has undergone a great many terrible trials, including her own death, to gain the wisdom that she uses to serve her community. Although she remains "Other", she is intimately

linked to her community and serves it with all her power and spiritual wisdom. In the darkest of times, she is the last resort, shining a light to bring her people back from the darkness.

The Hermit, as suggested by her name, may withdraw herself from society or community in order to, in the ensuing silence, find a greater understanding of the Other, whether that is the spirit world, the soul, nature or the inner processes of spiritual transformation. However, it is vitally important for the Hermit to return to her people, bringing them the gift of her wisdom and spiritual power.

Untouched by Christianity until the 18th century, the different peoples designated by the term "Inuit" possess a very recent oral history of shamanic practice. An Inuit shaman is an *angakkoq* (meaning "visionary and dreamer", [97] plural *angakkut*), and can be male or female. The call to become an *angakkoq* often comes in dreams [98] and thereafter a series of encounters that initiate the person as an *angakkoq* are undertaken. These initiations share similar themes, such as those of a female *angakkoq* called Teemiartissaq, who experienced "…searching for encounters with spirits in remote areas, the mountain and the grave site, receiving teaching from possible helping spirits, losing consciousness through interaction with the spirits, dreaming a travel to the underworld and meeting her dead brother, interacting with ghosts, facing fear of the spirits and being devoured and returning to life naked". [99] A common feature of all *angakkoq* initiation and training is that "…the *angakkoq* has to

---

[97] Mariko Namba Walter and Eva Jane Neumann Fridman eds. ***Shamanism: An Encyclopedia of World Beliefs, Practices and Culture***, p. 297. ABC-CLIO Inc., 2004.

[98] Angela Sumegi, ***Dreamworlds of Shamanism and Tibetan Buddhism***, pp. 28–30. State University of New York Press, 2008.

[99] Merete Demant Jackobsen, ***Shamanism: Traditional and Contemporary Approaches to the Mastery of Spirits and Healing***, pp. 57–8. Berghahn Books, 1999.

encounter spirits, overcome his fear and turn them into helping spirits, be devoured and rise again". [100] This is the same process by which the Hermit descends into the underworld – a realm of fear and uncertainty – to confront the darkness that resides within the soul of every human being and face their fear of it, dying to the world and themselves so they may be reborn and bring with them the wisdom that overcoming fear creates. It is for this reason that the *angakkut* are seen as "healed healers" or "wounded healers": they are those who have cured themselves of their fear and spiritual ignorance and in the process discovered the wisdom that they use to cure and guide others. [101]

An *angakkoq* possesses *qaumaniq*, "enlightenment", the capacity to see souls and spirits and to see through bodies, houses and the landscape to identify the causes of illness or other problems. Light plays an important role in this, as "…when a person becomes an *angakok*, a light covers his body. […] The stronger the light is within him, the deeper and further away he can see, and the greater is his supernatural power". [102] Despite this, it is suggested that the stark cold and darkness of a Greenland winter creates the shamanic attitude:

"But the cold and the darkness is what makes us think. And when the great darkness covers the land many hidden things are revealed and then the thoughts of human beings go along pathless ways." [103]

---

100 **Ibid.**

101 Andrei A. Znamenski, **The Beauty of the Primitive: Shamanism and the Western Imagination**, *p. 119. Oxford University Press, 2007.*

102 F Boas, p. 133, "**Second Report on the Eskimo of Baffin Land and Hudson Bay. From Notes Collected by Captain George Comer, Captain James S. Mutch, and Rev. E. J. Peck**" in Bulletin of the American Museum of Natural History *vol. 15, no. 2, pp. 371–570.*

103 An East Greenlandic man, quoted in Merete Demant Jackobsen, **Shamanism: Traditional and Contemporary Approaches to the Mastery of Spirits and Healing**, *p. 45.*

Angakkut are primarily healers and maintainers of balance in a chaotic, unpredictable world. Illness or misfortune are believed to be caused by the soul going astray or going to the land of the dead, and by the breaking of taboos by the community. The *angakkoq* can undertake a dangerous journey to the underworld, the realm of the dead, to retrieve a person's missing soul, [104] or is required to journey to another, non-ordinary reality to negotiate or do battle with spirits on behalf of the community. The most well-known of these soul-journeys is the descent beneath the sea to the realm of the Sea Mistress, or Sedna, who gave to humans the animals they could hunt for food. The breaking of taboos by a community was believed to stop her releasing the animals for hunting. The *angakkoq*'s journey to the Sea Mistress's home beneath the sea would be filled with dangers and obstacles, overcome with the aid of their helping spirits. When they reached her, they would find her with her back to the lantern that illuminated her home and her pool of hunting animals. She would be covered in filth, symbolic of broken taboos. The *angakkoq* would battle the Sea Mistress or comfort her, combing the filth from her hair and turning her towards the lantern. After this, the Sea Mistress would be appeased and the community would benefit when the *angakkoq* returned from their underworld journey. [105] Other shamanic journeys to "Other" worlds were undertaken for healing and soul retrieval, such as the journey to the Moon Man [106] and the spirit canoe of the Salish shamans. [107] It is through these descents into darkness, into the Other, that the *angakkoq* and the Hermit may shine the

---

104 Graham Harvey and Robert J. Wallis, ***Historical Dictionary of Shamanism***, *p. 113. The Scarecrow Press, 2007.*

105 *Mariko Namba Walter and Eva Jane Neumann Fridman eds.* ***Shamanism: An Encyclopedia of World Beliefs, Practices and Culture***, *p. 310–11.*

106 *Merete Demant Jackobsen,* ***Shamanism: Traditional and Contemporary Approaches to the Mastery of Spirits and Healing***, *p. 88.*

107 *Piers Vitebsky,* ***The Shaman: Voyages of the Soul, Trance, Ecstasy and Healing from Siberia to the Amazon***, *p. 44. Macmillan, 1995.*

light of their spiritual power and wisdom to bring about healing and transformation.

～ Revelation

Guidance from a spiritual source; seeking spiritual insight or wisdom; going within and reflecting to gain answers; being a guide for others; illumination in the darkness; going through a time of difficulty or darkness in order to achieve greater understanding; helping others with one's knowledge; the seeds of wisdom; introversion; meditation.

Negatively aspected…
Feeling isolated from others; being unable to find answers; feeling blind and ignorant in a situation; ignoring a spiritual calling; refusing guidance.

The Wheel
The cult of Demeter

Mankind is born from the before-gods, fragments of the great Titans that came before the heavenly ones; yet their lot is given to them on the plains of wheat and flower, fruit and tree. Through the turning seasons they live out their days and in their time they wear many faces. Like all creatures given life, they are at the mercy of change. It is as constant and reliable as the earth beneath your feet, as the sun's rising with every dawn. It surrounds you in the budding and the blooming and the dying, in birth, life, death and rebirth. It is my word and my embrace, my promise to mankind that there is nothing new under the sun, but all returns. I am Of the Earth and Of the Mysteries, and these titles are not opposed. I am the Mistress of Change, and have given to mankind the laws of the universe: that change will be your ever-present companion and by the rituals of change you will measure out your lives and come to know the mysteries of the soul's transformation. For your soul is as seeds of corn, descending into the earth to grow to their fullness surrounded by matter. Time and time again they will be freed from the soil and rise up towards the light, there to be threshed and ground and return once more to whence they came. Like the seasons, your soul will always walk a path of change. Descend into the chamber of my Mysteries and you will be shown the planting and the growing, the threshing and the consuming; then you will truly know how to walk on the roads of change.

~ Mystery

Held gently in the arms of bountiful Demeter, the Wheel shows us the truth of all things. Surrounded by nature, that ever-present reminder of the cyclical way of the world, the force of change

is displayed as a four-spoked wheel with the seasons within it. Demeter, as the Greek goddess of agriculture, watches over the seasonal changes of the earth and the changes that humans undergo throughout their lives, both mundane and spiritual.

Demeter had several mystery cults around ancient Greece. Although her most well-known mystery religion was that of the Eleusinian mysteries (see *The High Priestess*), which she shared with her daughter Persephone/Kore, each of her mystery cults around Greece had distinctive features and took on the nature of the areas in which they were located. In Mantineia, Arkadia, there was a sanctuary of Demeter and Kore in which a perpetual fire was tended; [108] in the Mysaion in Akhaia (a sanctuary of Demeter Mysia), the mystery festival for Demeter was performed over seven days, with the men withdrawing on the third day so that the women alone might perform that night's rites. [109]

On the surface, Demeter's cult worship appears to have been concerned with agriculture and the earth, ensuring a plentiful harvest. In Hermione, Argolia, she was called Khthonia – "of the earth" [110] – and the largest bull from the herd was sacrificed to her to ensure that "every farm in Hermione may thrive exceedingly". [111] One hymn calls upon her to also bring peace, "so that he who sows may also reap". [112] Sowing and reaping can be seen as symbols of the consequential nature of the

---

108 Pausanias, ***Description of Greece*** *8.9.2, trans W. H. S. Jones. Loeb Classical Library, Harvard University Press, 1933.*

109 ***Ibid.****, 7.27.9*

110 ***Ibid.****, 2.35.4.*

111 *Aelian,* ***On Animals*** *11.4, trans. A. F. Schofield. Loeb Classical Library, Harvard University Press, 1959.*

112 *Callimachus, Hymn 6 to Demeter,* ***Callimachus: Hymns and Epigrams, Lycophron, Aratus****, trans A. W. Mair and G. R. Mair. Loeb Classical Library, Harvard University Press, 1921.*

Wheel card: what goes around, comes around. Demeter was also called Horephoros – "bringer of seasons", [113] and in the Orphic Hymns she is addressed as:

"Goddess of seed, of fruits abundant, fair, harvest and threshing are thy constant care. […] rejoicing in the reapers' sickles, kind, whose nature lucid, earthly, pure, we find. […] Only-begotten, much-producing queen, all flowers are thine, and fruits of lovely green." [114]

The card image shows Demeter in her aspect as earth goddess, surrounded by flowers and wheat. The wheat was sacred to her and representative of the two gifts she gave to humankind; it also reminds us of the cyclical nature of the earth and therefore the universe – there is a time for everything to be born and for it to die, a time to sow seeds and a time to reap the harvest. Understanding the cycles of one's life allows us to more fully engage with it and accept the changes that are ever-present. The poppy that features among the brightly coloured flowers was worn by her priestesses [115] and was also a symbol of death to the ancient Greeks (see *Five of Cups*). The poppy was often planted or grew naturally among wheatfields and is therefore symbolic of the life-death-life cycle.

It was Demeter's role as mother that was most obviously celebrated in her mysteries: the Thesmophoria, held over three days and observed only by women, remembered her mourning for the loss of her abducted daughter and culminated in a feast for Kalligeneia, "beautiful birth", who is not otherwise known

---

113 Homeric Hymn 2 to Demeter 1 ff, **Hesiod, Homeric Hymns, Epic Cycle, Homerica**, trans. Hugh G. Evelyn-White. Loeb Classical Library, Harvard University Press, 1914.

114 **The Hymns of Orpheus**, Orphic Hymn 39, trans. Thomas Taylor. London, 1792.

115 Callimachus, Hymn 6 to Demeter.

elsewhere in myth and may be another form of Demeter. [116] In Kypros, keeping Demeter's festival was the duty of all mothers, who would make offerings to the goddess of the first fruits and sheaves of wheat from their harvest. [117]

It was Demeter who instituted the mysteries among man, [118] just as she instituted agriculture, both of which she taught personally to humans. The mysteries and agriculture were seen as "the two gifts", inseparable and equivalent. [119] Thus, she not only gave us the means by which the changing seasons could be harnessed to our material benefit, but the means by which the changing nature of the soul through life and death could be understood, engaged with and used to our benefit. Further, she was called Thesmophoros, ("Law-Giver"), as she first gave laws to mankind:

"Ceres [Demeter] first turned the earth with the curved plough; she first gave corn and crops to bless the land; she first gave laws; all things are Ceres' gift." [120]

Thus, like the Wheel, Demeter's mysteries of the changing world reveal laws of the universe: change is a law that cannot be broken. The myth of Persephone's abduction and return from Hades and the institution of the seasons thereby works on two levels: it explains the endless cycle of the seasons and the earth's growth and "death", and it acts as a metaphor for

---

116　Lotte Motz, ***Faces of the Goddess***, *p. 127. New York: Oxford University Press, 1997.*

117　Ovid, ***Metamorphoses*** *10.431, trans. A. D. Melville. New York: Oxford University Press, 1998.*

118　*Homeric Hymn 2 to Demeter 472 ff,* **Hesiod, Homeric Hymns, Epic Cycle, Homerica,** *trans. Hugh G. Evelyn-White.*

119　*Carl Kerényi,* ***Eleusis: Archetypal Image of Mother and Daughter****, p. 121 New Jersey: Princeton University Press, 1991.*

120　*Ovid,* ***Metamorphoses*** *5. 341 ff, trans. A. D. Melville.*

the burial of the body in the earth and the immortality of the soul. Since it has been suggested that Persephone (who was sometimes imagined as a stalk of corn, [121] or as seed) was the great secret revealed during the rites of Eleusis, [122] we can imagine that the mysteries of Demeter and her maiden daughter revealed to initiates the soul's nature as an ever-changing, cyclical thing, working on the same principles of change as the material world.

∽ Revelation

Changes; change as the only constant in the universe; the cyclical nature of life; what goes around, comes around; consequences; the turning of the seasons; change for the better; being at the centre of an ever-changing situation; consciously creating change in one's life.

Negatively aspected…
Uncertainty caused by a great deal of change; change needed but blocked or delayed; unwillingness to accept change; change for the worse; changed being forced.

---

121 Lotte Motz, **Faces of the Goddess**, p. 128
122 Carl Kerényi, **Eleusis: Archetypal Image of Mother and Daughter**, p. 26.

Justice

The ancient Egyptian concept of Ma'at

The pathway of righteousness is a tender balance of cosmic order and human will, of action and reaction, cause and effect. There is nothing you do in this web of a world that does not affect the whole pattern: pluck one strand and the whole shivers; break a connection and it weakens. The universe responds to your every movement and moment, breathing and bleeding with you in symbiosis; thus it maintains the order by which the seasons process, the sun follows its course in the sky and stars are born and die. This is justice: not only the human hand of judgement pronouncing punishment and reward for what is done and not done, but the equilibrium that perpetuates existence in the world maintained by divine and human will. Yet do not mistake this equilibrium for equality, for to treat all things in nature the same creates imbalance and need: the heart and the feather are in balance not because they are the same but because they are different. Mine are the mysteries that unfold beyond the veil of the balanced scales, for I am the fulcrum upon which the order of the universe rests and the gateway through which it manifests in the world. Know me and you shall live in truth and peace, you shall go forth in joy, certain of the rule that governs you; come to my halls and I shall show you the measure of the world.

∽ Mystery

The title of this card initially suggests notions of human justice, of judgement in a court of law, retribution, reward and punishment; it carries with it an inherently moralistic tone. Tarot cards, however, always work on more than one level; in the Justice card the human codes of law and moral behaviour reflect a higher order: the laws of nature and balance. However, like

the scales that form the main symbol of this card, this balance is not static: it is a continual process of subtle shifts and changes. Balance does not mean equality but an act of changing in response to necessity to maintain order. Along with this notion of cosmic order and balance comes the concept of "rightness" – not in the sense of being morally acceptable but in the sense of being in line with the balance of the universe.

To the ancient Egyptians this was represented by the concept of *ma'at*, which later became the goddess Ma'at, to whom a temple complex in Karnak was dedicated and of whom viziers, judges and scribes from the 5th dynasty onwards were the priests. In later periods, judges wore images of Ma'at to denote their duty. [123] The Karnak temple complex was used as a courthouse during the reign of Ramesses IX. Judges and viziers were also called prophets of Ma'at, [124] and the Pharaoh was her son, of her body, her beloved. [125] In the *Pyramid Texts* the Pharaoh is urged to be like Ra by repressing wrongdoing and causing Ma'at to stand behind him, [126] emphasising that it was through the Pharaoh that Ma'at, the force of order, manifested in the world and acted in human life. When the Pharaoh furthers the cosmic order in this way, "[t]he sky is at peace, the earth is in joy, for they have heard that the King will set right [in the place of wrong] the King [is vindicated] in his tribunal on account of the just sentence which issued from his mouth". [127] Numerous images show the Pharaoh giving offerings of a small figure of Ma'at to the gods, representing his willingness "to uphold the fundamental principles of world order that were established at

---

123 Seigfried Morenz, trans. Ann E. Keep, **Egyptian Religion**, pp. 117–125. 1973.

124 James Henry Breasted, **Ancient Records of Egypt**, vol. II and III, p. 233 and 385 respectively. University of Illinois Press, 2001.

125 **Ibid.**, vol. III, p. 74.

126 R. O. Faulker trans. **The Ancient Egyptian Pyramid Texts** 1582, p. 238. Oxford University Press, 1969.

127 **Ibid.**, 1775–1776, p. 260.

the beginning of the time". [128] Similarly, we may take more control of our lives if we follow the cosmic order and maintain its balance.

The word "*ma'at*" translates as "that which is straight" and was used in many texts to refer to rightness, order, law and truth. It also had connotations of something being genuine and steadfast. It has been suggested that the term has connotations of an instrument by which things were kept straight, a rule, and therefore the rules and laws by which human action was kept straight and governed. [129] Ma'at's opposite was Isfet, "violence/injustice", chaos personified. [130] As the opponent of chaos, Ma'at's importance for the balance of the universe is highlighted. As such, she is called "mistress of heaven" and "ruler of the gods": nothing escapes the eyes of cosmic order, all are subject to the laws of nature. [131] In the *Instructions for Merikare* it is further emphasised that life itself depends upon Ma'at: "Do Maat that you may endure upon the earth". [132] Everything in the universe moves in accordance with Ma'at; she set down the daily course of Ra, the sun, thus setting down the laws by which the cycles of the world take place. [133] In the tarot, all is at the mercy of Justice and its fine balance. We bring order to our lives through a process of balancing. We know that if we give too much of ourselves to one thing, for instance, we cannot give as much to another thing; if we direct our resourc-

---

128 Emily Teeter, ***The Presentation of Maat: Ritual and Legitimacy in Ancient Egypt***, *p. 1. The Oriental Institute of the University of Chicago, 1997.*

129 E. A. Wallis Budge, ***Legends of the Egyptian Gods***, *vol. 1, p. 417. Dover Publications, 1969.*

130 Jan Assman, trans. Rodney Livingstone, ***Religion and Cultural Memory: Ten Studies***, *p. 34. Stanford University Press, 2006.*

131 James Henry Breasted, ***Ancient Records of Egypt***, *vol. II, p. 387.*

132 Emily Teeter, ***The Presentation of Maat: Ritual and Legitimacy in Ancient Egypt***, *p. 2.*

133 E. A. Wallis Budge, ***The Book of the Dead***, *p. 5. Arkana, 1989.*

es to one avenue they are not directed elsewhere. We institute ways of dealing with excess and deficit. If we were to give ourselves and our resources equally to everything, we would not be productive.

The most memorable image of Ma'at that comes to us is the image that has lent itself to the card: she is often depicted with wings on each arm and an ostrich feather on her head. She is usually shown standing upon a wedge-like shape, which some have suggested to be a flute, others a cubit, or more specifically, the measure of a cubit. [134] In many of her appearances in funerary carvings she is shown in her role at the judgement of the dead, weighing the heart of the deceased, the seat of the soul, against her ostrich feather, symbolic of the cosmic order and "rightness". Those whose heart balanced with the feather could pass beyond to the starry afterlife, shown behind Ma'at in the card image. These individuals are depicted in tomb carvings "with baskets filled with grain as a sign of their material provisioning and the other with the feather of Maat as a symbol of their vindication in the Judgement of the Dead. They all have 'existence until its end', sheltered in Maat, while the condemned belong to the Place of Annihilation". [135] Those whose hearts were too heavy were devoured by Ammit. This states that the soul at death had to be in line with the cosmic order, truth and rightness, having spoken what is right and walked the path of balance. The deceased was expected to have been a human manifestation of the *ma'at* of the universe. When they did not achieve this, punishment was not the outcome, but rather being stuck outside of the afterlife, prevented from ascending by being devoured: stagnation. Only when order is achieved can change be experienced. Just like the fine balancing act of

---

134 E. A. Wallis Budge, **Legends of the Egyptian Gods**, vol. 1, p. 416.

135 Erik Hornung, trans. David Lorton, **The Ancient Egyptian Books of the Afterlife**, p. 63. Cornell University Press, 1999.

the scales, the balance of the universe is not static but an ever-present fine-tuning of action and reaction, creation and destruction.

Another aspect of the judgement of the dead over which Ma'at presided was the deceased's confession: not of guilt for sins committed but a declaration of the sins that had not been committed, called the 42 Negative Confessions in the *Papyrus of Ani*.[136] 42 "Maati goddesses" oversaw the confession, to whom the deceased had to address the confession. Thus, we are reminded that acts of goodness and rightness in the mundane world reflect the rightness of the universe. Not only does the Justice card govern the process by which we face reward or punishment for our deeds, but it also governs the criteria by which we decide what is "good". Just as Ma'at set the order of the universe in place and the laws of nature in motion, the Justice card charges us to set the order of our lives and maintain the laws we have set for ourselves, maintaining our checks and balances so that we might adequately respond to the changes of the world and create a world in which it is a blessing to live.

~ Revelation

Balance and equilibrium; maintaining order; rightness; truth and honesty; positive dealings with the law and justice; the laws of nature; cosmic order; notions of reward; fairness; staying on the "straight and narrow"; aligning one's self with a sense of purpose and cosmic order.

Negatively aspected…
Unfairness and imbalance; falsehood; negative dealings with the law and justice; notions of punishment; deviance.

---

136 Ibid., p. 418.

Hanged Man

The Sun Dance of the North American Plains nations

In every soul there is a storm bringing clouds and rain; night comes like a bride to her lover and surrounds the spirit in suffering. Give in, seeker. Become the bridegroom of your agony and let the rain purify you. This is the mystery of the ascetic, who through withdrawal from the sacred comes closer to it. These are the roads of the sacrifice that creates the world, the first offering to the gods of blood spilled on the earth. In your pain you must know that you, too, are a sacrifice; your power, your energy, your self might re-create that primeval act and rebuild the universe around you. Follow my dance, and I shall show to you the ways of suffering. For I am the Hanged One and the Holy One, the Scapegoat and the Tortured; it is my cries of pain that are the four winds and the sound of the storm; my tears that flow as streams and rain, replenishing the world; my blood that falls to nourish and revitalise all the creatures of the earth. Let your power be given up to that which calls to you: in becoming small you become great; after your agony you will know only joy and the ecstasy of divine light. Yet remember, mystic, that you can only give as an offering that which is your own: your Self.

~ Mystery

Two of the themes found commonly in the mystical and religious traditions of all cultures are represented by the Hanged Man: sacrifice and the "dark night of the soul". It is through sacrifice that we might come to understand worth; it is by undergoing the suffering and pain of spiritual anguish and isolation that we grow closer to the sacred. In the Hanged Man, the self is sacrificed to a higher power, we let go of control

and give in to that power. We come to understand that when it seems we have been abandoned by the gods, we are instead growing closer to them. Here, at the point between the midnight of the soul and the dawn of the gods, a young man from one of the Plains nations of North America offers his blood and self in sacrifice, enduring the exhausting mortifications of the Sun Dance.

In recent decades the practices of the Sun Dance have become more secretive in order to prevent misuse, abuse and appropriation by non-natives. The several ceremonies categorised as Sun Dance must be taught in the right way, preserving as they do much of the aboriginal customs, traditions and beliefs of this people. However, there are several accounts given to anthropologists from the late nineteenth and early/mid twentieth centuries of the dances and the beliefs and feelings of those who practiced them.

These ceremonies are also called Medicine Lodge [137] and Young Dog's Dance. [138] They are shared by several tribes, including the Arapahos, Cheyennes, Crows, Blackfeet, Sarsis, Teton Dakotas, Kiowas, Plains Crees, Plains Ojibwas, Sisseton Dakotas, Wind River Shoshonis, Comanches, Utes, Hekandika Shoshonis, Poncas and the Kutenais west of the Rockies. [139] Although there are differences in practice, the purpose of the rite and its features are frequently similar. The ceremony takes place over several days during which fasting is undertaken by the dancers and sometimes those witnessing. In some cases, self-mortification is practiced, in which the breast or back

---

137 George Bird Grinnel, "**The Cheyenne Medicine Lodge**" in **American Anthropologist**, New Series, vol. 16, no. 2 (Apr.–Jun., 1914), pp. 245–256.

138 George Bird Grinnell, "**The Young Dog's Dance**", in **The Journal of American Folklore**, vol. 4, no. 15 (Oct.–Dec., 1891), pp. 307–313.

139 Fred W. Voget, **The Shoshoni-Crow Sun Dance**, p. 89. University of Oklahoma Press, 1998.

of the dancers are pierced with skewers and tied to rawhide ropes that are attached to a centre pole outside or inside the Sun Dance lodge. According to some accounts, those making the sacrifice will often dance without food or water for two or more days and nights, or spend anywhere between an hour and a few days trying to pull themselves free from their attachment to the centre pole by ripping the skewers from their flesh. The Shoshoni call the lodge in which this takes place *taguwunexa*, "thirst-standing lodge", in recognition of the fasting and the physical exertion that takes place there. [140]

The purpose of the dance varies between tribes and individuals. The Shoshoni Sun Dance is called a "revitalisation cult" by Hultkrantz, [141] referring to its themes of seasonal renewal, growth and replenishment. For the Dakota it was a cultic drama, a recreation of the primeval action through which the earth was created. [142] When speaking to those who practice it a more personal motivation is found: it may be an act of thanksgiving, of prayer for happiness and strength, but most commonly it is an act of healing for others. People might undergo the ordeal as an offering to bring a loved one back from war unharmed or help a sick relative recover. [143]

This may seem at first to be a mundane act of physical endurance, but the symbolism of the Sun Dance shows otherwise. For the Shoshoni, the central pole from which the dancer is

---

140 Åke Hultkrants, p. 82, "The Traditional Symbolism of the Sun Dance Lodge Among the Wind River Shoshoni", in ***Religious Symbols and Their Functions***, pp. 70–95, ed. Haralds Biezais, Scripta Instituti Donneriani Aboensis, 1979.

141 *Ibid.*, p. 71.

142 Åke Hultkrantz, "The Traditional Symbolism of the Sun Dance Lodge Among the Wind River Shoshoni", p. 72.

143 Richard Erdoes, ***American Indian Myths and Legends***, p. 34. Pantheon Fairytale and Folklore Library, 1984.

suspended while pierced is a sign for the Milky Way, called *tugungu'himp,* "backbone of the sky", the path over which people travel when they have passed to the beyond. This is the channel between humans and the spirit world, the *axis mundi*, the "world tree". The lodge is a microcosm, "a sacred replica of the earth". [144] Those suspending themselves from the centre pole are symbolically hanging themselves in sacrifice from the backbone of the world, becoming the intermediary between the sacred and the mundane, their drama played out in the realm of the divine, encased in its own universe in which the sacrifice recreates the world.

The paint of the dancers also relates features of the ceremony. In the card image, lines on the dancer's face symbolise his tears of suffering. [145] Bands on his arms are symbolic of his prayers, [146] and the dots on the upper arms symbolic of the buffalo calf. [147] This identifies the dancer with the animal that was once a staple source of meat on the plains, linking the sacrifice of the buffalo for the tribe's physical nourishment with the sacrifice of the dancer for its spiritual protection. The sage crown and wristbands, worn by the Sioux, are purificatory. The white paint all over the dancer's body is traditional for many plains tribes.

A first-hand account of the Sun Dance ceremony by a Sioux medicine man, John Fire, who undertook it, reminds us of the pain felt by its dancers as well as the reasons for the bodily mortifications, shedding light on the process undergone in the Hanged Man:

---

144 Åke Hultkrantz, *"The Traditional Symbolism of the Sun Dance Lodge Among the Wind River Shoshoni", pp. 83–84.*

145 ***Ibid.**, p. 89.*

146 *George A. Dorsey, p. 159, **"The Arapaho Sun Dance: The Ceremony of the Offerings Lodge**", in **Publications of the Field Columbian Museum**, Anthropological Series, vol. 4 (June, 1903), pp. 1–228.*

147 ***Ibid.**, p. 163.*

"You are staring with your wide opened eyes into the scorching sun, the sunbeams are making you blind, they are burning into your scalp and filling you up with the insufferable brightness […] Dancing, dancing from the morning to the evening without food and drink until you almost pass out… Dragging, dragging the strap made of the raw skin fastened to the skewer, which is fastened deeply into your flesh. The skin must crack and you will free yourself and you will be bleeding from the chest […] Many people do not understand why we are doing this. The Sun Dance is a barbarian, savage and bloody superstition. But I think our body is the only thing, which really belongs to us. When we, the Indians, are giving our flesh, our bodies, we are giving up the only thing, which belongs only to us." [148]

☞ Revelation

Sacrifice and offering; learning what one values by being forced to give something up; letting go and giving in to a higher power; suspension of activity; a dark night of the soul; achieving mystical awareness through spiritual isolation or suffering; a time of difficulty and an ordeal resulting in increased understanding; seeing things from a different perspective.

Negatively aspected…

Being unwilling to give something up or make a sacrifice; detrimental isolation; being unable to see one's way through suffering; being forced into an ordeal unwillingly; the world being turned upside down.

---

148 John Fire, **Chromy Jelen: Lame Deer,** trans. Josef Porsch and Ladislav Horaček, p. 176, Paseka, 2004.

Death

The Mexican cult of Santa Muerte

All things must die. It is inevitable and unavoidable, yet this simple truth strikes terror into the hearts of so many. They cling to life, clutching it preciously to them, desirous of it. They want more of it – more life, more time – but there is no possibility of more. There is only enough. I am the boundary that defines what is enough. I am there when the last grain of sand in the hourglass falls, and I am there when the first glimmer of life sparks into existence, for that life is mine. It is only through me that you might have your beginnings. Every moment in the universe is a beginning and an ending; in truth you do not die once but countless times. There is no moment in time when you are not dying. I am Most Holy Death, that beautiful, skinny sister who brings profound transformation along the unknown road. I am shrouded in a bridal gown out of love for you, and in my skirts the seeds of life yet remain. Mine are the treasures of the world below and within: know death and you will know yourself; know the time of harvesting and you shall not truly end. Everything dies, and nothing dies. Yet know that each of you bears me as a burden for some steps along your road. I am the weight of the burden and its lifting, and you will weep at my presence and rejoice at other times. I am rich, for I have all the days of the universe in my halls, but I shall continue to take from you: accept and let go, and the pain of the sundering shall be nothing. Every step forward is a tearing away from the present moment, and you think nothing of these steps: why not also think thus of that greatest of steps into the unknown? Then I shall be by your side always, a companion, and there will be no fear to hold you back.

☙ Mystery

Death is a certainty. It is unavoidable and unknowable, feared by many above all things. In our time we experience not only our own death, but the deaths of loved ones, acquaintances and people we did not know but who were tied to us through commonality of language, culture, country or religion. Death is so much a part of every person's life and the life of everything in our universe that it is no surprise to see it in the Major Arcana of the tarot. Here, it represents transformation at its most foundational, for even in death nothing is destroyed, it just changes form. It represents both the physical death of the body and metaphorical deaths that we experience throughout life. It is at once beautiful and terrifying, unifying – for it is something we all have in common – and deeply isolating – for we are alone in our experience of our own death. It is no wonder that humankind's relationship with death is so conflicted and confused. Many cultures demonstrate the conflicted relationship with death by depicting it as both frightening and beautiful, and the Mexican cult of Santa Muerte – Holy Death – is a perfect example of this.

Although Santa Muerte is primarily worshipped and petitioned by devotees across Mexico and North America, there are undoubtedly followers spread across the globe; her cult has exploded into life in the past 10 years, estimated to number between 10 and 12 million followers. It is a living tradition, so the interpretation from its devotees of the symbols and practices of the cult vary and evolve to encompass new ideas and modern needs. Yet there are some themes that, no matter where in the world Santa Muerte is worshipped, are always found beneath her wings.

The cult of Santa Muerte has strong ties through its devotees to Catholicism, but in 2013 the Catholic church condemned it as "a blasphemy against religion". [149] Santa Muerte is considered a banned saint, but this does not matter to her devotees. She is instead a folk saint who personifies death, and, unlike a great number of folk saints, she does not appear to have once been a living person. Her origins are unknown, but several theories have been put forward, the most common that she is a Catholicised version of the Aztec goddess of death, Mictecacihuatl. [150] We know that Santa Muerte first appears in references in the Spanish colonial record in the 1790s, but then she disappears from record until the 1940s when she resurfaces as a magical mistress of love. [151] However, there are devotees of la Flaquita ("the Skinny Lady", one of her popular epithets) in their 70s who tell of altars in their homes as children, so while she only resurfaces into record in the 1940s – and exposure in the media occurs in the 1990s – we can be sure that the practice has been around for quite some time. [152]

Devotees have many names for this lady of death, all of which are affectionate and often familial in nature: la Huesuda (the Bony Lady), la Niña Blanca (the White Girl), la Madrina (the Godmother), la Hermana Blanca (the White Sister), la Niña Bonita (the Pretty Girl), la Dama Poderosa (the Powerful Lady), and more. Through these often ironic names, devotees acknowledge some of the more frightening aspects of Santa Muerte, who is always depicted as a skeleton, her gender denoted only by her clothing, which may be a nun's habit, a beautiful ballgown, or even a bridal gown, highlighting death's intimate connection with all of humankind.

---

149 *"Vatican Calls Santa Muerte, Mexico's 'Death Saint', Blasphemous"*, *Huffington Post*, 5 August 2013.

150 See R. Andrew Chesnut, **Devoted to Death**, pp. 28–31 for other possible origins of Santa Muerte. Oxford University Press, 2012.

151 *Ibid*, pp. 30 and 33.

152 *"Meet Santa Muerte, The Tequila-Loving Saint Comforting Both Criminals and the Marginalized"*, *Huffington Post*, 11 July 2014.

There are many details found in the depiction of Santa Muerte that tell us about her and death's role in our lives and the tarot. Most commonly, she is shown holding a scythe, a farm implement used for reaping crops, an item familiar to anybody who knows what the Grim Reaper looks like. This gives Holy Death the role of reaper of souls: we are all crops that grow throughout our lives and one day must die and be harvested.

The scales of justice are often found in images of Santa Muerte, perfectly balanced in one of her hands. This conveys an aspect of death as law, equilibrium and justice. It also shows death as the weigher of souls, though when devotees call upon Santa Muerte; she is a "supernatural attorney who represents her devoted clients regardless of the crimes they may have committed. Unconcerned with their guilt or innocence, she seals the best deal possible for her clients in a dysfunctional justice system fraught with corruption and incompetence". [153]

Many images of the Pretty Girl show an owl, symbolising great wisdom, darkness and death: in Aztec culture, *tecolote* (owl) would cry when death came. In the darkness of a death-transformation there is wisdom to be obtained. She is often surrounded by flowers, in particular roses, carnations and marigolds, the flowers used in Day of the Dead celebrations. Some figurines are made out of, or cloaked with, paper money, or it may be stuffed into her hands or laid at her feet. Many of Santa Muerte's followers petition her for material wealth; however, the symbolic association of the world's wealth with death is not a new one: the Romans, acknowledging the fact that death took people beneath the earth, named their god of death Pluto, "rich one", for the riches in minerals, gems and ores found there. Since all that dies returns to the earth in one way or another, death is indeed wealthy.

---

153 R. Andrew Chesnut, **Devoted to Death**, p. 178.

The Earth itself is usually depicted either held in one hand or beneath the feet of Santa Muerte, symbolising her complete dominion over the world. Nothing in the universe escapes her. "She is a global saint who rules over all human life, regardless of nationality, sex, age, or social class." [154] The universality of death is a point of celebration in the cult of Santa Muerte, as devotees frequently cite the equality of death as a way of building community. "In this cult there are no soldiers, there are no cops, there are no criminals, there are only brothers," says one devotee. [155] Another devotee said, "I think she's an angel sent from God. Like her name says, I think we're all one short step from life to death. Sooner or later, she takes the rich, the poor – everyone". [156] This miraculous, skeletal wonder worker is often turned to by those on the margins of society and whom organised religion has failed. She offers wondrous transformation and a rejuvenation of one's outlook on life. As death, she walks closely every day with her devotees, who have no reason to fear her. Death comes for us all, but to her devotees she comes as a friend, sister, mother and godmother. She is ancient: "Santa Muerte has always existed. She comes from our ancestors." [157] The cult of Santa Muerte, although devoted to a skeleton saint, is living and breathing. Her skeletal appearance might suggest otherwise to the uninitiated, but Santa Muerte does not bring dormancy and stagnation; instead, she is a "supernatural action figure who heals, provides, and punishes, among other things. She is the hardest-working and most productive folk saint on

---

154 ***Ibid***, *p. 67.*

155 *"**Condemned by the Catholic Church – Saint Death Gathers Devoted Followers**", 1 November 2014, https://www.youtube.com/watch?v=-JYYsaO84ZMg&feature=youtu.be*

156 *"**I Call Her La Flaca**", Faith in the Five Boroughs, http://faithinthefiveboroughs.org/video/la-flaca/*

157 *"**Condemned by the Catholic Church – Saint Death Gathers Devoted Followers**", 1 November 2014, https://www.youtube.com/watch?v=-JYYsaO84ZMg&feature=youtu.be*

either side of the border." [158] She is particularly well known for the profound and long-lasting transformation of alcoholics and drug addicts.

Many of the cults in the Major Arcana of the *Tarot Apokalypsis* are ancient and dead, but the cult of Santa Muerte, of death, is very much alive. True death is not about stagnation, but about transformation. The transformation in this card is a natural, gentle one, just as the cult has changed naturally with the needs of its followers; it is not the sudden, devastating transformation of the Tower. Death and the Tower are also opposites in another way: the Tower is liberation, being freed through the destruction of what has been built; Death is an obligation: we must die, for we come into life under pain of death. In order to be the receivers of life we must pay back at the end.

◈ Revelation

Natural endings; progression towards a conclusion; bringing something to a close; transformation; metaphorical death; letting go of a loved one; harvest; a reaping of results; considerations of mortality; change that must be accepted; a change of state; metamorphosis; one door closing and another opening.

Negatively aspected…
Refusal to accept change; stagnation; failing to reap a harvest through refusal to acknowledge an ending; fear of change; unwanted change; issues of mortality causing pain and suffering.

---

158 R. Andrew Chesnut, **Devoted to Death,** *p. 51.*

Temperance
Alchemy

The spiritual journey is one of unending transformation. There is no completion at its far shores, nor the final consumption of the fuel for its phoenix fires. Even the moment of perfect attainment produces the essence of change, for the spiritual accomplishment of one spreads like a wildfire through the web of the world and the hearts of all. Thus, the Stone of the Philosophers turns lead into gold, the gross into the sublime. Yet the journey to refine that miraculous stone is one of careful moderation, of the tempering of the heat of the sun and the coolness of the moon, the dryness of the day and the wetness of the night. Like the blacksmith's art of hammering and tempering the metal that will be forged into beauty and death, the alchemist's art shapes and transmutes the base in the vessel, undergoing many stages. The creation of the universe takes place within his alembic of Art, and the creation of Illumination in the vessel of his heart. But slowly, with measured grace and attentive care, must he approach the Great Work; there he shall rectify the base earth and find the hidden stone.

~ Mystery

Temperance appears like a moment of relief in a run of "dark" Major Arcana cards, beginning with the Hanged Man and ending with the Tower. Even though its outward appearance is one of beauty, it is as difficult and challenging as its companions. Here, we are charged to reunite that which we have separated and been taken apart in the process of the journey. What began in the Lovers with the marriage of the Sun King and Moon Queen now takes place on a deeper level: no longer are the two in union, for now they are truly one, an entirely new part of creation that is greater than the sum of its parts. The sacred

marriage bears its fruits and a continued, careful process of transmutation begins, during which the soul will continue to ascend. The card image portrays the mysteries of Temperance as the art of alchemy, though it bears mundane mysteries also: here is the art of blending different aspects of something to create something better, of manipulating the resources we have in a process of creation, of tempering our activities to ensure that, through moderation, we are productive.

The name of this card does not adequately convey the depth of mystery that it holds. Conjuring up images of quiet virtue and timidity, the title seems to ignore the mystical transformation of the soul that takes place herein, the process by which the base matter of the self can be transmuted into spiritual gold. However, temperance is the virtue most apt for the artform of the alchemical process. This process separates the quintessence (perfect spirit) from the unrefined, base earth, the "subtle from the dense, gently with unremitting care". [159] This is a gentle art, performed with prudence and temperance.

Alchemy is an eclectic practice bringing together elements of philosophy, art, science, astrology, magic and mysticism. It has roots in ancient Egypt, but its philosophy was deeply influenced by ancient Greece; its name derives from Arabic, it was made widely available by the Arabic world, and gathered to itself hermetic doctrines in Western Europe. As such, its history spans at least two millennia, though the form in which we know it today began in the 8th century with the Arabic alchemists. The card image shows a man in Persian clothing in a walled garden, referring to the Arabic influence on alchemy.

---

159 The Emerald Tablet of Hermes 7a, Fulcanelli translation, online at http://www.sacred-texts.com/alc/emerald.htm [Accessed 28 February 2016].

The aim of alchemy was the transmutation of something "lower" into something "higher", such as the transmutation of base metals (such as lead) into a precious metal (such as gold), the creation of a universal cure, an elixir of immortality, or the philosopher's stone. The philosopher's stone symbolised the perfection of the soul and the attainment of spiritual enlightenment. Just as the philosopher's stone could transmute base metal into gold, so our souls could be transmuted from a low state to one of perfection. The philosopher's stone was called "the most ancient, secret […] blessed sacred Stone of the Sages. It is described as being true, more certain than certainty itself, the arcanum of all arcana – the Divine virtue and efficacy, which is hidden from the foolish, the aim and end of all things under heaven, the wonderful epilogue of conclusion of all the labours of the Sages – the perfect essence of all the elements, the indestructible body which no element can injure, the quintessence; […] – the everlasting light – the panacea for all diseases – the glorious Phoenix – the most precious of all treasures – the chief good of Nature". [160]

The process by which the philosopher's stone is created, and therefore by which the soul reaches perfection, was called the Great Work, a term still used in many Western Mystery Traditions. It is the Great Work that is shown in the card, rather than its results – the philosopher's stone is not yet attained. The link between a physical process of chemical transmutation and a spiritual process is highlighted by one of the fundamental tenets of alchemy:

"What is above is like what is below, and what is below is like that which is above. To make the miracle of the one thing." [161]

---

[160] Anon, **The Sophic Hydrolith**, *quoted in* Cherry Gilchrist, **The Elements of Alchemy**, *p. 6. Element, 1998.*

[161] **The Emerald Tablet of Hermes** *2.*

This also means that what happens externally happens internally and vice versa. Thus, "the world is a reflection of the inner psyche, [...] in a very real sense each individual is responsible for everything that happens in the outside world. This is the key to understanding the true significance of humanity as a microcosm: as above, so below; as within, so without." [162] Through the gentle tempering of forces upon the base material, by which it will be transformed, we change the world by changing ourselves. The light glowing in the breast of the alchemist in the card image reminds us that through our mundane actions we transform our inner selves.

The Great Work is the process of the incompatible and conflicting opposites contained within the *prima materia* being gently guided towards a redeemed state of perfect harmony. The process is described in stages: "First we bring together, then we putrefy, we break down what has been putrified, we purify the divided, we unite the purified and harden it. In this way is One made from man and woman". [163] The elements that undergo the various stages of alchemical transformation are represented as man and woman, sun and moon, king and queen, red and white. In the Lovers card they were united; in Temperance they now harden, producing something new from their union. This is expressed in the alchemical formula *solve et coagula*. Where the Lovers is the *solve* part of the formula, the dissolving of two into one, Temperance is the *coagula* part, in which matter and spirit become perfected as one.

White and red roses surround the alchemist in the card. From the union of the Sun King and Moon Queen comes a child, alchemical material that must be heated until it "whitens", its

---

162 Francis Melville, ***The Book of Alchemy***, p. 53. Quarto, 2013.

163 Alexander Roob, ***The Hermetic Museum: Alchemy and Mysticism***, p. 125. Taschen, 2001.

first stage of perfection being attained; this material must be further treated until it reddens. The red rose grows from the white rose, and is the ultimate goal of the alchemical process. [164] The many stages it goes through include heating and cooling, which is an act of temperance – the heat must be tempered correctly in order to produce the correct results. As with many fine arts, a minor error will prove disastrous. Temperance therefore represents more than the virtue of the same name: it shows us a way of being and perceiving that can create spiritual transformation, opposite in practice and philosophy to other modes of transformation like those found in the Tower card, in which extremes produce profound change. One of the mysteries of Temperance is in knowing when the extreme is necessary and when moderation will lead to the goal.

∞ Revelation

Moderation and temperance; not taking things to extremes; tempering one's actions and those of others; gentleness and carefulness; undertaking a long process of transformation; blending many eclectic influences to create something; something that is greater than the sum of its parts; the first results being born from a process of spiritual transformation; spiritual transformation being caused through mundane action.

Negatively aspected…
Treating eclectic influences separately; separation; being immoderate and intemperate; rushing; going to extremes; spiritual transformation blocked by mundane activity.

---

164 Ibid., pp. 446–7.

The Devil

The imagined cult of the witches' sabbat

What are the howlings on the wind? What are the cries at night from the bedchamber? What are the strange figures beckoning in the darkness, calling you to the woods? Only you, my little one, only your deep, hidden secrets and desires, only your inner demons and fears made manifest. There is no devil here, only you; no evil except that which you make. It has been said that I speak only in lies, but the more terrifying thing is that I speak only in truth: I show what is uncivilised, yet exists within all civilised beings; I show what you want to ignore and disguise; I show you the animal within. I am that force of nature that calls you back to the wild and forces you to face that ugly beast of you, that you might become its master and not its prey. I demand that you dance for me and make a pact with me not because I desire your subservience but because you must learn what needs to be committed in order to fully realise your self. To know but one part of your being is the greatest danger – do not discount even the most repulsive, but learn how vital it is for your soul. If you do not, then your fears will control your perception and give themselves to the harm of others; your desires will become unnatural by virtue of being against the order of your self; and those parts of you that you will not accept will become the fuel of blame upon others. You see: this is the law of the strong.

ᛰ Mystery

As its name suggests, the Devil is a complex card that is often feared and reviled but which offers ways towards spiritual realisation as much as it offers warnings and temptations towards spiritual stagnation. Like the other "dark" cards of the tarot, it reminds us that the darkness is as much a part of illumina-

tion as the light, and here there are mysteries to be found also. These are the mysteries of the primal beast within, of expressing the animalistic and feral aspects of our personalities rather than repressing them; of learning the origins and nature of our fears so that they might not control us and be projected onto others; of recognising when we are our own worst enemy and when we are demonising others for our faults.

The card image shows the imagined cult of the witches' sabbat of medieval and early modern Europe, in which the mind's darkest fantasies and fears take control of reason and manipulate logic to nefarious ends. Here, we are at the mercy of our inner demons, often projecting them onto others in an infantile attempt at processing them. These inner demons, fantasies and fears became externalised as real demons and devils that tempted people to abandon civil society for immersion in the wild, dark woods, to taste forbidden fruit and experience strange ecstasies. It is notable that this is an imagined cult as opposed to one that actually existed (it has been shown repeatedly that confessions from so-called witches that claimed attendance at a sabbat were false and a mixture of folk beliefs and influence from interrogators). The Devil often shows us projections of our fears rather than reality and demonstrates how the repression of our fears and desires creates distorted perceptions.

The witches' sabbat varied in nature geographically and over the centuries, but maintained a few key features. Accused witches described being transported to meetings with other witches, devils and the Devil himself. The sabbat was sometimes a festival of perversions and desire and sometimes a formal rite in which witches would give obeisance to the Devil. It is suggested that the sabbat came about in its full form in 1428–9 in Switzerland and Italy. [165]

---

[165] Robin Briggs, ***Witches and Neighbours: The Social and Cultural Context of European Witchcraft***, *p. 33. Penguin Books, 1996.*

It became a "central feature of witchcraft doctrine among such subsequent western European demonologists [...]. At about the same time, it also seems to have become increasingly important in witch trials". [166]

Many confessions from witches, such as those in Germany, stated that they performed lewd, sexual dances at sabbats. [167] The same account describes how witches openly described "the dirtiest and the most obscene occurrences and deeds, with such liberty and gaiety, that they make saying it glorious, and take a certain pleasure in telling about it". [168] Sexual relations with the devil, appearing to the witch in the form of somebody they desired, also occurred. After the coupling had taken place the devil revealed himself to the witch and a pact was made. [169] In the seventeenth century, "witch-finder general" Matthew Hopkins used aggressive methods of interrogation to gain confessions from accused witches of having sexual intercourse with demons. [170] The overtly sexual nature of many features of the sabbat conveys the deeply sexual nature of the Devil card, which places value in the expression of lust and desire, recognising and affirming sexual needs and fantasies at its best, repressing them at its worst. The repression of sexual desire has been seen as one of the causes of the focus on sexual acts during the witches' sabbat, as interrogators projected their own repression onto the object of their revulsion: the accused witch.

---

*166 Bengt Ankarloo, Stuart Clark and William Monter, **Witchcraft and Magic in Europe vol 4: The Period of the Witch Trials**, pp. 8–9. The Athlone Press, 2002.*

*167 Brian Levack, ed. **The Witchcraft Sourcebook**, p. 106. Routledge, 2005.*

*168 **Ibid.**, p. 107.*

*169 Jonathan B. Durrant, **Witchcraft, Gender and Society in Early Modern Germany**, pp. 154–6. Brill, 2007.*

*170 Bengt Ankarloo, Stuart Clark and William Monter, **Witchcraft and Magic in Europe vol 4: The Period of the Witch Trials**, p. 79.*

Another way in which we project our inner demons and fears onto others, as represented by the Devil card, can also be found in a common accusation made of witches: that they caused male impotence and stole penises. [171] This highlights a negative aspect of this card: the act of scapegoating. Just as the Devil has been blamed for countless evils wrought by humankind, so those accused of witchcraft were blamed for the ills that befell an individual, community, or nature. [172] Witches were said to work magic during the sabbat to cause women and cattle to miscarry, blight crops and spoil butter and ale. This also presents witches as acting against the world. It reminds us that the Devil card represents the ways in which we act against our best interests, preventing our growth by projecting or repressing our fears.

The witches' sabbat, and the Devil card of the tarot, present to us an inversion of acceptable reality. Where we are raised to control our fears and emotions, often hiding or disguising them, the witches' sabbat revelled in them and the Devil card advises us to let them free so they cannot work their evil unseen. Where we try to be civilised and human, the Devil reminds us that we are still animals and that we have a bestial side that, if ignored, can manifest negatively. In the same way, witches' sabbats took place in wild locations and commonly inverted the acceptable morality of the time: the host of the Eucharist was stamped on, the name of the Virgin Mary defiled and traditional Christian baptisms were mimicked by devils to commit witches to infernal pacts. The infernal pacts made by witches during sabbats remind us of another aspect of the Devil: bonds and the ties that bind.

---

*171 Catherine Rider, **Magic and Impotence in the Middle Ages**, pp. 186–7. Oxford University Press, 2006.*

*172 Jonathan Barry, Marianne Hester and Gareth Roberts eds. **Witchcraft in Early Modern Europe**, p. 239. Cambridge University Press, 1996.*

These fantastical accusations thrown at supposed witches led to around 100,000 trials and between 40,000 and 50,000 executions between 1450 and 1750. [173] In the Devil card we see the danger of allowing reason to be subdued by fear and unprocessed, misunderstood, neglected desire. Desire and yearning properly processed and acknowledged – such as in the Lovers card – is healthy; here it is repressed and unhealthy. In the same way that the witch hunts of medieval and early modern Europe harmed a large number of people, victims of the externalised fears and desires of repressed individuals and fearful communities seeking a scapegoat, so we can harm others when we ignore the depths of our subconscious.

∽ Revelation

Accepting the wild, animalistic aspect of the self and life; processing fears and inner demons in a healthy manner; experiencing lust and desire; being bound to something one wishes to; something sexual in nature; flouting authority in a form of challenge.

Negatively aspected…
Demonising others; scapegoating; projecting one's fears onto others or a situation; not seeing the reality of a situation; something feeling unnatural; being bound to something unwanted; harming others through distrust, manipulation or guilt; sexual feelings and desires repressed and unprocessed.

---

*173 Robin Briggs, **Witches and Neighbours: The Social and Cultural Context of European Witchcraft**, p. 8.*

The Tower

Aghoris, the cremation-ground ascetics of India

For many lifetimes you might chant peacefully in honour of the gods, meditating on their great names on a gentle road to liberation. But I offer you initiation into the mysteries of destruction, incineration, of exposure to the most terrifying and repulsive so that you might stand and become part of the dance of destruction that stirs up this world. Come to the cremation ground to see how everything burns, how the universe is fed from the fires of the final sacrifice. My adorants, adorned with ash from the pyres, drink thirstily from skull cups, consuming pollution and food with equal acceptance; they have truth in their eyes. They know liberty and freedom, not fear, nor shame, nor desire, nor attachment. They have walked the paths among the corpses and vultures for so long that there is no terror for them. When I finally come for them – I, inexorable Great Time, the devourer – they will not weep and cling to the falsehood of "Self" and "I". For what are these constructs you have created but a vain attempt to escape death? Foolish. All dies. All that is created must be destroyed, and these bonds you have made will only make it more painful. Let go. Give in. Learn that you have walked among ghosts all your life. On the day I come for you, covered in ashes and dreadlocks, frenzied and dancing and accompanied by fearsome spirits, I will carry your skull as my cup. Let me take your hand as a Lord and Father, and your consumption in the great fire will be a swift and sweet release.

~ Mystery

"...the sight of [Shiva] is not terrible; it is wonderful. But the ego sees Him as terrible because He has come to rip Her

away from all Her attachments, and some attachments go very deep." [174]

Often seen as one of the most terrifying cards of the tarot, the Tower shows us a painful process of destruction and the world-changing re-evaluation necessitated by it. Lightning strikes, simultaneously illuminating us and causing our world to crumble. What we hold most dear, sacred and true is consumed by fierce and unstoppable fire; even the most fundamental things upon which we have built our lives crumble to dust. It is in this moment of utter devastation that we are liberated and given no-thing and no-self as a firm foundation upon which to build a new life. We walk now in the great cremation ground, surrounded forever by the consuming fire that renders to ash the illusion of attachment, and with it all our fears and weaknesses.

Many people experience the sudden devastation of the Tower without conscious decision when external events influence our internal processes. For the Aghoris of India it is a process that is consciously sought so they may be liberated from fear and the attachments that hold them in the wheel of suffering. Aghoris are ascetics devoted to the god Shiva who usually perform their rites in cremation grounds or live in them. They paint their skin with cremation ash and are often seen with matted hair or dreadlocks, wearing loin cloths (sometimes made from funerary shrouds) and necklaces of beads shaped like skulls. The sect is relatively recent, tracing its origin to Baba Kina Ram in the 18th century; he was visited by the deity Dattatreya, who offered him his own flesh as *prasād* (edible offering). [175] However, Aghoris do not all belong to the Kina Ram lineage, and the practices are widely varied.

---

174 Robert E. Svoboda, **Aghora: At the Left Hand of God**. Sadhana Publications, 1999, p. 101.

175 Ronald L. Barrett, **Aghor Medicine: Pollution, Death and Healing in Northern India**, p.33. University of California Press, 2005.

Aghoris most commonly worship the aspect of Shiva called Bhairava ("terrible", "frightful"). According to legend, Bhairava was created by Shiva from his brow when Brahma became egotistical, claiming to be the supreme deity of the Trimurti. Shiva created Bhairava, instructing him: "Worship him [Brahma] with your sharp-pointed and quick-moving sword." [176] Bhairava then cut off one of Brahmas heads – the head that was boasting – and Brahma was grateful for having his ego so painfully removed. Here, the purpose of the Aghori tradition is revealed: to destroy the ego and the illusion, attachment and fear it creates. The means by which this is achieved focus on the breaking of taboos, ascetic practices and exposure to pollution, both physical and spiritual. Through this, Aghoris aim to remove the artificial boundaries that have been set up by traditional morality and see beyond the illusion of duality. They share core Hindu beliefs about the soul: that it is trapped in a wheel of suffering (*dukkha*) through reincarnation (*samsara*), that one of the reasons for suffering and continual reincarnation is the acceptance of duality, and that once the illusory nature of duality has been realised and an attitude of non-duality (*advaita*) achieved the soul will achieve liberation (*mokṣa*). Aghoris further believe that every soul is bound and held back by eight *astamahapashas* – "great nooses" – including fear, anger, shame, greed, sensual pleasure and obsession. Aghori practices often expose the Aghori to stimuli that trigger these emotions in order to overcome them: they may go naked, exposed to shame to eventually remove it; they perform rites in cremation grounds where ghosts and spiritual pollution linger in order to feel fear and overcome it; they may perform certain sexual practices that help them overcome the pull of sensual desire.

---

176 *Shiva Purana* vol. 1, VIII. 1, pp. 57, ed. Professor J. L. Shastri. Motilal Banarsidass, 1970.

In recent years the Aghoris have reformed their sect in order to legitimise it, caring for the sick that nobody else will touch for fear of pollution and contagion: they care for lepers and perform miraculous healing for those affected by diseases that ostracise them from their community. [177] By ministering to leprosy sufferers – whose bodies are considered too polluted even for the cremation pyre – the Aghori demonstrates that he is beyond the duality of clean and unclean. Aghoris perform this service "as an exercise for overcoming their aversions". [178] Some sources suggest they take this care for the dead further, using their potent power of transformation and healing (gained through frequent exposure to pollution) to free the deceased from living the fate of a homeless ghost by consuming parts of the dead body. [179] The deliberate immersion in the taboo and polluted, that which would otherwise terrify and cause us to break down, is a way of removing fear and the illusion of duality. Just like the fire of destruction in the Tower card, this is a method through which all is made equal, yet it evokes primal fears. As such, the resulting process of destruction of boundaries is painful.

There is some suggestion that Aghoris perform *shāv sadhana*: meditation while sitting on a corpse. [180] It creates detachment from the physical world through exposure to something that should physically shock and repulse. The loincloth that Aghoris sometimes wear, taken from a cremation shroud, signifies that they live in a permanent state of death. [181] The location

---

177 Ronald L. Barrett, ***Aghor Medicine: Pollution, Death and Healing in Northern India.***

178 ***Ibid.***, p. 5.

179 Veena Das, **"Language and Body: Transactions in the Construction of Pain"** p. 78, in ***Daedalu***, vol. 125, no. 1, (Winter, 1996), pp. 67–91.

180 June McDaniel, ***Offering Flowers, Feeding Skulls: Popular Goddess Worship in West Bengal***, pp. 123–132. Oxford University Press, 2004.

181 Richard Burghart, **"Renunciation in the Religious Traditions of South Asia"**, p. 648, in ***Man***, New Series, vol. .18, no. 4, (Dec. 1983) pp. 635–653.

chosen for Aghori practices is also significant, representing the "...totality of psychomental life, fed by consciousness of the 'I'; the corpses symbolise the various sensory and mental activities. Seated at the center of his profane experience, the yogin 'burns' the activities that feed them, just as corpses are burned in the cemetery. By meditating in the [cremation ground] he more directly achieves the combustion of egotistic experiences, he evokes the terrible demons and obtains mastery over them". [182]

The act of cremation – used in the card image as the crumbling tower itself – in Hinduism is symbolically important for the deceased. Throughout Hindu life, fire sacrifices of food offerings (*yajna*) are made to the gods, and when building the sacrificial fire the first sacrifice of the creator god Prajapati, which helped create the world, is re-enacted. At important moments in Hindu life *saṃskāras* (life-crisis rituals) are performed, which usually involve fire sacrifice. Cremation of the corpse (*antyeshti saṃskāras*), the final ritual that a person will be involved in, is seen as the ultimate fire sacrifice to the gods and in its destruction the universe is recreated. [183]

One Aghori, Vimalanada, whose words were recorded by Robert E. Svoboda, reflected that incineration was the most important process for gaining truth, stated: "I don't believe in *Sampradaya* (sect), I believe in *Sampradaha* (incineration). Burn down everything which is getting in the way of your perception of truth." [184]

---

182 Mircea Eliade, **Yoga: Immortality and Freedom**, p. 296. Princeton University Press, 1970.
183 Ronald L. Barrett, **Aghor Medicine: Pollution, Death and Healing in Northern India**, p. 52.
184 Robert E. Svoboda, **Aghora: At the Left Hand of God**, p. 167. Sadhana Publications, 1999.

The cremation ground – a microcosm of the greater universe – is a world where everything changes, nothing is permanent, and every body burns. It is the great equaliser, a potent reminder that in the end even our most treasured ideas of self, fuelled by ego, will be consumed and crumble to ash. These cremation grounds are the home to Aghoris and to Shiva, also an ascetic, who is often depicted as dancing his great dance of destruction. As Mahakala, Shiva is worshipped as "Great Time", who is inexorable and brings death and destruction suddenly. When great changes comes for us, we cannot make them wait.

✥ Revelation

Destruction; devastation; sudden change; painful realisation; external forces acting upon a person to force them to change; turning life upside down; need to re-evaluate; everything being taken away; breakdown; destruction of the ego; liberation from what held a person back; release; freedom from fear through immersion in it; breaking down constructs that limit us; crisis; the house built upon sand.

Negatively aspected...
Refusing to let change happen; being unable to recover from a crisis; clinging to constructs despite them falling away; not cutting losses when you should; the captain staying on the sinking ship.

The Star

Cult of the Virgin Mary as Stella Maris

Child, there will come a time when the darkness of the world consumes you, a time of deepest despair where you are tossed upon the tempestuous seas, fearing for your life and your soul. Here you have lost everything, but there is one final thing you can give up: a prayer, humble and true. Here, in the darkest storm-ravaged skies, I shine my brightest and will not abandon you. When you call to me in earnest I shall pour forth the waters of salvation and blessing. I shall save you in body and soul, for I am the Mother of the World, the Star of the Sea, the Queen of Heaven and the Lady of Perpetual Help. I have walked in both worlds to bring you a road to salvation; I have known the bitterest sorrows that I might know mercy; yet I am inviolate and pure, that I might be a channel for grace and divine love. To my children I give assurance of blessing, as long as they remember that they are divine beings walking the world for a short time and when their road is ended they will continue. I promise them their higher selves, a calling more radiant and true, and ask only that they continue to rise, shining forth in the world. I am the light of dawn after the long night, the bringer of hope and joy; it is through me that all prayers may be answered. Let the sailor lost at sea call to me: I shall guide him home. Let the mourner turn her mind to me: I shall comfort her. Let those in darkness ask for my help: I shall draw them back into the light when all else is lost. I am the Mother of Miracles, and the waters I pour forth replenish the world.

∞ Mystery

"O you who find yourself tossed about by the storms of life, turn not your eyes from the brightness of this Star, if you would not be overwhelmed by its boisterous waves. If the winds of

temptations rise, if you fall among the rocks of tribulations, look up at the Star, call on Mary. [...] when you implore her aid, you will never yield to despair ; thinking on her, you will not err ; under her patronage you will never wander; beneath her protection you will not fear; she being your guide, you will not weary; if she be your propitious Star, you will arrive safely in the port." [185]

Devotion to Mary, mother of Christ, is widespread and old, going back to around the 4th century CE. [186] She is praised by many names and has manifested to her devotees across the world in many forms. The particular form of Mother Mary represented in the *Tarot Apokalypsis* as the Star is Our Lady, Star of the Sea, also known as Stella Maris. As Stella Maris, Mary is a sign of hope and guidance for those lost in the darkness; she provides mercy to those lost on the metaphorical seas of life's troubles and brings them safely to shore. Like the Star of the tarot, which comes directly after the terror and destruction of the Tower, she heals and soothes, offering renewal and peace.

She shares the title "Stella Maris" with Polaris, the North Star or Pole Star, by which sailors have navigated since ancient times. It arises from St. Jerome's Latin translation of Eusebius' *Onomasticon*: he translated the Hebrew name Miryam ("drop of the sea") as "Stilla Maris", which was later transcribed as "Stella Maris", a term that also made sense in Latin. [187] Perhaps a happy coincidence, as it fit with traditional ideas of Mary and later became a popular name for her. The first reliable use of this name is found in the 9th-century writings of Paschasius

---

185 St Bernard of Clairvaux, On the "Missus Est", Hom. II, **Sermons of St. Bernard**, p. 47. R. & T. Washbourne Ltd., 1909.

186 Chris Maunder, **The Origins of the Cult of the Virgin Mary**, p. 23. Burns and Oates, 2008.

187 Maurice A. Canney, **"Stella Maris" in "Revue de l'histoire des religions"**, vol. 115 (1937), pp. 90–94.

Radbertus: "Mary, Star of the Sea, must be followed in faith and morals lest we capsize amidst the storm-tossed waves of the sea." [188]

St Bernard of Clairvaux described Stella Maris as a "glorious star", casting her radiance over the whole world. She was "the star whose splendour rejoices heaven, terrifies hell, and sheds its mild and beneficent influence on the poor exiles of the earth. She is truly the Star which, being placed over this world's tempestuous sea, shines forth by the lustre of her merits and example." [189] The Star of the tarot is a kind, merciful and healing influence, purely beneficent in nature. The Virgin Mary in all her aspects is believed to grant miraculous healing and there are many collections of miracles attested to her. [190] Many traditional prayers ask her to grant protection, healing, grace, mercy and deliverance, and to intercede on behalf of the petitioner. The earliest extant example of a Marian prayer is the *Sub tuum praesidium*, found in a fragmentary papyrus from late ancient Egypt, thought to date to around the 3rd or 4th century CE, in which she is called upon in her merciful power:

"We take refuge in your mercy, Theotokos [Mother of God]. Do not disregard our prayers in troubling times, but deliver us from danger, O only pure one, only blessed one." [191]

A hymn dedicated specifically to Stella Maris (*Ave Maris Stella*) is used in the Liturgy of the Hours in the Catholic church, calling upon her to "break the captives' fetters, light on blind-

---

188 Paschasuis Radbertus, ***De Corpore et Sanguine Domine***.

189 St Bernard of Clairvaux, On the "Missus Est", Hom. II, ***Sermons of St. Bernard***, pp. 46–7.

190 See, for instance, Johannes Herolt Discipulus, ***Miracles of the Blessed Virgin Mary*** (1435–50). Trans. C. C. Swinton Bland. Routledge, 1928.

191 Sarah Boss, ***The Virgin Mary: the Complete Resource***, p. 130. Continuum, 2007.

ness pour, all our ills expelling, every bliss implore". [192] Here she has the power to liberate people from their bonds, shine light upon that which causes us blindness and confusion, revealing our way in the darkness, and remove that which troubles us, replacing it with joy. A popular Catholic hymn, *Hail, Queen of Heaven, the Ocean Star*, written by Father John Lingard in the 19th century, invokes the purity of Stella Maris, calling her "gentle, chaste and spotless Maid". Like the Star of the tarot she is a figure of unwavering purity, and it is from this purity that she is able to shine such powerful blessings of healing upon us. The hymn also calls her "guide of the wanderer here below", referring to her role as the North Star, by which we can navigate through life's waters. It petitions her to pity the sorrows of the petitioner, calm their fears and soothe their misery with hope. [193] Like the Star in the tarot, Mary is a source of hope for those who call to her for aid.

Romanos the Melodist wrote a hymn to Mary evoking symbolism of water and light to call upon her powers of purity and mercy:

"Rejoice, for you caused the refulgent light to dawn!
Rejoice, for you caused the river of many streams to gush forth!
Rejoice, living image of the font!
Rejoice, remover of the stain of sin!
Rejoice, laver that washes the conscience clean!" [194]

Like the Star, Mary is a cleansing pool ready to baptise her devotees and remove their ills. After the darkness of night she

---

192 ***Liber Hymnarius***, *translated from the Latin at http://www.ourcatholicprayers.com/ave-maris-stella.html. Accessed 1 August 2015.*

193 *https://en.wikipedia.org/wiki/Hail_Queen_of_Heaven,_the_Ocean_Star. Accessed 15 July 2015.*

194 *Version by Andrew Harvey, quoted in* **Spiritual Writings on Mary**, *p. 230. Skylight Paths Publishing, 2005.*

brings a new dawn, offering promise and renewal. Symbolism of water is commonly given to Mary in descriptions, such as in Bernard of Clairvaux's writings: "Before the birth of Mary, a constant flow of grace was lacking, because this aqueduct did not exist". [195]

One of the powers of the Star is in bringing two different worlds together: it reunites the spiritual and material realms, allowing people to live equally in both. Through nourishing the material realm with the waters of the spiritual realm, a fuller and more blessed life can be lived. The 12th-century mystic Hildegard of Bingen wrote a hymn to Mary saying "light burst from your untouched womb like a flower on the farther side of death. The world-tree is blossoming. Two realms become one", [196] seeing in her the union of mundane and divine.

The power of the Star is to pour spiritual blessings into the everyday world. It is an undoubtedly fortunate card, being associated with "wishing upon a star" and the common practice of referring to great celebrities or experts in their field as "stars". No matter the trouble or darkness, no matter how lost we are, with the Star we can always find our way. Here is our guiding light, hope in the darkness, and an opportunity for healing: here is Our Lady, Star of the Sea, granting us her miraculous mercy and forever extending her hand to those who ask her for help.

∽ Revelation

Hope, light in the darkness; guidance in times of trouble; refreshment, renewal, rejuvenation; blessings being given; unexpected good fortune; a time of healing; spiritual guidance;

---

195 *Ibid.*, p. 107.

196 Hildegard of Bingen, in ***Symphonia***, in ***Hildegard of Bingen: Devotions, Prayers & Living Wisdom*** ed. Mirabai Starr, pp. 50–1. Sounds True Inc., 2008.

finding one's path after confusion; returning to the world after seclusion; nourishing one's spiritual self and path; uniting the spiritual and material worlds; allowing the spiritual to inform the everyday world; a guiding star; intercession; being pulled away from danger; mercy, grace, and salvation.

Negatively aspected...
Ignoring offers of help and healing; refusing to see the hope in the darkness; giving up hope; being lost; difficulties reconciling one's spiritual life with one's everyday life; separation of spiritual and material world; request for help refused.

The Moon
The cult of Hekate

When light fades and the silver paths of the moon snake across the dark earth, the people shall call out for their mother in her waxing and waning, calling her thrice down: torch-bearer, key-bearer, child-bearer. I shall come then to rest at the dreaded crossroads of night, standing sentinel for the lost and the seeking. The baying of my hounds warns and guides as one, my torches blazing in their eyes, showing the way down to the caves of the mysteries. Follow their howling in the moonlight, seeker, lost one, and you shall find the place of my secret rites. There I shall take you into my embrace as a mother, whisper to you in your blindness of the nocturnal and the Other, the dangerous and the liminal. In words like the hissing of snakes and steam I shall teach you of the womb and the tomb, the way to birth through death, the power of the hidden and the ways of magic. You shall descend into me, into the earth, there to be shown the most sacred: the virgin, the bitch and all the rest. Take up my torch and throng the caves with my mystics, howl in the darkness and seek the crossroads of the earth, there to find the undulating workings of the universe in its tides. For I am terrible and fearsome of countenance, queen of witches, fire-breather, mistress of ghosts, and I am the Maid and the Mother, Saviour and Light-Bringer. Through my mysteries you may learn to walk the night-roads of descent and fear not the dark nor the shadows therein.

∽ Mystery

A card of flux, shadows, magic and feminine mysteries, the Moon shows us the dark roads of the subconscious, the half-dreamed and the almost nightmarish. At night, by only the light of the moon, the familiar becomes strange and the way uncer-

tain. By the light of the moon we might catch enough light to be guided through the darkness, secret trysts are made and the nefarious beings of the night emerge. It is here, at the liminal crossroads, that we might participate in the secret rites of Hekate.

Hekate was given many names and epithets that express her nature and her mysteries: Enodia ("of the ways") and Trioditis ("of three ways") stood at the crossroads; Dadouchos ("torch-bearer"), Phosphoros ("light-bearer") and Propolos ("companion" or "guide") illuminated the way into and out of the underworld for Persephone and for initiates; Brimo ("terrible") revealed Hekate's fearsome face; Propylaia ("before the gate") stood at the liminal points of the world; Chthonia ("of the earth") and Aedonaea ("of the underworld") made her home in the realm of the shades and Hades; as Kleidouchos she bore the keys to the world; and Kourotrophos ("child's nurse") gave Hekate a mothering face.

We know little of Hekate's mystery cult, which was shrouded in secrecy. We are given brief images of her mysteries being attended/celebrated by "torchbearing mystics" on the island of Samothrace [197] at night. Initiates into her mysteries were believed to be protected against terrors and storms. [198] Accounts say that they took place in a cave, suggestive of the entrance to the underworld, into which initiates would probably have descended to be shown her sacred mysteries. [199] It is as mistress of the underworld that she was commonly invoked in magic, where she is presented as a fearsome mistress of the dead:

---

197 Nonnus, ***Dionysiaca*** *Vol. 1, 13.400 ff, trans. W. H. D. Rouse. Loeb Classical Library. Harvard University Press, 1940.*

198 *Suidas,* ***The Suda****, ed. D. Whitehead. Adler number: sigma, 79. Online at http://www.stoa.org/sol/*

199 *Hans Dieter Betz,* "***Fragments from a Catabasis Ritual in a Greek Magical Papyrus****" in* ***History of Religions****, vol. 19, no. 4 (May, 1980), pp. 287–95.*

"O nether and nocturnal, and infernal, Goddess of dark, quiet and frightful one, O you who have your meal amid the graves, Night, Darkness, broad Chaos: Necessity, Hard to escape are you; you're Moira and Erinyes, torment, Justice and Destroyer, and you keep Kerberos in chains, with scales of Serpents are you dark…" [200]

However, she was not feared in such invocations but respected, her aid sought because she was so powerful and had command over the realm with which sorcerers often worked: Hades. As dread goddess of the underworld she was associated with various animals that represent power as well as danger, such as snakes. She is often described as having snakes at her brow, on her head, or for her hair and accompanied by baying hounds:

"Hekate Brimo … hearing his words from the abyss, came up … She was garlanded by fearsome snakes that coiled themselves round twigs of oak; the twinkle of a thousand torches lit the scene; and hounds of the underworld barked shrilly all around her." [201]

This terrifying countenance, despite the fact that she was also called "Maid" and depicted in artwork as beautiful, demonstrates her otherness and her rulership over the dangerous, liminal and shadowy. However, Hekate had also a kindly face as child's nurse (Kourotrophos) and mother. She was depicted with a child in her arms on coins and engraved gems, in poses reminiscent of Isis sucking Horus, and shown in theriomorphic form as a whelping Lacadaemonian bitch on the seal of a ring from the 6th century BCE. [202] This maternal role arises in part

---

200 PGM IV. 2855-2862. **Greek Magical Papyri in Translation**, trans. Hans Dieter Betz. London: University of Chicago Press, 1986.

201 Apollonius Rhodius, **Argonautica** 3.1194, trans. E. V. Rieu. London: Penguin Books Ltd., 1971.

202 Rudolph Reitler, "**A Theriomorphic Representation of Hekate-Artemis**" in **American Journal of Archaeology**, vol. 53, no. 1 (Jan.–Mar., 1949), pp. 29-31.

from Hekate's identification with the moon (Porphyry goes as far as to say "the moon is Hecate" [203]). The moon was seen as a generative force through which souls came to earth. [204] The fertile moon of Kourotrophos meets with the fertile earth in Hekate Chthonia's rulership of the underworld, giving her both a shadowy, terrifying face and one of birth and motherhood. To many, she is therefore the fearsome mother, the frightful parts of womanhood, the fluctuating nature of feminine mysteries.

At Eleusis she was Dadouchos and Propolos, Persephone's guide and companion on her journey to and from the underworld, using torches to light her way. She is shown on an Athenian vase in this role with torches raised. [205] In the *Greek Magical Papyri* she is described as carrying twin or triple torches or baskets of fire. [206] Just as Hekate is given the role of guiding Persephone out of the underworld in the Mysteries (see *The High Priestess*), so do her torches guide the magician and mystic to and from a liminal state, between the land of the living and the land of the dead, and in their own ascent out of the womb/tomb and descent back in. Further, she also guards those who tread the dimly lit paths of the mysteries and secret rites, for she was frequently associated with dogs. Dogs in ancient Greece and Rome were not used as guides for travellers, but as hunting dogs and guard dogs. The type of dog usually shown with/as Hekate was known for its loud baying, used to pro-

---

203 Porphyry, **On Images** 8, trans. Edwin Hamilton Gifford. Online: http://classics.mit.edu/Porphyry/images.html

204 Porphyry, **On the Cave of the Nymphs** 8, trans. Thomas Taylor. London: John M. Watkins, 1917.

205 Gisela M. A. Richter, "**An Athenian Vase with the Return of Persephone**", in **The Metropolitan Museum of Art Bulletin**, vol. 26, no. 10 (Oct., 1931), pp. 245–8.

206 For example, PGM IV. 2441–2621, which gives her "untiring flaming fire in triple baskets" and calls her "fire-breather"; PGM IV. 2708–84, which says she walks on fire; PGM XII. 1–13, in which she comes carrying torches. **Greek Magical Papyri in Translation**.

tect farms and homes from thieves. [207] As Phosphoros she also watched over the trysts of lovers at night-time, bringing enough light in the darkness by which they might see each other.

As the Moon, Hekate has a multitude of faces that shift from one to another as easily as the moon changes in the sky. She rules over the shadowy and liminal parts of the earth, lights the way on the dangerous roads, guides us through the mysteries, teaches us her secrets, terrifies and protects. She bears the keys to the mysteries, opening up the way before us that we might enter the realms of otherness and darkness.

~ Revelation

Otherness, the Other; feminine mysteries; secrecy and mysteries; secret meetings and trysts; a journey (physical or metaphorical) through uncertain or untested areas; the unknown; the subconscious; magic; descent; investigating the taboo or dangerous; female biology; the key to a mystery.

Negatively aspected…
Secrets being kept maliciously; not being able to trust a person; danger in unknown places; risks as a result of a new path; refusal to adapt to change; difficulties with aspects of the feminine; madness.

---

207 Virgil, ***Georgics** III. 404ff*; Varro, ***De Re Rustica**, 1.19.3*.

The Sun

The Roman cult of Mithras

Open your eyes, mortal, and they will be blinded; keep them closed and you shall surely die. You cannot live without light – not light from the stars, from the moon, or even the sun, but pure and holy light, white-hot and scourging: fiery truth-light from the realms beyond the sun. It is from here that all truth comes and it is here from which your soul descended into birth, trapped in that rock of a world, a womb-tomb in which you will truly die without my salvation. I am the revelation of the universe in its glory; I am the Earth-Shaker, Bull-Tamer, Equinox-Pusher; where I step I burn the life in my path, yet all grows beneath me. I reveal myself to you and the sevenfold rays of light illuminate you, that I might bid you to take the first step of the ladder that will lead you to the truth beyond truth. I make open to you the doorway of the temple that you might descend into its starry cave and in the darkness see the mysteries illuminated. I destroy the force that holds your soul here, striking away the chains that bind you. I may burn you, you may turn your face from my light, but you will soon know that you are my Soldier, and you will share a feast with your Brothers of the Sun in my name. Let all elements of earth, air and rushing fire be obedient unto me: I am the mighty one who possesses immortal fire; I am the one who begets and destroys; come forth and follow. For I am the moment of revelation, the mystery that is revealed at the end of All, and that which is found in the centre of All.

~ Mystery

"What further then shall I say? You foreign priest and partner of Mithra, you will worship Mithra alone as the sun, whose light penetrates and illuminates, as you imagine, the secret shrines." [208]

---

208 *Hegemonius*, **Acts of Archelaus** *ch. 36.*

The Sun may convey small mysteries of the everyday world but also the deeper mysteries of the soul, initiation, revelation and illumination. While every Major Arcana card initiates the reader into a mystery, the Sun represents the moment in which illumination occurs when mystery is revealed. It is the awe-inspiring, wondrous realisation that is initiation's aim, which was physically represented in many mystery initiations in the Graeco-Roman world by an unveiling/revealing of a cult icon. This icon was often an image of the god to whom the cult was dedicated but may also have been an item that was symbolic of the mystery being conveyed (as in the rites of Eleusis – see *The High Priestess*).

The Roman cult of Mithras, active from around 1st century BCE to the 4th century CE, offered revelation of the truth of reality. It was a solar cult, Mithras being a god of the sun. Its members were from many walks of life but it was popular with soldiers, who saw in Mithras one of their own. It is clear from the numerous locations of Mithraic temples (called *mithraea* pl. or *mithraeum* sing.) that the cult was widespread and popular. The extant accounts of Mithraic beliefs and practices in most cases come from Christian writers who may have been sensationalising their descriptions but which prove useful in confirming conclusions reached from iconography.

The cult of Mithras had a strong focus on planetary symbolism and foundations in Neoplatonist philosophy. Its seven grades of initiation were each associated with one of the seven classical planets, as shown by a fresco found beneath the church of Santa Prisca, Rome, and we know that they represented an upwards ascension, depicted in the *mithraeum* of Felicissimus at Ostia, which showed the symbols of the seven planets in a ladder ascending upwards. This series of initiations for cult members suggests a focus on spiritual evolution and the continued process of realisation and illumination. The early Christian theologian, Origen, wrote of the link between the cult of Mithras and Plato's philosophy of the birth and ascension of the soul through the planets, giving us an insight into the wealth of symbolism for the soul's illumination found in the cult. He identified two heavenly spheres in Mithraic belief, one fixed and the other of the planets, through which souls ascended on a road with seven gates and a final gate at the summit. [209] The Emperor Julian also wrote of the mysteries by which Mithras "leads souls back again to the courts of light". [210] These initiations through the planetary gates refined the soul of the initiate until they reached a final gateway.

The cult's use of caves, or underground temples that were made to look like caves, gives us further insight into the nature of the mysteries that took place there. The roofs of the caves or temples were often painted to look like the night sky. These "caves" may have been seen as representations of the world fabricated by Mithras – the mundane, material world in which the soul currently resides. [211] Plato's Allegory of the Cave – which seems to have been accepted by the cult of Mithras – makes the cave symbolic of the mundane world, a world of shadow, a poor reflection of the truth of the soul and the universe. [212] The soul, through initiation, could take part in rites within the mundane world – a microcosm – that they could then ascend out of into the macrocosm, or noetic realm.

This iconography of the soul's ascension is akin to that of Mithras' ascension in the "rock birth" figures found in many cult

---

209 Origen, **contra Celsum VI. 21–22**
210 **Oration to the Mother of the Gods** in **Two Orations of the Emperor Julian**, trans. Taylor, Thomas.
211 Porphyry, **De Antro Nympharum 6.** *For other accounts of the worship of Mithras in a cave or cave-like temple, see Tertullian,* **De Corona 15**.
212 Plato, **The Republic**, *514a–520a*.

temples, [213] in which Mithras is represented as being born from a rock with both arms upraised. This rock – like the *mithraeum* and cave – represents the world. [214] It seems that the Mithraists believed in a mundane world of shadow and illusion, a cosmic world of planets, in which could be found the sun, and the hypercosmic world of truth, in which could be found the hypercosmic sun. Scenes from various *mithraea* depict both Mithras and Sol/Helios together, which seems odd if we assume that Mithras is the sun god (Sol and Helios were the gods of the sun in Roman and Greek mythology). It is suggested that this is because the Mithraists believed in two sun gods. [215] Mithraists saw Sol/Helios as the visible sun and Mithras as the hypercosmic sun located in the *hyperouranios topos* (the place beyond the fixed stars, a realm described in Plato's *Phaedrus* [216]). In this threefold cosmology, the moon ruled over the lowest realm (earth), and served as a mediator between this world and the cosmic and hypercosmic worlds. [217] Further, the moon was a force by which the soul achieved birth (descent). This leads to one of the most important symbols of the cult of Mithras: the bull-slaying scene, in which Mithras stabs the neck of a bull. It was this image that was found in the innermost part of the *mithraeum*, so is likely to have been the one revealed during initiation. With the understanding that the moon was the force that brought souls to birth (therefore confining them to the mundane world), Porphyry shows us that the moon is symbolised by a bull:

---

213 See, for instance, the St. Clement/Rome bas-relief (Cumont, **Mysteries of Mithra,** fig. 30 p. 130).

214 See, for instance, Clauss, **The Roman Cult of Mithras,** p.62-70. The snake that is so often depicted curled around the base of the rock represents the earth also.

215 David Ulansey, **Mithras and the Hypercosmic Sun.** Studies in Mithraism, ed. John R. Hinnells, pp. 257–264.

216 Plato, **Phaedrus,** 246D6–247E6.

217 Sarah Iles Johnston, **Hekate Soteira: A Study of Hekate's Roles in the Chaldean Oracles and Related Literature,** p.29. Oxford University Press, 1990.

"... to the moon also as presiding over birth they gave the name of bee, especially since the moon is a bull and the moon culminates in the Bull, and bees are bull-begotten. And souls when they come to birth are bull-begotten..." [218]

By killing a bull, Mithras is killing the force that holds the soul in the mundane world, allowing it to pass through the gates of initiation and ascension, through the cosmic world and finally into the hypercosmic world: apotheosis. Such an illumination is not gentle but sudden and shocking. Following the half-light of the Moon in the Major Arcana, the Sun burns away shadow and illusion, almost blinding us with its radiant truth. It is for this reason that Mithras was depicted in a white tunic with a golden crown, often with a red cape – the colours of divine fire.

The image of the card is inspired by the Mithras Liturgy, a theurgical rite in which the magician aims to achieve union with Mithras. He is shown here as revealed to the magician, who has caused his soul to be lifted up, breathed in the sun's rays and been given a vision of the visible gods; he has seen the sun's disk expanded and its gates opened so that he may travel through them, ascending beyond the visible realm to the cosmic realm, where Helios has appeared to him and led him to the gateway to Mithras, who finally appears in full revelation. [219] There are also elements in the card taken from other representations of Mithras, including a bas-relief from Modena in which he is wrapped by a snake (this image appears in several places) with the ring of constellations around him. Here he is also rock-born, representing the ascent of the soul from the earth and Mithras' power to offer it to initiates. He holds his traditional fiery torch and bears a gladius, the weapon of a Roman soldier.

---

218 Porphyry, **De Antro Nympharum**, ch. 18.
219 PGM IV. 475–829. **Greek Magical Papyri in Translation**, trans. Hans Dieter Betz.

This Roman cult of Mithras, a solar cult and series of initiations that offer the soul ascension from the lunar realm, finds its natural place in the Sun card of the tarot. For no other Graeco-Roman cult do we have so much evidence for a focus on revelation and illumination. Mithras is the sun beyond the sun, the truth beyond truth, the ultimate revelation, and the bliss that comes therefrom.

❧ Revelation

Illumination, revelation, truth being revealed; the harsh light of day; realisation; achieving a great understanding; the natural state of the soul is one of illumination; liberation from illusion; rising above the shadows; speaking truth to others; showing others the right way; happiness, bliss; celebration and victory; a time of growth; improvement and movement forwards; a burning desire for truth.

Negatively aspected...
Delayed improvement; seeking illumination in the wrong place; painful realisations; a truth that hurts.

Judgement
The Great Flood

Even the universe grows old and weary; in its age it cries out for renewal. Just as the soul yearns to rise out of its tumultuous waters of creation to be made anew, so the world seeks liberation from inertia. In this, you and the universe are one and the same: both must be made new, both must be pulled from stagnation and evil, both must be flooded by the divine waters of birth. I am the Deluge, the force of overcoming that must in turn be overcome. I am the Chaos that will destroy chaos and usher in the age of peace. I am the hand of God that crushes the unrighteous and makes the way for goodness of heart. Know me and fear me, for my mystery is as deep as the unending ocean; it calls to you inexorably, urging you to rise, to direct your heart to the call of your higher self, to turn to the goodness of your heart as a compass and guide. I am the judgement of the righteous over the wicked, the destruction of evil and the bane of death. In my purging waters there is only life, renewing and replenishing, the breaking of chains and the urge to ascend above all limitations to the heavens.

☙ Mystery

It is not always through mystical practices and initiations into mystery religions that we achieve revelation and spiritual evolution. Mythology plays a vital role in our spiritual landscape, often acting as the foundation upon which the mysteries of initiation are founded; mythology is the language through which a mystery is revealed and experienced; it links our human endeavours and experiences with those of the gods, heroes and ancestors, creating a timeless thread between the past, present and the future. In the Judgement card, we show not a mystery religion or mystical practice but

an almost universal myth, a motif, of spiritual evolution and rebirth: the Great Flood.

Judgement represents a fundamental experience of human life: evolution and rebirth. It is so vital for our spiritual health that no single mystical practice or mystery religion could illustrate it – every initiation, every revelation, is a process of rebirth. The soul is reborn out of darkness, out of a state of death and inertia; in alchemical terms, it rises out of its state as a base metal and is transmuted into gold. In the card image, the people in the lowest part of the card are white, their skin corpse-pale; some are actually dead, their bodies dashed against rocks by the great waves. Those who have pulled themselves from the waters are pink-skinned, alive and rising; those at the pinnacle of the card, taking the final leap off the foundation of earth towards the glowing heavens, are golden like the philosopher's stone.

The Great Flood myth is found in a large number of cultures, the most familiar to the Western world being that of the Old Testament, in which God sent a flood to wipe out mankind, which had become wicked. [220] In this story, one man (whose heart is not wicked) and his family survive the flood, saving a pair of each animal and repopulating the earth. In the same book, the world and all creatures were created out of the chaotic waters, [221] raising parallels between the waters of origin and the waters of rebirth. In the Judgement card, it is from a state of darkness and origin that we are reborn so we might rise above it.

A Great Flood is found in ancient Sumeria too. As above, the gods decide to wipe out mankind, but one man hears of the plan

---

220 *Genesis 6: 5–7.*
221 *Genesis 1: 1–2.*

and builds a boat in which to survive the violent floods. After seven days and nights, the sun shines for the first time and the man, Ziusudra, prostrates himself in praise to the gods. [222] Ancient Greece had its own Great Flood, referenced by Plato in various works as "the great deluge of all", [223] as well as a tale of a great flood in which Deucalion, the son of Prometheus, survives a flood sent by Zeus to destroy mankind by building a chest in which he and his wife survive. [224] In several texts of Hindu mythology there is a great flood from which the Manu (first man) of that age, his family and seven sages escape, having been warned by Matsya, the fish-avatar of Viṣṇu. [225] The *Kalevala*, the Finnish mythological epic, has one rune (verse) that refers to a flood of blood that covered everything. [226]

Chinese myth tells us of the Great Flood of Gun-Yu, a natural disaster rather than an act of divine punishment, which was eventually overcome by a culture hero, Yu, who went on to found the Xia dynasty. This story offers a mythological origin for civilisation, as the result of fighting against the flooding was great inventions and improvements in agriculture, husbandry and land management. As such, it represents the evolution of humankind out of a chaotic state into a higher one of order. [227] One commentator has pointed out that in this flood myth, "they employed water as an image for the dissolution of all distinctions, and thus

---

222 James B. Pritchard, ***Ancient Near Eastern Texts Relating to the Old Testament***, *pp. 43-4. Princeton University Press, 1969.*

223 *Plato,* ***Laws*** *III. 677a;* ***Timaeus*** *22;* ***Critias*** *111–2.*

224 *Ovid,* ***Metamorphoses*** *I. 262-416, trans. A. D. Melville, pp. 9–13. Oxford University Press, 1998.*

225 *James G. Lochtefeld,* ***The Illustrated Encyclopedia of Hinduism***, *pp. 228–9. The Rosen Publishing Group, 2002.*

226 *M. Kuusi, K. Bosley and M. Branch eds. trans.* ***Finnish Folk Poetry: Epic: An anthology in Finnish and English***, *p. 94. Finnish Literature Society, 1977.*

227 *Lihui Yang et. al.* ***Handbook of Chinese Mythology***, *p. 117. Oxford University Press, 2005.*

presented the taming of the flood as a process that recapitulated in the age of men, and, through human action, the creation of the world". [228] Similarly, the Judgement card of the tarot shows how we may transform ourselves from a state of base, ignorant wildness to a state of golden, enlightened awareness. It also allows us to recreate, through our own choices and actions, the world in which we live and move. It reminds us that every action we take and thought we have will be directly reflected in the world and, just as the gods of the Old Testament and ancient Sumer sought to destroy what they saw as an imperfect world, we can "destroy" that which is imperfect in our lives, breaking the chains of the base and sweeping it away. This is the process through which we can achieve a clean slate.

That nearly all Great Flood myths have a culture hero who survives the flood or seeks to tame it reminds us that at the centre of this vast, cosmic occurrence there is human will. The Judgement card often presents itself in vast events that are difficult to comprehend (initiation into the mystery religions being one of them), but its focus is on human activity as a means of survival: rebirth and spiritual evolution is not a passive journey but one of active will and energy. The culture heroes of these myths represent "the human craving for life" [229] as well as the experience of having one's "true calling": they are called upon by the gods to be the beings from whom the rest of creation will be rebuilt. This true calling, the spiritual quest or realisation of one's purpose, is represented in the tarot by the Judgement card, which calls us to become better than we are. It is representative of our higher selves and gives us a sense of direction and spiritual purpose in our

---

228 Mark Edward Lewis, ***The Flood Myths of Early China,*** *p. 16. State University of New York Press, 2006.*

229 *David Leeming*, ***The Oxford Companion to World Mythology***, *p. 138. Oxford University Press, 2010.*

lives, challenging us to direct our will towards a distant goal of evolution.

To many, the title of the card poses difficulty. It, like the Great Flood narratives of many cultures, brings with it notions of a wrathful deity punishing human beings for wrongdoing. Indeed, sometimes the Judgement card refers to morality and the codes by which we live, our sense of goodness and an understanding of what is right. This is because a moral code is one of the means by which we evolve spiritually – it is a guide for better living. The purge of the unrighteous during the Great Flood myth can be seen as symbolic of our purging of that which is too base for us, too low: that which holds us back from spiritual liberation. At the centre of the Great Flood motif are themes of rebirth from the violent waters, humankind overcoming and rising above the chaos of destruction and death and the goodness of just one human heart ensuring the eventual recreation of the world.

∼ Revelation

An experience or process of rebirth; rising above; climbing out of a state of chaos or inertia; finding one's purpose; having a "calling"; the call to the spiritual life; gaining increased awareness; a heightened sense of understanding; transformation; pulling oneself out of a base and uncontrollable situation; morality and a sense of what is right; achieving freedom, listening to the higher self; serving one's higher needs, purging that which is holding one back.

Negatively aspected…
Refusal to accept a calling; being trapped or chained down by a person, situation, or outlook; feelings of going backwards; regression; a morally bad choice; ignorance; being kept in the dark.

The World

The Sophia of Valentinian Gnosticism

You have walked the long road, seeker of wisdom, with your feet on the firmament of the earth; but do you see the place in which your head resides? Do you see the starry canopy in which the angels call you back to your place of birth? You are a being of divine origin, one star among the company of stars above, with a blood-tie to the earth below: you are the very force and process through which the universe might know itself; you are the means by which the sacred is exalted. All things share in your divine spark: by exalting that which is above, you also exalt that which is below, no thing is separate from another thing, yet they are fragmented from the great One. This is the triumph and completion of the world and the soul's journey: it has separated from the heavens so that it might come to know the plethora of manifestation into which it is born, so that it might know reunion with the whole. Your soul is a cauldron of synthesis, in which the sacred and mundane dance and embrace. When you have opened your eyes to this truth, you may see me in all my glory: resplendent with my prostitution among the company of mortals, for I am Wisdom, and am to be taken by all. My mystery is that of the beginning and the end of all things, of the purpose for the journey and the attainment at its completion. I am the first and the last, the fallen and the exalted. I am your birth right. Now, seeker, you have reached the end, and thus you can see the beginning.

≈ Mystery

At the end of the Major Arcana we are given the World. It shares with the Fool the paradoxical nature of first and last, beginning and ending, for it is the goal attained at the end

of the journey, the cause of the journey and the process by which it is travelled. As with many of the higher cards of the Major Arcana, its spiritual applications seem more natural than its mundane meanings. At its simplest, the World represents the wisdom that has been gained over the long journey to attainment. Here it is shown in the form of Sophia, the divine feminine of Valentinian Gnosticism.

The Valentinian sect of Christianity, originating in the 2nd century CE and continuing for around 600 years, is now defined as "gnostic", a term used to signify forms of early Christianity that did not become orthodox or ancient religions that viewed the material world as created imperfectly. In the case of the Valentinian school, the world, while imperfect, contained divine essence and was created as a means through which redemption and reunion with the spiritual world could be attained. The Valentinian text, *Apocryphon of John*, presents a myth in which a feminine force called Sophia, "wisdom", is part of a pair in one of a series of aeons, created by an ineffable spiritual force above all things. She "wanted to bring forth a likeness of herself without the consent of the Spirit [...] and without her consort". [230] When she did so, her creation was crude and ignorant; she named him Yaldabaoth, hiding him from the other aeons and the Spirit in a cloud. Yaldabaoth thought he was the only being; he drew power from his mother, creating new aeons beneath him. He created the material world and man in seven days but it was not until he blew the breath that was Sophia's power into his creation that man moved and gained strength. [231] Due to her act, Sophia "fell" from her position in the aeons, re-attaining a position there, albeit lower, after pleading for redemption.

---

230 James M. Robinson ed., **The Nag Hammadi Library in English**, p. 110. New York: HarperSanFrancisco, 1990.

231 **Ibid**., p. 116.

The gnostic text *Pistis Sophia* tells of Sophia's ascent back up through the aeons following her fall into chaos. Sophia's ascent and reunion with the divine is complete when she states, "For the Light is with me, and I myself am with the Light". [232] This text also states that Sophia's "light-energy" will be drained by the beings in this chaos. In the same way, when we forget our divine origins and the sacred spark within us and others, our light begins to fade.

Sophia's fall is the descent of the soul into matter. This, and her repentance and redemption, created the three parts of the universe: matter from her suffering, soul from her repentance and spirit from her gnosis. [233] Sophia needed a place in which unformed spiritual substance could grow to maturity – this place was the material world. She used Yaldabaoth to create human beings and through her instructions Yaldabaoth blew the spiritual seed emanating from her into each one. Just as the external world is made up of matter, soul and spirit, so each person is made up of the same, a microcosm of a divine plane. According to the ancient writers, spirit was secretly given to Yaldabaoth so that he might, unknowingly, pass it onto each soul he created, so that the body created for that soul might carry the spirit. [234] This Valentinian teaching reminds us that we originate from the divine; it is our inheritance and our birthright to seek reunion with it. The World represents the womb in which the gnosis to achieve this is gestated and the process through which we may learn to synthesise the mundane and divine elements of our lives and selves in order to transcend them. Thus, Sophia holds a

---

232 *Pistis Sophia* 159: 116, trans. G.R.S Mead, p. 97. J. M. Watkins, 1921.

233 David Brons, **The Valentinian View of Creation.** *The Gnostic Society Library. Online at: http://www.gnosis.org/library/valentinus/Valentinian_Creation.htm.* Brons cites Ireneaus' **Refutation of Heresies** *6:25–27 and* **Excerpts of Theodotus** *43:2–46:1.*

234 *Irenaeus,* **Against Heresies** *1:5–6.*

flaming heart in her right hand, symbolic in alchemy of the *anima mundi*, the World Soul, [235] an intrinsic connection between all living things on the planet.

Through this myth, the Valentinians understood "our own consciousness has emerged from a primordial wholeness and proceeded into alienation and chaos. Yet even in our confused state, we still sense a connection […] with a higher, transcendental self. Thus, like Sophia, we are split in two: our human personality abides in confusion and alienation, while our eternal self partakes of wholeness and wisdom". [236] This dual nature of the soul is illustrated in the card by Atlas, a man holding up the world, and by the double-edged sword held by Sophia.

Sophia does not only appear in Valentinian cosmology; reverence for her can be found in the Old Testament as wisdom to be sought after: "Acquire Wisdom, never forget Her, do not desert Her, She will keep you safe. Love Her, She will watch over you". [237] Philo treated Sophia as the divine mother, an attribute or emanation of the divine father, whom he called "the husband of Wisdom". [238] She was Mother Wisdom who nurtured humankind, so it is not surprising that alchemy depicted her as the World Soul, nourishing all facets of creation. The *Aurora Consurgens*, attributed to St. Thomas Aquinas, depicted the process of alchemical transformation as a liberation of Sophia – and therefore each soul – from her imprisonment in the material world. [239]

---

235 *Robert Place, in correspondence, January 2016.*

236 *Stephan A. Holler,* **Gnosticism: New Light on the Ancient Tradition of Inner Knowing***, pp. 39–40. Quest Books, 2002.*

237 *Proverbs 4:5–6.*

238 *Asphodel P. Long,* **In a Chariot Drawn by Lions: The Search for the Female in Deity***, p. 46, 162. The Women's Press, 1992; Raphael Patai,* **The Hebrew Goddess***, p. 98. Wayne State University Press, 1990.*

239 *Stephan A. Holler,* **Gnosticism: New Light on the Ancient Tradition of Inner Knowing***, p. 51*

Other gnostic texts make reference to Sophia or another divine feminine being like her. *Thunder, Perfect Mind*, from the Nag Hammadi Library discovered in 1945, is a revelatory speech by an unnamed feminine force who many scholars have suggested is Sophia. The speaker gives numerous paradoxical statements highlighting the nature of Sophia and the World card:

"For I am the first and the last. I am the honoured one and the scorned one. I am the whore and the holy one. I am the wife and the virgin. [...] I am the silence that is incomprehensible and the idea whose remembrance is frequent. I am the voice whose sound is manifold and the word whose appearance is multiple. [...] I am the union and the dissolution. I am the abiding and I am the dissolution. I am the one below, and they come up to me." [240]

Just as the World card is the conclusion of the journey of the Major Arcana and the cause of the journey, so these lines present dichotomous concepts that, when meditated upon, create a point of synthesis between them. At the culmination of the Major Arcana, we can synthesise all that we have experienced and learned, thereby gaining wisdom.

～ Revelation

Completion, culmination and conclusion; high achievement; victory and triumph in attainment; reaching the end of a journey; synthesis of all that has been learned; gaining wisdom through experience; breaking through to a new stage of one's journey; claiming one's sacred birth-right and inheritance; realising one's place in the universe; realising the sacred and divine in the self.

---

240 James M. Robinson ed., ***The Nag Hammadi Library in English***, *pp. 297, 298, 301.*

Negatively aspected…
Delayed attainment; a journey of struggle; feeling trapped in one's life or body; a hint of something greater than one's current situation; being afraid to move on.

Minor Arcana

Each suit of the Minor Arcana depicts a different ancient civilisation: the Khmer Empire of Cambodia (Pentacles), the Greek and Roman worlds of the classical to Late Antique period (Cups), the Norse of Northern Europe (Swords), and ancient Egypt (Wands). Each of these civilisations had deeply profound and complex ideas of the sacred, which they expressed in art, architecture, literature, religion, ceremony and the little rituals of daily life. These cards show important aspects of the lives of these cultures, from mourning customs and ceremonies for inauguration of a king, to cosmology and social customs. Many of the cards show how people from these cultures interacted in their daily lives with ideas of the sacred and its manifestation in the mundane world. Looking at ancient cultures in this way reminds us that our everyday lives are not separate from the sacred, and that the divine permeates the fabric of our existence on every level. In the modern world it is easy to forget this, but we can learn from those who walked this earth before us how to reclaim the magic of existence.

The Minor Arcana ("Lesser Mysteries") often relate to the everyday world in which we act, to our daily concerns and duties, and to how other people affect our lives. As the sacred manifests in the mundane world, however, they can still present images of spiritual concerns and experiences. They generally do not depict the "big" life experiences like the Major Arcana do.

Each suit of the Minor Arcana is associated with one of the four elements: Earth (Pentacles), Air (Swords), Water (Cups) and Fire (Wands). These elements manifest in our lives in their own way, which in turn gives to each suit an area of concern:

Element	Suit	Area of life
Earth	Pentacles	Money, work, health, home
Air	Swords	Study, learning, communication, the mind
Water	Cups	Emotions, social life, spirituality, romantic life
Fire	Wands	Ambitions, energy, drive, creative pursuits

Numbered 1–10, each of the cards of a suit also have numerological associations, as follows:

1	Initiation, ego, self, beginnings, unity, raw energy
2	Duality, partnership, duality, division, conflict, balance
3	Teamwork, creativity, group, family
4	Manifestation, grounding, the mundane, stillness, stability
5	Destruction, aggression, imbalance
6	Reunion, peace, harmony, re-balance
7	Fluidity, flow, uncertainty, unreliability
8	Certainty, setting down in stone, heaviness
9	Fruition, results, the inevitable direction
10	Conclusion, transformation, moving on

The numerological and elemental associations of each Minor Arcana can be interpreted together to give a brief understanding of some of the meanings of each card. For instance, the stillness and stability of the number 4 is expressed in the suit of Swords as mental respite; the destruction and imbalance of the number 5 can be seen in the suit of Cups as emotional loss.

Ace of Wands

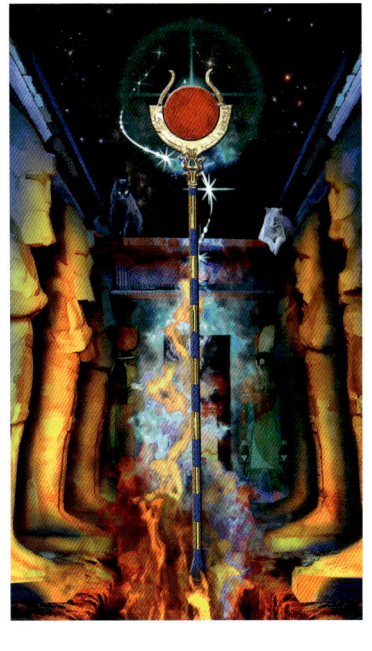

You were born from the desire of the Universe to be not One but Many. To give you form you were raised from the red earth, but to give you spirit you were pulled from the stars. Your Becoming is inspiration in its truest sense: at the moment you took your first gasp of air you inspired, sucking deep of life. This first inspiration taught you to want, yearn and desire; you know unconsciously that you need to feed the fire within as much as you need the air to breathe and the ground beneath your feet. I am the vigour that pulses through you, the implacable and tenacious desire to live and thrive, demanding and desirous of everything the world has to offer. I am your need to consume and to rise towards the heavens. Your birthright is not beneath you or passed down in legacy: it is above you, inside you and all around you. You are not a creature of clay, but one ensouled and enshrined, and your place of origin and destination is beyond all that you can see. You will deviate from this knowledge as you tread the years, but a moment will come that reminds you. This is true inspiration. You will forget that you are star-born, and the darkness around you may overwhelm you. But the sun does not die at midnight and you must remember that you have the magic of all of creation within you; you are a god in human form, enthroned in your place upon the world. I am the burn-

ing flame within you and the fuel that feeds it so you may thrive; I am the energy you expend and create and the driving force behind all things. You seek divine inspiration, but to be inspired is not to be gently coaxed into the attaining of desire: it is to be set on fire.

~ Mystery

Although ancient Egypt had several creation myths, most of them agree that in the beginning there was chaotic, dark water and that the world began when the sun rose for the first time over this ocean. This was called "The First Occasion". [241] Out of darkness rose light. The sun, and the force that caused it to rise, would remain important symbols throughout the ancient Egyptian world for millennia.

The Ace of Wands is the tarot equivalent of the sun rising on the first day: it is the force of vital spark and generative power that kickstarts all processes of creation; it is thereafter necessary for the perpetuation of existence. It is energy in all its forms and is even more necessary than breath or food: for there to be a need for those things the necessity for that which sparks the creation and perpetuation of life at its most basic must be fulfilled. Elementally, the Ace of Wands is associated with Fire; therefore, it is the "highest" (but also the most abstract) of the elements – it is closest to spirit yet the most fundamental force for us all. On an abstract level, the Ace of Wands is the energetic forces in our lives, power, a sense of self, personality and ego; on a more mundane level it is all the forces that we engage with that allow us to move forward and create: drive, desire, ambition, will, power, inspiration, yearning and passion. The Ace of Wands, on a spiritual level, is also paired with the Ace of Cups: the former is the divine phallus, penetrating into the divine womb, the Ace of Cups – this is Will entering the Soul, a divine union that births form and success. It is this force that the Princess of Wands wields.

---

241 James P. Allen, **Middle Egyptian: An introduction to the language and culture of hieroglyphs**, p. 126. Cambridge University Press, 2014.

In the ancient Egyptian world, the all-permeating force that was vital for all acts of creation was called *heka*, "magic", and it was personified as a god with the same name. This god was depicted as a young man wearing a headdress of two upraised arms with palms forward. [242] The hieroglyphs of his name included the wick hieroglyph for the letter "h", which is often used to represent the concept of eternity, and upraised arms, which represent the divine life spirit of each person (their *ka* and the creating and sustaining power of life). Sometimes the wick ideogram looked like two snakes being held in somebody's arms, and Heka was sometimes depicted as snake-headed. For the ancient Egyptians, all things possessed *heka*, magic, including the gods themselves, and this they held in common with humankind. As *heka* was spelled with the ideograms for eternity and the spirit, it was seen as a force that activated the *ka*, the part of the human soul that is the personality and represents a person's vital essence.

This magic of activation and vital essence was present before the beginning of creation, before the gods, and before duality:

"...to me belonged the universe before you gods had come into being. You have come afterwards because I am Heka." [243]

This fits with the attributes of the Ace in the tarot: it exists as a moment before duality (the Two of its suit), before anything is fully formed; as such, it is also a fundamental force that permeates its suit, making possible the engendering and multiplication of its suit. In the cosmogony of Heliopolis, this force was not only magic but passion and desire: the god Atum was a self-engendered being who created the "Other" (Shu and Tefnut) through masturbation (thus fulfilling the role of the Ace of Wands as the divine phallus).

---

242 *An example of this depiction of Heka can be seen in Stephen Skinner,* **Techniques of Graeco-Egyptian Magic***, p. 34. Golden Hoard Press, 2014.*

243 **Coffin Texts**, *spell 261.*

Magic was not only a force of creation present at the beginning of all life, but also a force that allowed the deceased to ascend to the stars. The dead were often buried with spells written on their coffin lids, on their funerary wrappings, or with amulets upon them, which would help them overcome the obstacles and challenges in the immediate afterlife that might prevent them from ascending and becoming one with the Imperishable Stars (see *King of Wands*). Thus, the magic and power of the Ace of Wands brings us to birth from the stars, stays with us through life and allows us to return to our origins at death.

Even the sun god Ra needed Heka to follow this cycle of birth, life, death and rebirth. Just as the deceased had magic to ascend to the stars after death and be born anew, so Ra needed that magic to rise from the Duat – the underworld – every dawn to be born as the rising sun: Heka accompanied Ra on his Boat of Millions of Years, along with Sia (perception) and Hu (the word of creation, the sound that Atum uttered upon ejaculation at the creation of the world). [244] In some versions of this, when Ra descended into the Duat he met the mummified Osiris. They joined together, becoming re-energised. Both were reborn with the new day. [245]

Ra's descent into the underworld at night was part of a four-stage cycle that happened eternally: he would then be born anew as the youth Kephri/Kephra ("he who comes into being") at dawn, become Ra at the height of his power at midday, and then Atum ("he who completes") at sunset, before entering the underworld at midnight once more. These stages are shown in the next few cards of the Wands suit, with sunrise being found in the Two of Wands, midday in the Three of Wands, and sunset in the Four of Wands.

---

244 *E. A. Wallis Budge,* ***The Gods of the Egyptians***, *vol. 1, p. 180. New York: Dover, 1969.*

245 *Allen, James P.* ***The Essential Guide to Egyptian Mythology***, *p. 28. Berkley, 2003.*

These cards, beginning with the Ace, represent the general process for all projects or goals we set, and ideally they return to the Ace each time, where lessons can be learned, energy renewed; thus, we spiral onwards and upwards into each new cycle.

The Ace of Wands represents the archetypal primal chaos that is also the darkness of nighttime, the underworld, the place in which rebirth and creation may occur. The sun/vital essence/magic/power not only creates from this place but repeatedly returns to it to be renewed and reborn. It is a self-perpetuating life cycle of energy creation and transmutation, forming the basis of all our endeavours. Without it we would not have been born from the stars, life would not be sustained, and we would be unable to harness and direct the primal power of drive, passion, vitality, energy and will that allows us to use the same power as the gods: *heka*, magic.

◆ Revelation

The initial spark of creation or desire; energy in all its forms; power; vitality and creativity; a primal urge, yearning, or desire; ambition in its earliest but most powerful stages; the beginnings of a creative project; ambition and drive; the setting of goals; will and the direction of will towards a goal; divine inspiration; creating now rather than in the future; the self, ego or personality; a fiery force; energy that is forceful but difficult to direct.

Negatively aspected...
Uncontrollable, destructive energy; ambition that is stunted or directed negatively (often linked with a sense of self or personality that is destructive); weak power or drive; lack of passion; passion that burns others; creative projects blocked or delayed; weak sense of self.

Two of Wands

The sunrise ushers in a wealth of opportunity and in its golden pathway I walk, the Son of the Morning, eager in my tread and desirous of the horizon. I have dreamed of many things and the stories of others have taken root in my heart, tugging insistently with the cry of "Now! Now is the time!". I have known and danced the ways of One, focused and passionate, but without a goal I have nothing. Over the rolling red sands I now send my goal, directed towards the horizon I seek,  *bearing with it my hopes, plans and ambitions. I have set it in motion: I cannot fail, for failure is only found through inaction and refusal of opportunity. If you are offered a sweet-smelling flower, will you take it and enjoy it? If the gods gift you with great foresight, would it not be against nature to fail to use it to your benefit? Make plans if you are able; consider the many paths of possibilities before you; make the choices you are blessed with; send your hopes far away and wait with eagerness to see what they become. They, like you, are youthful in the beginning, headstrong and uncertain of anything but the horizon ahead. But childhood does not last forever: growth and expansion beckon. I offer the mysteries of discovery and enterprise. Their revelation is carefully planned and eager.*

~ Mystery

All the Twos share a kind of duality, highlighting the difference between One Thing and Another Thing (or The Next Thing). In the case of the Two of Wands, we see the movement from the focus and initial spark of the Ace of Wands to an extension of that idea and drive. Since the suit of Wands is associated with Fire and therefore with a dynamic process of creation, we can imagine that in the Ace we have conceived an idea and the passion with which to fuel it, and it has been busy powering up and fuelling itself, the need and drive growing greater and more difficult to contain, until it finally bursts out in one focused beam of energy. Now we have a goal, something to aim for; the initial point of focus has become a line from point A to point B; a plan has been formed for reaching the finishing line. Being in the suit of Wands puts this extension in the realm of ambition, passion, goals and drive – this is the movement forwards, the direction of the will into a focused and driven goal.

What follows in the suit of Wands is a creative process, with the Two showing us the extension of the idea, the testing of its boundaries and the discovery of what the creative process offers. The Three presents a return on these initial pursuits, with maturity granting us insight and experience and our horizons expanding to the point where we are the masters of our destinies. In the Four we see the time to celebrate and enjoy the fruits of our labours and in the Five challenges present themselves in order to shake up what may have become stale. To show this process, the *Tarot Apokalypsis* develops the story of a man and his endeavours from the Two of Wands to the Four of Wands. The time of day in which each card is set tells its own story also, tied firmly to the New Kingdom mythology of the sun god Ra's journey across the sky every day.

Ra was given four faces to reflect the four stages of the sun: in the morning, at sunrise, he was Kephri/Kephra, "he who comes into being"; at midday he was Ra, strong in force and power having climbed to the heights of the sky; in the evening, at sunset, he was Atum, "he who completes"; and at midnight he entered the underworld where he battled against the forces of evil. Many of the tombs in the Valley of the Kings depict this journey, showing it as taking place over twelve hours, with each hour being a different stage of his journey.

Here in the Two is a young man, still wearing the traditional ancient Egyptian side-lock of youth. He is not yet out of his teen years, but he has taken on the responsibility and mantle of adulthood and set his intentions towards becoming a successful merchant. He has purchased (probably with the generous donations and loans of friends, family and investors) a caravan of camels and sent them on their first trade run. Like many ancient Egyptians, he will trade with Punt, Lebanon or Afghanistan, and his caravans will cross between the Eastern Deserts and the Western Deserts of Egypt. They will return laden with cedar wood, ivory, precious lapis lazuli, incenses and myrrh.

To embark on such a trade run requires careful planning, as well as a lack of fear of what the unknown horizons might hold. A heart set on discovery and the unique pushes new endeavours in the right direction.

It is morning in this card; the sun is rising over the sand dunes, indicating promise of new beginnings and opportunities. The old saying goes "The early bird catches the worm" and the young entrepreneur of this card is not wasting a minute of this day – he sees every day as a new opportunity to grasp in both hands.

~ Revelation

Entrepreneurship; new business plans and projects; start-up plans moving forward; the logical extension to the next step; taking a risk with a goal in mind; goal-setting; affirmation; being driven forwards; taking opportunities; creating opportunities for one's self and others; expanding horizons; outcome is unknown but the path is certain; having the world at one's fingertips; plans for the future; expansion; extension.

Negatively aspected…
Opportunities missed; time rushing by before a chance is taken; new business plans or projects stifled in the early stages; lack of direction; lack of drive; fear of new horizons; preferring comfort over adventure; lack of a plan; poor organisation.

Three of Wands

Some would tell you that the midday sun will harm you, that its heat will take away your breath and shrivel you, that it creates deserts and dry husks; but I tell you that it is a living god, breathing life and power into those that stand proud before it. Do not listen to those that would put you in shade: do not prize mediocrity over greatness and achievement. Allow yourself to stand in the sun and accept its light completely. Before the day is done, you shall have success. I am Ra of the risen  *and the resplendent light, established at my highest and seeing all from the pinnacle of the sky. May you follow in my ways and see the entirety of your creation before you; may your empire be as grand and as lasting. For you must carry with you the sure knowledge and challenge that great things are not born in an instant, great ideas not invented in a moment, great people not born great. Creativity, the ability to expand and extend ideas and energy into the world, is what makes greatness. Dare to know! Dare to be! Dare to experience. But be patient and brave. Doubt is your failure, success is your proof. I am Ra of the Two Horizons, but even I must descend. May you live in greatness accompanied by the knowledge that your fate is to die. Let this certainty goad you onto more greatness, for you do not know how your days are numbered or how many dawns are given to you.*

ᴥ Mystery

In the Ace of Wands we saw Ra at the beginning of the world, the creation of the universe, the midnight just before the sun rose for the first time over the nascent form of the earth. From this the Two of Wands came, extending from the point of origin and expanding its horizons. Ideas sparked, creativity was generated and movement following a desire to explore. Endeavours were begun as Kephrer, the aspect of Ra at the rising run, arose in the morning. Now, Ra rules at his pinnacle as the midday sun, shining his all-encompassing majesty over the Three of Wands, in which endeavours pay off, projects are completed, experience is gained and dominions expanded.

The man in the card is the same young man from the Two of Wands, lacking the side-lock of youth, grown in years, wealth and experience. His camels, which set out in the Two of Wands, are returning laden with treasures that he will use to further his trade dominion. Before him three slaves – bedecked in gold similar to their master – show the young man reverence and have laid before him sacks of spices and incenses. They have also presented to him a chest filled with his profits and fine dyed materials. Most of these materials are dyed a stark purple, a colour seen in the ancient world as a status symbol. Called "Tyrian purple", its colour did not easily fade and instead became brighter when worn and exposed to sunlight. The dye was sold at high prices, so only the richest could afford it. [246] The Three of Wands brings with it the concept of experience and rulership from the foundation of experience, influence over others and a thriving dominion. Just as Ra, the midday

---

246 *Athenaeus, The Deipnosophists*. 12:526. *Harvard University Press*, 2000.

sun, ruled over the Two Lands of Egypt, so the man in the card rules over all that he has grown and cared for. Like the purple dye of the cloth, this man's dominion will not easily fade, but will grow stronger as his days lengthen: time, in the Three of Wands, is one of the greatest resources any endeavour can be given. It takes time to grow a business, gain power and complete a project. The time it would have taken in ancient Egypt for a single trade run could be months or even years and carried considerable risk over great distances. However, the further out one reaches into the wider world, the greater one's rewards.

With this card comes increased experience and an expanded dominion over others, an area or place. The young man from the Two of Wands has been successful in his endeavours and is receiving the fruits of his labours. He now owns slaves, but it is worth noting that in Egypt slaves often lived a better quality of life than peasants, being looked after by the household or temple in which they served. In ancient Egypt it was morally virtuous to be kind to one's slaves. In the *Book of the Dead* one of the 42 Negative Confessions that the deceased must be able to pronounce in good faith was that he had not "domineered over slaves". [247]

The young man wears blue scarab designs on the arm rings on his biceps. The scarab design was a popular amulet in ancient Egypt, generally coloured blue or green and suspended from cord or string. The beetle rolled dung into balls in which it would lay eggs, which would later hatch as larvae – a phenomenon that was seen as an analogy of the sun, or Ra, rolling across the sky and being reborn each day. The majority of surviving examples of scarab amulets date to the New Kingdom king Thuthmosis III (1504-1450 BCE) and bear his throne

---

247 *E A Wallis Budge, trans* **The Book of the Dead,** *Brit. Mus. No. 10477, Sheet 22.*

name *Men Kheper Re* ("the appearance of Ra is established"). It is here mentioned because of its association with Ra as a ruler over a kingdom, just as the merchant in the card rules over his small empire.

In the background the sun is at its height: it is midday, the hottest part of the day. This merchant has grown to manhood not through age but through reaching a prime in his life, achieving through his experience and applied wisdom the goal he set out towards. Physical age, while sometimes being a limiting factor, does not necessarily prevent somebody from achieving great things. It is only a matter of hours before the sun reaches its pinnacle every day and shines gloriously over its kingdom.

∞ Revelation

Success and achievement that still has further to go; reaching a pinnacle that will lead to further ideas and creativity; success sparking inspiration; projects that were started long ago coming to fruition; one's ships coming in; experience influencing a situation or providing a useful resource; the height of one's creative power; teamwork with others to create something; inspiration applied and the results it can offer; business and projects seeing great success.

Negatively aspected...
Arrogance, not knowing one's boundaries; not trusting experience; immaturity; disrespect for others in a team; poor teamworking skills; creative block; reaching a goal but not knowing where to go next.

Four of Wands

I have made my inexorable journey across the sky and with the sunset have begun to descend. But do not know me as weak or fading, for the path I have wrought in fire and urging will wind its way across the landscape of the universe for aeons to come. My work is done, yet it is not yet done; my completion is not the end but merely a foundation for greatness. Beneath my feet I have set steps leading down and a firm platform rising to the heights. Before me is arrayed the harvest of my labours, and I see with joy what my accomplishments have wrought. This is the essence of joy in abundance: to see your work and know its virtue, to form it and manifest it, to consolidate its power and fuel it for the journey ahead. For Work begets Work, just as my descent into the dark begets another birth. I am the Prince of Uniting: in me are chaos and order, love and war together; their union creates life and power. The sunset calls to me and bids me look upon my lands and their abundance, feel the support of the red earth beneath my feet, and know that though I am at an ending there are many more dawns to come. Until then, I celebrate and proclaim my joy for the world: Behold what I have wrought!

☙ Mystery

Since the initial burst of energetic creation in the Ace of Wands, this fiery suit has been growing increasingly powerful. The nascent spark of an idea and urge was expanded in the Two, its horizons and potential tested, and plans for its growth made. With the Three this direction bore fruit and experience was gained; now in the Four, power, will and the creative urge are given manifestation. Since the Fours of the tarot are associated with the manifest world around us – the four corners of the earth, the four winds, the four directions, the four elements – and are part of the Emperor's domain, each of them represents varying ways in which their suit is made firm, stable and manifest. For the suit of Wands, Earth interacts as fuel and a firm foundation on which to burn. Power is consolidated, mastery certain. As it is a card of manifestation it brings with it celebration and thanksgiving, particularly on a community level. Now is the time to enjoy the fruits of one's labours.

It should be noted that the Four of Wands, although sharing with the Six of Wands an aura of celebration, is very different in meaning to the later card. In the Six, great victory and heights of achievement are celebrated. In the Four, great heights have not yet been achieved: it is simply the firm foundation and consolidation that allows for this ambitious victory.

The card scene is one of celebration and consolidation of power. The new Pharaoh has been crowned and lauded by the people, who give thanks at the base of the temple in which the coronation is taking place. The wands of power surround him at the four directions, adorned with flower garlands, and the Pharaoh carries the crook and flail of kingship, items that are frequently depicted in ancient Egyptian imagery either held crossed over the chest of the Pharaoh or by gods associated with kingship, such as Osiris. The Pharaoh is undergoing a baptism, administered by the gods themselves. This scene is depicted frequently in imagery from ancient Egypt, and shows Set and Horus each pouring water in the form of ankhs over the head and body of the new Pharaoh. [248] The ankhs represent eternal life, or the breath of life, and as a symbol they are usually held in the hands of deities or kings/queens of Egypt. That it is the power of the ankh with which the Pharaoh is being baptised reminds us that although this card offers stability of one's desires, creative urges, projects and power, it does not indicate their completion: there is more life in them yet. Given the descriptions of Set in the *Prince of Wands*, the question of what he is doing here, side-by-side with Horus and baptising the Pharaoh with the breath of life, might be raised. Set and Horus are, in many texts, enemies contending with each other for dominance and kingship, and Set is set up as a chaotic, contentious force of challenge. However, the reconciliation of these two deities in imagery may indicate a reconciliation between Upper and Lower Egypt at some point in history, or simply between the forces of authority and chaos, civilisation and wilderness. This reconciliation is a marrying of two powerful aspects of the world, now given over to the establishment and consolidation of power and the creative urge. It also brings stability to the community.

The timing of this scene is vitally important: it is taking place at sunset, during the time of the harvest following the annual Inundation of the Nile. During the Inundation the Nile would flood, allowing its rich minerals to be deposited on the land, which was enriched by these nutrients. When it receded, the crops would grow and the harvest be plentiful. These crops can be seen in the card image, rising tall behind the Pharaoh, the red Nile snaking into the distance. As this is a card of comple-

---

248 Eugene Cruz-Uribe, p. 216, "*Seth, God of Power and Might*" in *Journal of the American Research Center in Egypt*, vol. 45 (2009), pp. 201–226.

tion, it is set at sunset, a time for enjoying what has been experienced and learned throughout the day and to ready oneself for night-time. In the cycle of the sun god Ra across the sky every day, his aspect at sunset was Atum, "he who completes". There are different versions of the ancient Egyptian creation myth depending on where and when the myth originates, but in most of them Atum plays a vital role. In some versions he created himself, and set himself upon the first mound of earth. He then created Shu and Tefnut (the god of air and goddess of moisture respectively) from his spit or, in some versions, his semen. Later, his tears became the first humans. This aspect of Ra depicted in the sunset of the card reminds us that, just as Atum consolidated and manifested the world, so we may consolidate and manifest our power, projects and creativity.

❧ Revelation

Completion of the initial stages of a project; firm foundations for a creative project or goal; stability and certainty in one's spiritual or magical life; certainty of life-calling; energies grounded and manifested; consolidation of power; celebration of completion; thanksgiving; gratitude; harvesting the first fruits of one's labour.

Negatively aspected…
Projects stuck and unable to move forward; creativity being oppressed; the completion of the first stages of something still yet to be reached; lacking a firm foundation for one's goals, ambitions and desires; lack of gratitude.

Five of Wands

Only fools seek contentment. In doing so, they abandon themselves to the pits of nothingness; they let their fires fade to cooling embers, suffocate their flames with the earth of too much stability. When the darkness of chaos comes for them they will turn aside their faces, they will lie peacefully and be overrun. But you, warrior, know the joys of battle and the hunt; you revel in the testing and the challenge. You would welcome the forces of destruction and chaos, pushing aside peace and its  *sickly stability. What great man ever arose without challenge? What great leader became such in a time of peace? Yet those without eyes to see do not look upon our hunt with favour, seeing only the sport and showmanship, wanton destruction and war for its own sake. They will wither away simpering into an ignoble fate: their names will not be remembered. For now is a time of war and great uprising. Now is the time for muscles to be tested and strained, youth to be initiated into adulthood, blood to be spilled and wounds to be taken, so that you may know the fire that courses through your veins. You are alive and there is a great challenge to face. Set aside peace, put aside luxuries and soft, sweet things: this is a time for blade and spear, blood and bone. This is the time of making.*

❧ Mystery

After the creative process that unfolded from the Ace to the Four of Wands, we are given a stark reminder that completion is not the end, stability is not guaranteed, and contentment is the enemy of innovation. As with all the Fives of the Minor Arcana, destruction and challenge reappear to throw things off balance. For some of the suits this has a constructive purpose, but for others it leads to pain. Here in the Five of Wands we see five young men undertaking the dangerous hippopotamus hunt. The male hippo spreads his jaws wide in aggression and the men drive their spears into its mouth. One man, wounded on his left thigh and arm, stabilises himself with the end of his spear; another demonstrates his physical prowess by flexing his muscles. In this card we find the renewed fight against destruction and the welcoming of it as an opportunity to test one's mettle, demonstrate one's power and keep oneself on top form.

The scene takes place at night, completing the sun-cycle of the first five cards of this suit. Following the celebration and gratitude at sunset in the Four of Wands, where the day's events were reflected upon and experiences harvested, Ra now descends into the underworld as the sun dips below the horizon. There he faces many challenges and is aided by various deities and underworld beings, travelling through the twelve hours of the Duat (underworld) on his barque. In the seventh hour he faces the adversary Apep (also called Apophis), known as Enemy of Ra and Lord of Chaos, the embodiment of chaos. [249] With the aid of Isis and Set, he does battle against the being that would consume him. Images of this nightly battle are common in ancient Egyptian art and tombs, and depict spears being thrown by

---

249 E.A. Wallis Budge, **The Book of Am-Tuat,** pp. 139–160. Kegan, Paul, Trench, Trübner & Co., 1905.

figures on the boat at Apophis, who is shown in the form of a giant snake.

These images are very similar to the popular hunting scenes found from the Predynastic period onwards, [250] though the hunted being is not Apophis but a bestial manifestation of chaos, and the hunter is not Ra but the Pharaoh or other royal figure. These hunt images frequently made the hippopotamus the prey, showing it half-submerged in water, with hunts taking place on boats in marshland. The great number of examples of the hippo hunt scene residing today in museums around the world attests to the popularity and importance of the theme it represented. [251] The choice of hippo as prey is notable: the male hippo was seen as an embodiment of evil and chaos. They were aggressive creatures that capsised the boats of fishermen and emerged onto land at night to graze on precious crops. Diodorus Siculus, writing in the first century BCE, stated that were the hippo to produce more young every year, agriculture in Egypt would be completely destroyed. [252]

These hunts were not undertaken for food. Hunting represented less than 2% of the food intake of ancient Egypt. [253] Diodorus Siculus also stated that hippo meat was "tough and difficult to digest". [254] As such, a hippo hunt was symbolic,

---

250 *Khaled Daoud, p. 36, "Notes of the Tomb of Niankhnesut, Part 1: Reliefs & Inscriptions" in **Bulletin of the Egyptian Museum**. SCA Press, 2006.*

251 *Stan Hendrickx and David Depraetere, p. 818, "A Theriomorphic Predynastic Stone Jar and Hippopotamus Symbolism" in **Egypt at its Origins: Studies in Memory of Barbara Adams. Proceedings of the International Conference**. Peeters Publishers, 2005.*

252 *Diodorus Siculus, **Historical Library**, vol. 1, chapter 35.*

253 *Willeke Wendrich **ed., Egyptian Archaeology**, Blackwell Studies in Global Archaeology, 1993.*

254 *Diodorus Siculus, **Historical Library**, vol. 1, chapter 35.*

ritual and recreational. It gave a chance for weapons practice and demonstration of skill and prowess; it represented control over chaos; [255] it signified the power of royalty to protect their people from danger; [256] and it demonstrated the divine power of the Pharaoh. [257]

It is suggested that by leading the hunt of a hippo, the Pharaoh embodied the role of the gods who overcame evil. There is extant ritual text concerning the hippo hunt, in which Horus himself is the hunter, and rejoices in his successful hunt. [258]

The hippo hunt operated on many levels, from pest control to sport, recreation and ritual. No matter its purpose, it would have been a dangerous undertaking, and those who took part were able to demonstrate their skill and bravery, perhaps showing off to others or using it as a way to maintain physical strength, skill and stamina. In the Five of Wands, this is welcomed as a test, an opportunity not to keep destruction at bay but to keep peace at bay. When there is nothing to fight against, no reason to battle and be tested, purpose and drive gives way to laziness and empty ritual.

∾ Revelation

Challenge; a return to instability after a period of peace; destruction leading to creativity and innovation; a demonstra-

---

255 *Stan Hendrickx and David Depraetere, p. 815, "A Theriomorphic Predynastic Stone Jar and Hippopotamus Symbolism", p. 815.*

256 *Wolfgang Decker,* **Sports and Games of Ancient Egypt.** *Yale UP, 1992.*

257 *Miroslav Verner, "****A Statue of Twert (Cairo Museum no. 39145) Dedicated by Pabesi and Several Remarks on the Role of the Hippopotamus Goddess.****" **Zeitschrift für Ägyptische Sprache und Alterumskunde** 96 (1969), p. 53.*

258 *Quoted in Dorothea Arnold, p. 24, "****An Egyptian Bestiary****" in* **The Metropolitan Museum of Art Bulletin**, *New Series, vol. 52, no. 4, (Spring, 1995), pp. 1; 7–64.*

tion of skill; a test; ritual or symbolic battle; a conceptual or figurative fight; putting oneself in dangerous or uncertain situations; a rekindling of passion or purpose due to having something to fight for/against; uncertainty and instability; destructive forces; chaotic forces.

Negatively aspected…
Being unwilling to take on a challenge; becoming lazy instead of taking action; inability to grow or change due to fear; not having the energy to fight; contentment as the enemy of innovation; empty contests and showmanship.

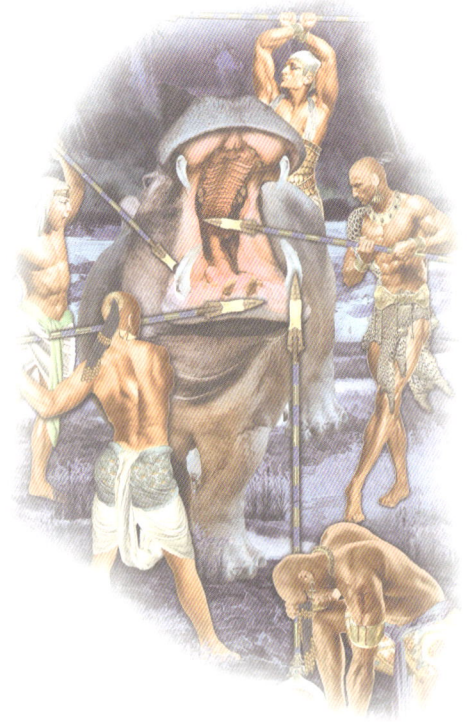

Six of Wands

True success and greatness is as blinding as the sun: stare too long and it will burn both certainty and devotion into your heart. Do not be fooled by those who let words of victory drip from their tongue as carelessly as dew falls from flowers in the dawn: they have not known greatness, and make it a shadow in their own image. But they were weak challengers, and I will always rise. I am the ruler by achievement and dedication; my striving does not cease as long as the sun rises and falls. With ev-  *ery dawn I am made anew in my jubilations, praising the name of Greatness so that I may be great; with every dusk I know the establishment of my success. For all the moments between, which span the length of the sky, I celebrate and continue to strive for more, for there is no barrier to my desire for accomplishment. Now is my time. I am Great of Name, born to Eternity, blessed by the divine light. Warrior of the Sun, Child of its fiery rays, I reflect the light of truth to others and they look to me for guidance. I see my victory established before me in the faces of those who love me; I hear their cries of celebration acclaiming me, claiming me as their own even as they are mine. My certainty of success serves them, as to inspire confidence one must be supreme in faith in one's self: perfect, one, and eternal. I am the one whose voice inspires rejoicing, and who am inspired by that rejoicing; I am the leader and the one who follows the people; I am great, and the great shall live forever.*

∽ Mystery

The Six of Wands is a card of true greatness, success and an almost divine authority. Those represented by the card lead a "charmed life" and everything they will comes to pass. This card is a force to be reckoned with, a victory, and acclamation from others. In short, it is the state of being that most people in the Western world strive for. However, it can also be a card of very brief victory, of the leader who comes out on top following great struggle, only to be deposed later in another struggle. It is also a card of strong ego and deeply rooted sense of self, as well as a certainty of a truth. The way in which this certainty is acted upon dictates whether the card may be as positive as it seems, or whether it also carries a burden.

Two of the most well-known faces of ancient Egypt can be seen in this card: Nefertiti and Tutankhamen. The former was a wife of King Amenhotep IV, later called Akhenaten, and the latter the son of Akhenaten by another wife. Amenhotep (circa 1380BCE–1336 or 1334BCE) ruled as king of Egypt for 17 years. There is some speculation that Nefertiti ("Beauty has Come") (1370BCE–circa 1330BCE) briefly ruled as the successor to her husband after his death, with the name Neferneferuaten. Akhenaten's son, Tutankhamen, would rule after Neferneferuaten for nine years with his wife and half-sister Ankhesenamun. The reign of Akhenaten and Nefertiti is particularly interesting to historians because it was unknown until the 19th century CE, when the city of Amarna was discovered. Following his reign, Akhenaten had been wiped from history by those who came after him – a backlash against the monotheism he established in place of traditional Egyptian polytheism. The city of Amarna (named Akhetaten, "Horizon of the Aten") was built swiftly by Akhenaten at the beginning of his reign, and was abandoned just after his death. It served as the centre for the worship of the Aten, represented by a sun disk from which rays of light with hands emanated. Where previous polytheism possessed a cosmology and eschatology in which the human soul was intimately connected with stars, ascending to them after death, the monotheism of the Aten was solar-centric, with worship taking place in temples open to the sky. Akhenaten oversaw the construction of some of the most impressive temple complexes in ancient Egypt. The swiftness with which Akhetaten was built is amazing even by today's standards: after just two years of construction the royal family took up residence in the new city. Each day Akhenaten rode along the Royal Road through the city to the palace in his chariot, mirroring the progress of the Aten through the sky, in order to emphasise his proximity to the new godhead. [259]

It is easy to imagine the success that Akhenaten must have felt when the city he had planned and built was completed, and when the worship of the Aten became established. Before him stretched an eternity of his name being remembered, a legacy to withstand the ravishes of time. With the growth of his monotheism, Akhenaten gradually shifted his relationship with the Aten from that of a worshiper and dutiful son to that of the living embodiment of the divine force – a sun king in all his glory. Texts that mention Akhenaten, such as hymns to the Aten, reaffirm his close relationship with the Aten. They praise together the greatness of the Aten in all its life-giving power and the success of Akhenaten as the son of the Aten, a great ruler and intermediary between the Aten and the people.

---

259 *Alastair Sooke,* **"Ahkenaten: mad, bad or brilliant?"** *in* ***The Telegraph****, 9 January 2014.*

The *Hymn to the Aten and the King*, written during Akhenaten's reign, shows the close connection between the god and the king, for the success of one was the success of the other. It portrays the Aten giving "jubilees" to the king, shining its light upon him, giving to him not just his own lifetime but also the Aten's lifetime. When the Aten dawns, it gives Akhenaten eternity; when it sets it gives him infinity. [260]

In these texts Nefertiti is also praised and she appears beside her husband more frequently than any other queen on record. Many of the images depict her performing actions more often given to a king: smiting an enemy, driving a chariot and leading worship. This suggests that she enjoyed a status higher than many ancient Egyptian queens. She is praised in one of the boundary stelae that dedicated the city of Akhetaten to the Aten as "great in the palace; the fair-faced, adorned with the two plumes; the mistress of joy, endowed with favour, at the sound of whose voice one rejoices; the Great Wife of the King whom he loves, the Mistress of the Two Lands: Nefer-nefru-aten Nefertiti, living forever". [261]

Tutankhamen, who would later rule, is shown here as a boy, at an age when Akhenaten would either have been dead or would soon be. This would have been a time when Nefertiti's power was great, perhaps even a time at which she ruled as the Pharaoh. They are both carried along the Royal Road on a litter born by priests, showered with beautiful flowers, arrayed in their finery; behind them obelisks bearing their great names stretch to the open sky and sun, and the image of the sundisk – the Aten – shines down on them. This royal family is

---

260 Miriam Lichtheim, ed. ***Ancient Egyptian Literature: vol. II The New Kingdom***, p. 93. University of California Press, 2006.

261 Miriam Lichtheim, ed. ***Ancient Egyptian Literature: vol. II The New Kingdom***, p. 49.

truly blessed: loved by their god, loved by their people, and loved by each other. However, in his own reign Tutankhamen would reject the religious revolution that his father instigated, returning polytheism to the temples. This reminds us that although the Six of Wands is a card of great success and victory, acclamation from others and divine blessing, victory is often fleeting and revolution will always come again. The card that follows in this suit, the Seven of Wands, is one of struggle and turmoil.

Akhenaten is an example of both great success and certainty of truth that overrides all other possibilities, resulting in a blind conviction in one's own version of truth. Although Akhenaten seems to have ruled fairly and given his subjects good lives, his religious revolution can be thought to have pandered to his idea of his self above others.

⇛ Revelation

Success, victory, triumph; acclamation from others; awards being given; promotion both in career and of one's agenda; a charmed life; accomplishment and great achievement; victory after a struggle; rising above; being in charge of one's own life; being looked up to or looking up to another; a hero; hero worship; something to be proud of; certainty of success.

Negatively aspected...
Ego overruling logic; being too self-centred; controlling others with one's power; stepping on the toes of others to achieve success; too much pride; pride comes before a fall; certainty of one's own truth leading to it being imposed on others; resting on one's laurels.

Seven of Wands

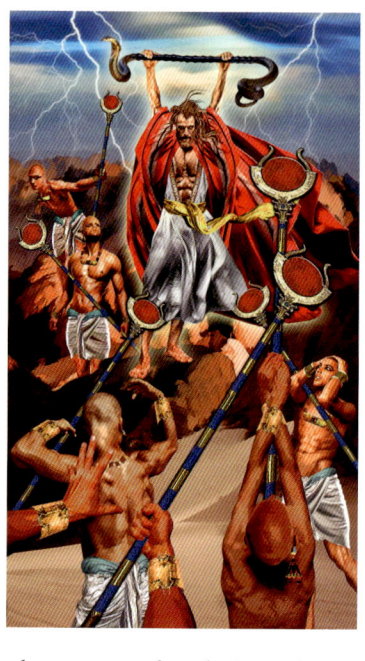

The leader stands tall and proud above his people. Yet when his weight bears down upon them, when his word crushes and threatens, when his hand no longer protects but wounds, we must stand against him. We may be weak, we may be burdened and filled with fear, we may challenge the majority, yet it only takes a single grain to tip the scales. The cowards say that one alone cannot stand, but walk the path over the burning mountains with me and I shall show you how to fight the battle of the freedom fighter and rebel, how to lift up the oppressed and give voice to the unspoken. I shall show you how to topple kingdoms and destroy the bonds of slavery. Those who would disparage and curse you I shall pit against your strength alone and you shall know the power of revolution. This road you walk is one upon which you are low and unworthy, upon which you are trampled and thrown down, but from the pain of the hot sand you have nothing to lose and everything to gain: what more can they do? Pain is pain, sorrow is sorrow: it can only give rise to a refusal to accept it again. Take up your weapons, warrior, take up your strength and all the many wrongs done to you: they are your sword and your shield; they shall strike down your oppressors and protect you. No battle is truly lost if you will its success.

◈ Mystery

Following the victory of the Six of Wands, we come to the Seven to be reminded that revolution will always come. It is not many steps for a glorious leader to become an oppressor, and in the Seven somebody takes a stand against oppression and fights for liberty. The person taking on this role is usually an underdog, somebody at a disadvantage and fighting against almost impossible odds. That which they fight against is engrained and systemic, deeply wounding and controlling; there are many others who are unable to fight for themselves, looking to the figure of the Seven of Wands to fight on their behalf. In this way, the Seven of Wands represents a freedom fighter, a rebel for a good cause, a campaigner, a protester and somebody fighting because there is no other choice. Those who are given no way out of a fight often fight the hardest.

The relations between the peoples that inhabited the ancient Egyptian world were not always peaceful or equal. We know from images created by the ancient Egyptians that they viewed Nubians, for instance, as their inferiors. According to the Old Testament of the Bible, the Israelites lived in Egypt for 430 years and were enslaved by the Egyptians. Slavery in ancient Egypt was normal; slaves were treated well and could often earn their freedom and become part of the family that they served. However, the *Book of Exodus* states that the Israelite slaves received cruel treatment from the Egyptians. The Pharaoh (not named), fearing that their rising numbers might pose a threat of them allying with his enemies, ordered all male Hebrew babies to be thrown into the Nile. [262] It was in this cruelty that Moses was born. His mother built a small boat for him and let him sail down the Nile, where he was discovered by the Pharaoh's daughter, who took him from the river and named him her son. When Moses had come of age, he killed an Egyptian

---

262 *Exodus 1: 9–16.*

who was beating a Hebrew slave. [263] He fled to Midian to escape those who would capture him for the crime and returned after many years, having been given a command by God to bring his people out of slavery, "to lead them out of Egypt, to stand up for them". [264]

Moses frequently expressed doubt that Pharaoh would listen to his appeal and that his people would believe him, demonstrating the seeming futility of the task that was put before him. So God gave his brother Aaron's staff a miraculous power that would show that Moses had been sent by God: it could turn into a snake. The two pleaded with Pharaoh for the freedom of the Israelites. When Moses demonstrated the miracle to Pharaoh, the Egyptian magicians also threw down their staffs in magic, but Aaron's staff consumed them. [265] The card image shows Moses bearing this miraculous staff, the Egyptian sorcerers reacting to it: some try to draw down their own magic, some look angry and are readying for a fight, another looks amazed. Those who oppress often don't expect to be fought against, taking for granted their power. This, in itself, can be enough of an advantage for the one who is fighting to make a difference.

In response to the initial request, Pharaoh ordered the slave drivers to make the work of the Israelites harder. This reminds us that when we stand up to those who oppress us, we should expect them to fight back. Eventually, after a continued struggle, Pharaoh agreed to release the Israelites. However, Moses' struggles did not end there: his people wandered the wilderness for 40 years before reaching the Promised Land, and Moses died within sight of it.

Moses was written about extensively, and there are many representations of his personality and commentaries on his life. Two

---

263 *Exodus 2: 11–12.*
264 *Exodus 3:7.*
265 *Exodus 7: 10–12.*

of the most striking are those of Josephus, who portrayed him using the same literary techniques used to portray Greek heroes, and Philo, who portrayed him as a Platonic philosopher-king. [266] In the Midrash he is said to have undertaken another battle on behalf of the Israelites: he ascended to heaven to receive the Torah, for which he battled angels. [267] Another Midrashic text states that Moses grew horns in order to fight the angels and God watched the fight and "rejoiced greatly at how the lamb was battling the lion". [268] Here, Moses is presented as the gentle lamb, battling against a creature far greater in strength and prowess. The Seven of Wands shows us somebody at a disadvantage battling against overwhelming odds. Sometimes the thing being fought is external to us – injustice, bullying, unacceptable treatment or physical limitations – and sometimes its source is found within us.

∽ Revelation

Standing up for oneself; fighting against overwhelming odds; valour and courage in the face of adversity; standing up for others; being a voice for those who have none; fighting against injustice; sticking to one's principles; a freedom fighter; rebellion for a worthy cause; having nothing to lose and everything to gain; demonstrating one's strength and will against a majority.

Negatively aspected…
Unwillingness to stand up for oneself; expecting others to fight; accepting injustice and oppression; being overcome by one's own weaknesses; cowardice.

---

266 *Louis H. Feldman (p. 305),* **"Josephus' Portrait of Moses".** *In* **The Jewish Quarterly Review***, vol. 82, no. 3/4 (Jan.–Apr., 1992), pp. 285–328.*

267 *Petirat Moshe, quoted in Rimon Kasher,* **"The Mythological Figure of Moses in Light of Some Unpublished Midrashic Fragments",** *in* **The Jewish Quarterly Review***, vol. 88, no. 1/2 (Jul.–Oct., 1997), pp. 19–42.*

268 **Ibid***.*

Eight of Wands

What greater joy is there than to soar above all, riding the winds of ambition above and beyond the mountains of expectation? Many cry out to those who take to flight, warning them against the soaring, predicting a great fall; some watch in envy at the flight they dare not make. A very few precious souls— warriors and hunters all— resolve to scale those great heights, trailblazing a new path into the horizon. If you walk my burning path I will show you how to train your sights and set the course of your greatest desires. Where the sun rises, you will rise higher; where the falcon flies, you will fly faster; where the lion roars, your war-cry will drown it out. You may ignite with the joy of it, with passion and intent, and like the flaming arrow your soaring will further fuel the source of your desire. You will fly straight and true to your goal, but remember that the beginning requires an explosive burst of focus and will, energy and passion. Without this your path will be cursed by the earth, slow and steady, stable and dependable, yet utterly uninventive. We do not advance through reinvention. Dare to know, dare to set your sights upon the heights, dare to become a warrior of the flaming arrow and a hunter with the falcon's speed. Set aflame the arrows of your desire and release them to flight into the very heavens!

≈ Mystery

The Eight of Wands is an explosive unity of the elements of Fire and Air. As air feeds fire, giving it the oxygen it needs to sustain itself and grow, so the mental focus and agility of Air symbolically feeds and increases the passion, ambition, will and intent of the suit of Wands. This fiery suit has been a rollercoaster ride so far: beginning with the first spark and growing into a great desire, becoming manifest and finding its way to conflict, discovering greatness and the need to protect it, and now the energy that was bogged down and struggling to sustain itself reaches a crescendo and can burst forth with all its might. Perhaps it is the struggle of the Seven of Wands being released that causes the Eight of Wands to fly so fast and free.

This is a card of great ambition, of geniuses and mad inventors. It is the card of those who dare to break free of the mould given to them, and who set their sights higher than anybody could expect. They demand everything of the world and go out to seek it: here is the explorer, the adventurer and the trailblazer. Nothing can stop the passion, will and pure focus of the Eight of Wands: its arrows fly fast and true.

In the *Tarot Apokalypsis*, a young man, possibly of royal descent, joins in target practice with two animal companions by his side: the fierce lion and the far-seeing, swift falcon. The bow was the principal weapon of the ancient Egyptian army, and there are many surviving images of soldiers and royalty alike undertaking archery practice and fending off enemies with it. The skill required to use a bow well can be seen on the face of the archer, who is focused and calm, determined and certain. While the lion by his side looks up to the heights to see the other arrows already flying overhead, the archer focuses solely on his target. It may be distant and seem unattainable, but he knows that with the correct application of tension and skill released at the right moment he will hit his target.

Flying as swiftly as the fiery arrows with which it currently shares the skies, the peregrine falcon has been released to hunt. This falcon is one of many birds of prey native to Egypt and is sacred to Horus, the youthful god of war and symbol of the Pharaoh (see *King of Wands*). The hieroglyphic sign of its name, *hr'w*, denotes "one far up/high", and Horus himself was frequently called "Falcon". This bird is known for its speed of flight, which can reach up to 242mph, making it the fastest member of the animal kingdom. It is frequently used for hunting and has keen eyesight. As the sacred bird of Horus, it also reminds us to make war on the world by assaulting it with our endeavours, leaving as many great works after we are gone as possible.

The lion, like many big cats, represents the force of will and strength of ambition required to fuel the flames that are carried to the heavens by the arrows. Yet it focuses on the arrows that have already been loosed rather than the current target. Such distraction is common, as we watch the achievements of others in admiration, forgetting to make ourselves great also.

The greatest danger with the Eight of Wands is that it explodes so quickly into life, pushing ever onwards to new heights, full of energy and never stopping, that it may quickly run out of fuel and burn out. Those who do too much, who just keep going as long as they have a goal, direction and passion, often do not realise they are at risk of burning out because they are so caught up in their efforts and adventure. However, until that moment they are a wonder to behold, a star blazing an unchartered trail of greatness.

❦ Revelation

Ideas of greatness, ambition, high hopes and expectations; a great drive and passion for a single thing; single-minded focus; all of one's energy put into a single goal or direction; impetus; momentum; events carrying one forward in unexpected ways; force of will and desire driving one onwards; trailblazing and unchartered territory; speed of action; quick bursts of energy; an explosive push towards one's goal; a straight path to one's goal.

Negatively aspected…
Burnout through a large amount of activity over a short period of time; being unable to stop; being caught up by the momentum of external events; too much energy with too little focus; great expectations without a firm foundation; a desire to be noticed by others.

Nine of Wands

Few pathways are straight and easy to tread; the most ambitious of roads lead through fire and blood. I speak of the road of battle and struggle, of the tensing of muscle and flexing of sinew and flesh, of the lungs filled with heat and the heart pounding. Know that the pain is not unending, that the fight must flow like the ocean's tides, moon-kissed and ever-changing: now it is deep water, overwhelming and drowning; soon it will be drawn back into its swell. Then must you rest, for your blood flows free. Then must you gather your strength once more, remaining certain in the knowledge that your time of battle will come again, and you must meet it with fervour and fury. There is no ending to the struggle when you walk these roads, only the briefest of moments of calm. Walk by my side, warrior, for I can show you the way of conserved force and the opportune strike. My name is strength in weakness, action in stillness, conflict in peace and my blessing is the price due in the shifting sands of battle and the grasping of power. Yet do not grow complacent, for the battle is never won: fight on!

✑ Mystery

As we near the end of the suit of Wands, we find that our energy is depleted, sent off in all directions, used up along the way. Now we have a fight continuing before us, a challenge yet to face before completion can be achieved, so, wounded and weary, we urge ourselves onward once more. However, unlike the Ten of Wands, in which we carry heavy burdens that oppress us, this final push towards the finishing line is no burden: it is an opportunity for greatness and the price we must pay if we are to reach our goals. Here in the Nine of Wands we find the fine line between exerting all our force and conserving our energy; it presents the necessity to wait for the opportune moment in which to strike. To some, it might look like our waiting is weakness, yet it is in this time that we conserve our energy, build up our strength and ready ourselves to fight on. This unity of stillness and action is symbolic of the cyclical nature of power represented by this card. While many of the cards in the suit of Wands see power as a thing to be grasped that can be forever held, the Nine of Wands shows us that power waxes and wanes like the moon; instead of trying to hold onto it we should respond to its flux. In this way, we will not fight impossible battles and our energy will be conserved for the right moment.

This constant shifting of power is clearly seen in the rises and falls of Cleopatra VII Philopater (69–30 BCE), commonly known as Cleopatra. Her continual struggle for dominance – first over her brother and then with the power that Rome held in Egypt – never allowed her to achieve her goals. Her life was one of perseverance, every move made with her goal in mind. She desired sole rulership of Egypt in a time when a woman could not rule without a male co-ruler (in this case, her brother Ptolemy XIII, who was 10 years old when he became co-ruler with 18-year-old Cleopatra). She wished for alliance and power with Rome during a time when Rome's rulership was contested. She hoped for her son with Caesar to be acknowledged as his heir and, when that did not come to pass, to expand her dominion through her alliance with Mark Antony, aiding him in his fight against his fellow triumvir Octavian for rulership of Rome.

Cleopatra originally ruled with her brother, but not long after they were married (according to Egyptian custom) she made her first push towards independent rulership by removing his face from all coinage and dropping his name from official documents. This sole rulership was ended less than two years later and Ptolemy XIII became sole ruler of Egypt. Although Cleopatra tried to raise a rebellion, she was forced to flee with her sister Arsinoë. Staying to fight further would have been foolish. [269] While in exile, Cleopatra waited for the right time to strike, which presented itself when Ptolemy XIII offended Caesar by having Pompey, Caesar's political enemy, beheaded. Cleopatra quickly took the opportunity to ally with Caesar, [270] becoming his mistress. Their union produced a son named Caesarion. [271] Caesar backed Cleopatra's claim to the throne instead of annexing Egypt, defeating Ptolemy in 47 BCE in a series of battles, one of which partially destroyed the Library of Alexandria. This siege of Alexandria is shown in the card image, with Cleopatra standing defiant and still against the chaotic fire and destruction.

After Caesar's assassination, during which Cleopatra was visiting Rome with her family, the queen returned to Egypt. Not long after this, the co-ruler that had been enthroned by Caesar, Ptolemy XIV, died in suspicious circumstances, and Cleopatra, once again sole ruler of Egypt, backed Mark Antony and Octavian and the Caesarian faction. She named her son co-ruler of Egypt by her side. The relationship that ensued between Cleopatra and Mark Antony is the stuff of legend, held as an example of devoted love; however, it is likely that it was as much a political move for Cleopatra as a romantic one. Mark Antony helped her further secure her rule and his success in the Roman civil war allowed

---

269 Appian, **Civil War** 2.84.
270 Plutarch, **Life of Caesar** 49.
271 Suetonius, **The Divine Julius Caesar** 52.

her to expand her power. [272] At the height of her rulership she was given the title "Queen of Kings", with her enemies in Rome beginning to fear that she would establish universal dominance. [273] However, a few years later Antony and Octavian went to war with each other, and Antony committed suicide after suffering defeat. Cleopatra, who would have been captured and humiliated in Rome, followed him. She was the last Pharaoh of Egypt, and following her death Egypt became a province of Rome.

Cleopatra's life reminds us that even when we are surrounded by enemies or in the heart of a war, wounded and struggling to survive, a show of force – even if we don't intend to act on it – can be enough to scare our enemies and give us an opening of which to take advantage. It also tells us that even when we are at our weakest, we can consolidate our energy in order to fight anew later.

∼ Revelation

Perseverance; a time of apparent defeat during which one can consolidate one's energy; waiting for the opportune moment; stillness and patience in battle; being wounded yet fighting on; a lull between conflicts; the ebb and flow of power; power easily won and lost; a show of force to disguise one's weakness.

Negatively aspected…
Striking at the wrong time; not conserving one's energy; accepting defeat; feeling unable to continue in a struggle; feeling overwhelmed; weakness; losing power.

---

272 Plutarch, **Life of Antony** 2.21.1–3.
273 Ronald Syme, **The Roman Revolution**, p. 274. Oxford University Press, 1962.

Ten of Wands

If you believed that this path would be an easy one, that you would tread it lightly and briefly, then your will was overridden by foolishness. My mysteries are those of the arduous, long road, the struggle towards culmination, the straining towards fulfilment. They are the burning fire in your muscles and lungs as you push ever onwards, burdened and tiring. They are the knowledge that even in the suffering and exhaustion there is an end at which the fires of your ambition and passion yet burn. Know that although the sun's light fades and you no longer feel its presence, a small spark of will still burns within you: it has pushed you to this point, given you strength and energy to overcome, and now it cries out in the darkness for you to take one more step… and another… over and over again, promising you with each urging that this next will be the last. It is not. But you need to believe it will be in order to press forward. This is my blessing, worker: that you shall know struggle and burden during your great work, that you shall strive onwards despite it. It is not in the culmination that you triumph, but in the continuing even as every piece of your being yearns to stop.

◈ Mystery

The suit of Wands has become more arduous the nearer it comes to completion and fullness. Like the suit of Swords, we do not experience the culmination of this suit in the same blissful fulfilment as we do the suit of Cups and Pentacles. This is because, for the fiery, energetic suit of Wands, the multiplicity of the Ten – being furthest away from the focus and oneness of the Ace – is a danger. Energy, passion and ambition thrive with focus and single-minded direction, but falter and become weak when spread over several areas. The Ten of Wands, therefore, shows us the final push towards completion rather than the completion itself; there is more work still to do, yet we are exhausted, our energy – stretched so thin – depleted, our will – now unfocused and distracted – wandering away from our purpose. At this stage, when every part of our being is crying out to give up and stop, shrinking away from the pain of pushing on, we would welcome the sweet relief of not having to continue. Here, we are in danger of abandoning all our hard work thus far because we believe we cannot carry on. This card also represents the burdens we carry, both voluntary and involuntary, all our duties and the things that we believe rest on our continued performance and effort.

In the card image we see a man dragging the capstone of a pyramid up to its final resting place. It is important that it is the capstone that he has taken on as his burden, for this is the final piece of the pyramid to be put in place: his work is almost done. The sun sets overhead and the torches around him have been lit. Even as the light fades his will still burns strongly, urging him onwards. He screams in agony and expended effort as his muscles strain against the ropes of his burden – it is clear that this task is taking every ounce of strength he has, every piece of his will and self. He wears a simple loin cloth, inspired by images from ancient Egypt of builders at work.[274]

---

274 Hilary Wilson, **People of the Pharaohs: From Peasant to Courtier**, p. 37. Michael O'Mara Books, 1997.

It is often wrongly thought that slaves built the pyramids. In fact, most of the workforce was made up of conscripted peasants who did the work during the annual Inundation of the Nile, when they would have been unable to work their farms. They were paid for their work with food. The pyramids that they built are some of the most well-known and impressive monuments to this day, a testament to the greatness of the work. Like the work of the suit of Wands, building a pyramid was a lifetime's goal: it ensured its user's ascension to the stars after death. By taking part in the building of such a monument, "the labourers and craftsmen sought to ensure their own eternity through service in constructing the royal tomb". [275] In the Ten of Wands we have the chance to complete a *magnum opus*, our Great Work, and we must remember that nothing ever worth doing was easy. However, we might consider also that the man in the card is busy finishing somebody else's *magnum opus*, taking the hard work and burden onto himself so they don't have to. Thus, the Ten of Wands can also show us our martyr complex, our feeling of needing to take on the burdens of others and negatively affect ourselves in doing so.

⇛ Revelation

Burdens, duties and responsibilities; the final push towards completion; one's *magnum opus* or Great Work; a long-desired ambition almost attained; hard work and effort; the need to apply oneself and devote oneself to a task; a great challenge.

Negatively aspected…
Exhaustion; a martyr complex; doing too much at once; being unable to finish something due to lack of energy or will; being exploited by others; an uphill struggle.

---

[275] Rosalie David, **The Pyramid Builders of Ancient Egypt**, p. 58. Routledge, 1996.

Ace of Swords

What must come before the Word? What must come before the Thought? What must come before Memory? What cannot be seen, yet must come before the Seeing? I am speech, but I am silent; I am spoken of, yet I am ineffable. I am the most basic principle necessary for the step from nothing, from chaos to something. I am Order and I am Law. It is upon my principles that the planets move in their cosmic dance, stars die and are born, and from the seething of time you emerge. I give life to your breath, your ideas and your words; it is only by my holy rede that you may say anything at all. For what is speech or thought but the ordering of chaos from unformed instances? With that speech you have called me by many names, but imagined me across the world as the great Tree, the roots of order reaching down beneath the earth to realms you cannot name, the branches stretching above the heavens beyond your kenning. I am Yggdrasil, Odin's Gallows, the chief and most noble of trees, for it is at my roots that the gods must convene to sit in judgement, one foot upon my foundation of cosmic order and one in my source-springs of Fate and Wisdom. I am the primordial image and prototype of law; I am the blade of impartial judgement that must be used to cut to the truth. I am the axis mundi, the great pole of this world, upon

which you build all ideas and conceptions. I am the very bones of a universe upon which you hang the sinew, muscle and skin of your notions; I am the bare branches of a tree that you bring to leaf, bud and bloom with thought and idea. Thus, you may wield me and become a creator of worlds.

～ Mystery

There is not a single culture or religion in the world that does not have some form of cosmology or concept of the order of the universe at the foundation of its understanding. This assumption of cosmic order is necessary for further assumptions to be made, and it is upon this foundation that we build everything else. This refers not only to religion or myth: science too must build its cosmology (or, more appropriately, paradigm) within which it may refer to the laws it has set and decide upon the questions that it wants to answer. [276]

In the tarot we find this vital cosmic order in the Ace of Swords. Here is the idea that underlies all knowledge; not the seed of an idea, but the necessary preposition or presupposition that allows for the seeds of ideas to be born. The Ace of Swords is, therefore, associated with order in its many forms. Being the key to its suit, it is also the element of Air at its purest, ready to be experienced in its many forms through the rest of the suit. As such, the Ace of Swords represents all mental processes – thought, communication, perception, listening and observing. Since it is not yet applied to the world it is also completely objective.

With these processes and the cosmologies we build we are able to form a complete picture of the world around us and within us. In Norse myth and saga, this *axis mundi* is represented by the tree Yggdrasil, "Ygg's horse", Ygg being one of Odin's names. It is

---

276 *For a study of science as paradigm-based, see Thomas Kuhn,* **The Structure of Scientific Revolutions**, *first released in 1962.*

also called the World Tree. The sources agree that it is gigantic in size: its branches stretch into the heavens and its roots delve into three water sources of great power. This tells us that the tree encompasses the universe (it is said to hold within its branches the nine worlds). One of its roots goes down to a spring in Hvergelmir, where the dragon Níðhöggr lives and chews at the base of the tree and where countless snakes seethe. [277] Another root goes into Mímisbrunnr, Mimir's well, and another to Urðarbrunnr, the well of Urðr (Urd). It was at Mimir's well, filled with "wisdom and intelligence", [278] that Odin (see *King of Swords*) sacrificed his eye for a drink from the well; this drink gave him knowledge of all things. At Urðr's well the three Norns live, and these maidens weave fate (called *ørlǫg*) for humans. [279]

The names of these maidens are telling: Urðr means "that which has come to pass", Verðandi is "what is happening" and Skuld means "debt" or "owe", denoting that which shall come to pass. These three set down laws, decide fate, and carve runes on wood from which they set the laws. That they create laws for the world as well as for humans (fate, *ørlǫg*) reminds us that the cosmic order we create applies to every aspect of the universe, without and within.

Yggdrasil, then, takes up from its roots the most important sources of wisdom, knowledge, law, order and fate in Norse cosmology. It should not be surprising that the tree that symbolises the principles that hold up the universe is fed by knowledge and order. The Norns continue to keep the tree alive by watering it with water from Urðarbrunnr; [280] thus, we are reminded that ideas and principles, upon which we base all other

---

277 *Gylfaginning 16*, **Prose Edda**, trans. Anthony Faulkes. Everyman, 1995.
278 *Gylfaginning 15*.
279 *Voluspa 20*.
280 *Gylfaginning 16*.

hypotheses and knowledge, must be continually fed with more knowledge, gained through insight, observation and experimentation.

We learn from the Eddas that Yggdrasil is conceived of as a place where the gods hold court each day. [281] The *Poetic Edda* states that this holding of court is for the gods to sit as judges. [282] It seems fitting that the gods should use the base of the tree of cosmic order as the seat of their judgement, for it is only with the foundations of law, order and wisdom that they can do so. It is for this reason that the King of Swords wields the sword at all – specifically, he wields the Ace of Swords, and thus is able to make his decisions and judgements with complete objectivity, logic and knowledge. It is perhaps for this same reason that it was upon Yggdrasil that Odin hanged himself for nine days and nine nights, sacrificing himself to himself, to gain the knowledge of the runes. [283]

Odin's ravens, Hugin and Munin ("thought" and "memory") can be seen in the card image, reminding us of the gallows god (here represented by the hangman's noose) who peered into the depths from his place of sacrifice and took up the runes. They are also symbols of observation and learning, as they who travel across the world every day and report back to Odin with information.

The runes on the card are another form of cosmic order: they are the building blocks of words and expression of ideas (they are the letters of an alphabet). They also represent, as a complete set, all aspects of the universe in its cosmic order. It is from these constituent parts that we may write the loftiest of hypotheses,

---

281 *Voluspa 15.*
282 *Grimnismal 29–30.*
283 *Havamal 138–141.*

the most in-depth theses, the most touching poems or the most persuasive arguments. They are the beginnings of history too, for it is through writing that most of history comes down to us.

Creatures live in the branches of Yggdrasil, just as concepts of cosmic order are populated by constantly moving, shifting and interacting ideas and narratives. In its tallest branches perches an eagle, and between the eyes of that eagle lives a hawk. This eagle "has knowledge of many things" [284] and his messages are carried down the tree by the squirrel Ratatoskr to the dragon Níðhöggr. In the *Prose Edda* it is simply messages that the squirrel carries, but in the *Poetic Edda* he tells slanderous gossip and perpetuates enmity between the eagle and dragon. Interpreters have commented on the chattering of squirrels and their swift, inquisitive movement, as well as the ease with which they scale trees, pointing to concepts of swift communication and constant feedback between heaven and earth. No parts of a cosmology exist in isolation, and our knowledge cannot be formed or sustained if it is not continually informed with new information, or – like the eagle and the dragon – tested and tried in enmity.

There are also four stags that live in Yggdrasil, called Dáinn ("the dead one"), Dvalinn ("the unconscious one"), Duneyrr ("thundering in the ear") and Duraþrór ("thriving slumber"). Some commentators have suggested that these stags are the four winds, and their biting of the leaves of the tree is the winds ripping the clouds apart. [285]

Upon Yggdrasil the saga of all the gods and humankind plays out, and history unfolds. From its roots come wisdom

---

284 *Gylfaginning* 16.
285 Magnússon, Finn, **Eddalæren og dens Oprindelse,** p. 144. Copenhagen: Gyldendal, 1824.

and knowledge, and it touches every aspect of the universe with order and wisdom. It is a symbol of pure thought, initial conception of an idea, which can be later built upon. The Ace of Swords presents to us everything we need to seed an idea, let it grow into a tree and then fill out its branches: the high-flying eagle of wisdom with the keen-eyed hawk between its eyes, seeing all and missing nothing; communication from the ever-chattering squirrel, carrying messages between above and below; the eternal process of creation and destruction created by the worm gnawing at the roots and the Norns watering them, a process that is necessary to keep ideas fresh and avoid stagnation and fundamentalism; it shelters the powers of past, present and future, and sets down laws while leaving room for that which has yet to be. It is upon this thought-birthing place that we may surrender ourselves to the process of discovery.

∽ Revelation

A unified idea, principle, or concept of the world around us; unifying principle; cosmic order; organisation of otherwise ineffable concepts; the necessary foundations for knowledge; paradigms; logic; observation; communication, thought; ideas; ideas at the very nascent stages; thought before action; wisdom and knowledge; giving logical form to something; providing expression for an idea; the beginning of a process of discovery; law; objective truth.

Negatively aspected...
Lack of organisation of thoughts and ideas; ideas based on poor foundations; chaos; blockage of communication; disorder of the mind; a weak mind; lack of ideas.

Two of Swords

The sword is sharp and deadly; it has the power to create or destroy worlds. Yet it is not only a point: its two edges define it and draw it from the abstract to the manifest so that you might feel its weight. Its balance dictates the ease with which you wield it, for balance in all things is a blessing. The road of the sword is one of careful thought and strategy, of consideration and logical extension; for this, the mind must always be ready. You must not fear the choice that unfolds before you, nor falter at pronouncing it, yet rush not into your words. In that moment before you have declared your word, entire worlds can be created or destroyed. In that moment the universe unfolds before you with the lines of cause and effect presented to your inner eye: learn to read this map with care and attention and you will soon walk the thresholds of balance and duality with joy, welcoming each new moment of before-speaking. Man was not made to know the future, but he might glimpse the myriad of possible worlds and futures awaiting manifestation at the moment he steps from his high seat of vision and makes his first move.

✥ Mystery

In the Ace of Swords the necessary presupposition that allowed for seeds of ideas to be born was formulated; now in the Two we see that initial seed idea extended to logical consideration. Here is an idea that can be analysed, discussed, disagreed over and taken to a logical – if only theoretical – conclusion. It is not yet acted upon. The Two of Swords is the moment of the first step over the precipice from nebulous seed of an idea to a fully formed and logical idea, from impulse to speak to the first word being spoken. It is therefore a card of liminality, the threshold, choice and duality. The two swords crossed above the head of the man in the card image represent this duality taking the form of equally significant or attractive ideas that require consideration and an eventual choice.

The man in the image is a player of hnefatafl, or tafl. He carefully considers all the moves of the pieces on the board and their outcomes, his brow furrowed in thought. This is the logical process that takes place in the mind before a choice is made and at some point soon the man will make his first move of the game. "Tafl" is a name given to several versions of a Northern European boardgame played on a board of odd numbers of squares. It is a strategy game in which the king (placed in the centre square at the start) must reach one edge of the board. His eight defenders are arrayed around him and can assist him in this task. The attacking force – which outnumbers that of the defending kingsmen – can capture opposing pieces by flanking them on two sides, except for the king, which must be flanked on all four sides. If he is flanked thus, the game is won by the attackers. [286] A variant of the game, called Tablut, was recorded by Carl Linnaeus in 1732 in Lapland, and it is this version that

---

286 Sten Helmfrid, **Hnefatafl—the Strategic Board Game of the Vikings**. [pdf] Online at < http://hem.bredband.net/b512479/Hnefatafl_by_Sten_Helmfrid.pdf> Accessed 18 November 2015.

is shown in the card image. [287] Tafl was played not only by mortals but by the gods, [288] reminding us that the art of strategy is all-pervasive on all levels of our lives.

Tafl, like any game of strategy, is a peaceful means of learning tactical skills, critical thinking, decision making and how to weigh up the outcomes of several options. It invites the player to consider the logical conclusions of their ideas and examine each thought as it arises, transforming it from gut instinct or intuition into reasoned choice and decision. It emphasises the importance of the moment before commitment is made to a choice, that moment which is transitive and liminal. The act of strategic decision making requires objectivity and distance, and thus the colours of the card are cold, grey and icy. The crossed swords hang above the tafl player's head just as the weight of his first decision presses down on him.

~ Revelation

Choice; duality; a liminal state; being at a threshold; needing to make a choice; uncertainty in the face of many possibilities; logical consideration of options; a pause to consider the potential outcomes of a decision; strategy; objectivity in approaching a choice; willingly making a decision, a peaceful reconciliation of opponents; agreements, contracts and accords.

Negatively aspected...
Being stuck between a rock and a hard place; being forced to decide; being unable to see clearly the possibilities or the potential outcomes of a decision; lack of choice.

---

287 Nigel Pennick, ***Traditional Boardgames of Northern Europe***, *p. 8. Cambridge: Valknut Productions, 1988.*

288 ***Voluspa*** 8, ***Poetic Edda***.

Three of Swords

To love and to think are not gifts: they come with a price: that you must perceive and feel loss and grief. To unite the grief of the heart with that of the mind is the particular curse of humankind, yet it might transform into a blessing. Your heart may be shattered and pierced, your soul wounded, but think – such a simple thing! – and you can be pulled from the churning waters and perceive the greater need. You could be consumed by the bale-fire, or let it enlighten you. This is not a time for  *your pain and sadness. This is the time when necessity drives you out of pain and into realisation. You do not have the luxury of drowning. I am the sorrow of the world for the greatest things; I am the mother mourning the children of every woman. Grief cuts and grief hurts, but I am the more terrible pain felt not in the heart but in the very being: the knowledge of the world's impermanence should drive more fear into your heart than the realisation of your own death. For even the most concrete of minds must begin to falter under the weight of that fearsome, awesome knowledge: that all is futile and for naught. Even now I can hear you raging against this with every fibre of your being, proclaiming your importance as loudly and fully as you can… But this will bring only more grief. The pain you feel rooting you to the spot is mine: existential and excruciating, yet powerful. For what can one do in the face of it? I offer you the power of the only thing you can do: have compassion. Do not sorrow with the world but for the world, and a light brighter than before will burn, fuelled by your sorrowing, transformed into compassion, reflected in the knowledge of what is at stake.*

⇜ Mystery

Grief can be personal, often accompanying big life changes, losses and transitions. It can also be felt by a person, community, nation or culture in response to more abstract concepts, or for somebody not personally known to the griever. This kind of grief can wound us just as deeply, as it recognises that some of our most deeply rooted and valued beliefs have been lost, undermined or threatened. In the tarot there are two cards that deal with grief: the Five of Cups and the Three of Swords. It is the Five of Cups that deals with personal grief; the Three of Swords shows it on a larger scale. As it is found in the suit of Swords, the suit of the mind, this is grief not only felt but truly considered, often caused by a perception or realisation. Where the Fives of the tarot all bear an imbalanced, destructive and dividing influence, the Threes are more lofty, being closer to the source (One/Aces) and the root issue. As it follows the Two of Swords, in which a fine balance is struck within the liminal moment before decision, the Three is representative of thought extended to its logical conclusion, leading to existential crisis. The Three of Swords reminds us that the logic of the world, in its stark yet most truthful form, is painful, and points to the realisation of the harsh truths of the world. As the Three is so close to the source, and as it is in the suit of Swords, allied with the cold distance of the mind, it offers an opportunity to react in a very different way to the Five of Cups. It asks us to take our pain, existential dread and sorrow, and apply it to the bigger picture. It asks us to consider everybody else who feels pain and suffers as we have. The Three of Swords can be found in those who, through their compassion, walk among the sickest, poorest and most downtrodden people so that they may help them, or in those whose sorrow extends to the environment and spearhead causes to protect the natural world. In this sense, the loss of something so precious that it strikes us with the deepest, most cutting grief can remind us of our core values: what is important to us? What do we value?

The card image is stark and bleak. The three swords in the image are stained with blood to represent the hurt and pain associated with this card; around them is an icy, snowy landscape indicative of the feelings of being frozen and unable to move that often accompany existential grief and suffering. At its worst, the Three of Swords answers the question "What am I to do? How will I go on?" with a resounding "Nothing. You can't". Yet behind the clouds a little sunshine can be seen, and the blood from the swords falls onto white roses, symbolic of innocence being marred by hurt yet remaining intact: nothing will go untouched by sorrow in its life, but it does not need to be destroyed by it.

Up the blade of the middle sword is a mistletoe plant. It was from this plant that was fashioned a sharp spear that killed Baldr, the Norse god of light, spoken of as the fairest and most beautiful of all the gods. He was so beautiful that light shone from him. [289] His death is seen as the death of the light, the sun, or some notion of truth and goodness. It is said in the Eddas to be "the greatest mischance that has ever befallen among gods and men". [290] It is his death that is given as one of the events that leads to Ragnarök, the end of the world. It is also the event that makes it clear that Loki (see *Prince of Swords*) is no longer

---

289 Snorri Sturluson, **Prose Edda**, Gylfaginning 22, trans. Anthony Faulkes. London: Everyman, 1995.

290 **Ibid**, 49.

an uncertain ally to the gods, but instead bears malicious intent and will fight against them at Ragnarök. Just like the Three of Swords' more global sorrow and concerns, Ragnarök brings pain and destruction to an entire world, rather than just individuals. It also ushers in a new world, in which humankind is born again from two surviving humans, and three young gods from the Aesir survive to rebuild the realm of the gods.

The death of Baldr is a story that puts grief at centre stage. First, Baldr dreamed of his death, which caused his mother, Frigg, to seek an oath from everything that could harm him not to do so. When she had done this, the gods threw a party at which they played a game: throwing weapons at the now invulnerable Baldr. Loki was unhappy that Baldr could not be harmed, so he disguised himself as an old woman and spoke with Frigg, discovering that everything in the world made the oath except the mistletoe – a tree she thought too young to seek an oath from. So Loki found this tree and fashioned a spear (or arrow) from it. He found Hódr, Baldr's blind brother, and said that he should test his brother by doing as the other gods did: as he did so, he handed Hódr the spear of mistletoe. In some versions of the tale Loki guided Hódr's hand, but in others he threw it without guidance; in all versions it pierced Baldr's heart and he immediately died.

As the gods sent Baldr to his funeral pyre, they sent Hermódr as an emissary to Hel to ask for his return. Hermódr explained that Baldr was so well loved and so painfully grieved that Hel should return him. Hel agreed, on the condition that every living thing wept for Baldr, and none gainsaid that he was sorely missed. So Hermódr rode out once more, and every living thing was asked to weep for Baldr. All did so gladly, except for the giantess Thökk, who many say was Loki. So Baldr – the beautiful light – was condemned to death.

It must have seemed unthinkable to the gods that the best of them should suffer this fate, but it is the harsh truth of the Three of Swords that even the most sacred and beloved ideas, ideals, beliefs and constructs must, in the end, be destroyed. The test that Hel sets for Hermódr suggests that although grief may feel all-consuming it serves a purpose. The Three of Swords has a vital function: grief and sadness out of love for others, and love for a suffering world. The story has one more facet that we must remember when we face the Three of Swords: that which doesn't seem harmful may still be so. Just as the seemingly young and harmless mistletoe was overlooked and turned against Baldr, and just as it was an apparently innocent question from a negligible old woman that gained the truth that would kill the god of light, so the smallest of details, if neglected or ignored, may cause us great pain.

Revelation

Existential crisis, pain, suffering, sorrow; realisation of painful and difficult truths; revelations that cause suffering; the suffering of others and the world; feeling anguish at the suffering of others; compassion; heartache and heartbreak; feeling frozen and incapable in the face of inevitability.

Negatively aspected…
Being stuck in a vicious cycle; unable to move on from grief; lack of compassion; focusing on one's own suffering to the detriment of others or other parts of one's life; being too focused on details; missing the bigger picture.

Four of Swords

The creative mind knows no end of trials and sorrows; within its halls there are infinite doors, and not even the keenest mind can walk them all. Yet you, thinker, try. You let yourself fall through the mansion of your mind, often not knowing which way you are being led, tempted by this, coaxed by that, pulled in one direction and then another. All this is the necessary journey of those who perceive and express ideas. But you have come now onto my road, and it is dark and silent; no creatures of the imagination and phantasms of duty shall haunt you, nor shall the wildness of your mind send you howling through the forest, hunter and hunted at once. My blessing is that of peace, of the dark, waiting womb in which all things must gestate; my mystery is that of the greatest possibilities arising from the quietest mind. Stop for a moment and be still: listen, rather than think. It is here, in the indefinable moment of absolute blankness, that your mind can be free. It is here that the very heartbeat and lifeblood of the source of your ideas can be touched, heard and felt; it nourishes and renews you, sustains you and gives form to your ideas as a mother gives form to her child. Mine is the womb of mystery from which all possibilities grow; mine is the mantle of darkness beneath which you might gestate your most precious of thoughts.

ᛜ Mystery

After generating the initial seed of an idea in the Ace of Swords, extending it to its logical conclusion in the Two and becoming aware of its consequences and the necessary pain that awareness brings in the Three, the Four of Swords offers an opportunity to rest. This rest is not necessarily a physical one, as it is not the body that has been tested by the journey thus far; rather, the rest is a mental one, during which the silence of the mind's everyday worries, conclusions, tasks and planning allows for the growth of new ideas, unhindered and secure. All the Fours of the tarot have the power of manifestation, solidity, growth and slow but certain progress. In the Four of Swords this power becomes a womb of ideas and thoughts, a time for gathering one's thoughts and the gestation of inventions. It is the time taken out of being busy and trying to act that allows us to solve problems and see situations from a new perspective. It is the musings on a concept that give rise to a wealth of new ideas and applications. It is the silent, peaceful time before the flurry of activity required to express ideas.

In the card image a young woman rests by a fire she has built in the forest. It is night-time, and the stars blaze in the sky above the tree canopy. By her side, sleeping, is a tame wolf, and dangling idly from her fingers is a quill pen. There is a full sheet of writing already completed beneath it, and she stares into the distance deep in thought, possibly reflecting on what she has already written or considering the ideas she wishes to manifest next on paper. On a tree nearby is a wooden shrine to Freyja, the goddess of magic, fertility, death and beauty. We can imagine the peace, solitude, relaxation and warmth that the scene depicts, hear nothing but the gentle breeze through the trees and the crackling of the fire. Perhaps these, coupled with the even breathing of her animal companion, lull the woman into a meditative state, trance-like, in which the flames of the fire take shape and the stars above become tapestries of stories.

The woman is a writer – a skald. Her role is to keep histories, tell stories and perpetuate sagas. It is her words, both spoken and written, that inspire others to greatness and express the important values by which her people live. Her mind must always be full of the weight of this great responsibility, of tales and facts, history and names, new ways of telling a tale and methods of holding an audience. The wolf that sleeps by her side represents this whirlwind of thoughts, this wild mind, made calm and tranquil. The darkness of the forest represents the subconscious and the quiet mind into which the woman is able to sink; it is womb-like and peaceful, yet teeming with life just as the quiet mind is teeming with possibility awaiting birth. We are reminded that it is often in this kind of environment – dark and quiet – that our own minds become relaxed and reflective. In our modern world it can be difficult to seclude ourselves, surround ourselves with the natural world and find a place that is truly quiet. Instead, we naturally surround ourselves with a constant influx of new information and attention-grabbing technology that, while useful, also distracts and can burden the busy mind.

The shrine to the goddess Freyja, a recreation of a 6th-century bronze image from Sweden, that has been set up against a tree shows that in her solitude and meditation, the woman is devoted to and protected by this goddess. As the Four of Swords is an inherently fertile card, offering the soft, dark earth in which the seeds of ideas can grow and from which fully grown ideas can be harvested, Freyja offers her blessing of growth and power. This dark, silent forest can be seen as her womb, in which her devotee rests. Here, in the magical moment of contemplation, when the mind stops, the greatest of ideas spring forth and the mind is truly enriched.

∽ Revelation

Relieving mental stress and anxiety; relaxation; taking a break from worries; meditation and contemplation; trance-like states; taking time to consider; planning ahead to give oneself enough time for relaxation; quietening the mind; removing external stimuli; letting go of focus on many goals or duties to enable a deeper understanding of them; gestation and manifestation of ideas and thoughts; solidifying plans and ideas; the blank mind leading to inspiration.

Negatively aspected…
Writer's block; difficulty generating new ideas; not having time to relax mentally; ignoring the need to calm one's mind; being distracted easily; mental stress and exhaustion; progress of intellectual goals or projects being slowed or blocked.

Five of Swords

Contest is the fuel of the mind; destructive attacks are the means by which ideas are formed strong and new. For no great idea was born of peace, agreement or acceptance. There is a path for all words, and this path is dark and sharp: here are the words of cutting and breaking, striking and sneering. Know that by walking this path you may take up weapons and battle, performing your superiority to others, but you might also fall by the weapons of another: no man can be 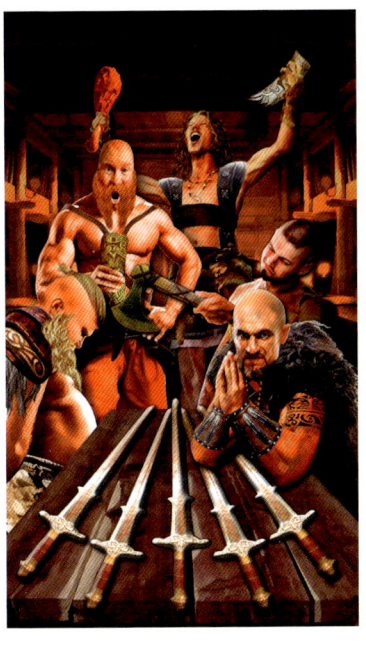 *spared the sharp tongue of insult or the injury of threat. But throw your words to the fire and speak of your greatness: boast your past achievements and swear your future glory – fill the world with your hot words! No man may gainsay them until you have proven your weakness. Yet make good your hastily spoken oaths, for true weakness lies in the broken vow and softness of speech. Do not coddle those for whom your words are pain or poison: they may fall alone into ignoble obscurity. Proclaim your distinction above others, shout your future excellence, listen not to the detractors: for truth begins in what is spoken, and thus you will drive yourself forward in the war of dominance.*

~ Mystery

"Quite enough senseless words are spoken by the man never silent; a quick tongue, unless its owner keeps watch on it, often talks itself into trouble." [291]

The destructive nature and challenge of the Fives of the tarot manifest in the suit of Swords as verbal challenges, insults, boasting, ideas pitted against each other and egos warring for dominance. In the Five of Wands the challenges allowed for renewed creative force, but in the Five of Swords there is no creative output; instead it is a performance of bravado, proclaimed self-importance and one-upmanship. In some contexts this can be constructive, providing a space in which to blow off steam or engage in ridiculous yet fun self-aggrandisement. In other contexts, however, it can take a nasty turn, with the deprecation of others and bullying words as a means to make oneself sound better in comparison. It is in the Five of Swords that we also find the means by which people try to gain advantage over others, not always fairly. In many cultures there are practices and traditions that allow for this sort of behaviour in a designated setting. For the Anglo-Saxon and Norse-speaking peoples, a special place was reserved for the traditions of flyting (from the Old Norse *flyta*, "provocation"), an exchange of insults, and *bēot*, a ritualised form of boasting. Flyting could occur in person at feasts and in other contexts, or through written communication; *bēot* was always undertaken in a feasting hall. A flyting contest was as much about demonstrating one's prowess as a wordsmith as it was about insulting the other person. In some cases it was also done for the entertainment of others, offering up the contestants as the subjects of ridicule. [292]

---

291 *Hávamál* 29, **Poetic Edda** trans. Carolyne Larrington, p. 18. Oxford University Press, 1996.

292 Geoffrey Hughes, ***An Encyclopedia of Swearing: The Social History of Oaths, Profanity, Foul Language and Ethnic Slurs in the English-Speaking World***, p. 173–4. M.E. Sharpe, 2006.

There are a great number of recorded examples of flytings, both between men and the gods. The flyting verses of the skaldic poet Egil Skallagrimsson against king Eric of Norway and queen Gunnhild are preserved in *Egil's Saga*, along with other examples. [293] The most famous example of a flyting is found in *Lokasenna* in the *Poetic Edda*, in which Loki, seeking to bring malice to a feast of the Aesir from which he had been excluded, speaks flyting verses against each of the assembled gods in turn, twisting their replies to him to attack them again. [294] His verses are at once clever, insulting, funny (for the reader), rude and profane, presenting an image of the gods not as divine, powerful beings but as quarrelling, jealous, lust-driven creatures. This event instigates the binding of Loki beneath the earth, making him an enemy of the gods. The first flyting verse spoken by Loki is a stark reminder of how our own words can be turned against us, as well as how speaking rashly or too much can work against us:

"You know, Eldir, that if you and I should contend with wounding words, I'll be rich in my replies when you say too much." [295]

The *bēot* was a more civilised practice, yet like flyting it relied on exaggerated words being spoken that could harm the speaker later. The term *bēot* may have had three meanings: threatening/menace, danger, and a boasting promise. [296] It consisted of oath-making over a mead-horn at feasts (often a "grave-ale", a feast for the new lord following the death of the old). While this was a solemn occasion, the grander and more difficult the subject of the boast the better, for the oath-maker would get greater glory

---

293   *Egil's Saga* 56–57, trans. W. C. Greeb, 1893.

294   *Lokasenna* 3–65, **The Poetic Edda** trans. Carolyne Larrington, pp. 85–95. Oxford University Press, 1996.

295   *Ibid.*, 5.

296   *Stefán Einarsson*, p. 980 "Old English Beot and Old Icelandic Heitstrenging" in **PMLA** vol. 49, no. 4, (Dec., 1934), pp. 975–993.

when it was achieved. However, there are several examples from the literature in which an oath made at a *bēot* put the oath-maker in a bad situation, such as Hrafnkell having to kill a man he did not wish to in *Hrafnkels saga Freysgoða*. [297]

It is easy for people to speak in ways they later regret. Boasting and inflating one's self-importance at the expense of others can also be fuelled by the mean encouragement of those witnessing the performance. The Anglo-Saxon poem *The Wanderer* gives advice on avoiding the pitfalls that can be created by such practices:

"A man must wait when he speaks oaths, until the proud-hearted one sees clearly whither the intent of his heart will turn." [298]

❦ Revelation

Intellectual contest; insults, threats and verbal attacks; meanness done to others as performance or entertainment; gaining advantage over an opponent; putting somebody at a disadvantage; destructive words; boasting; issuing a challenge; egos fighting; bravado, one-upmanship; feelings of self-importance.

Negatively aspected…
Inability to rise to an intellectual challenge; being the victim of verbal assault; weak ideas that do not stand up to testing; refusing to engage to competition.

---

297 *Ibid.*, p. 988.
298 *The Wanderer* 70ff, online at http://www.anglo-saxons.net/hwaet/?do=get&type=text&id=wdr [Accessed 10 November 2015].

Six of Swords

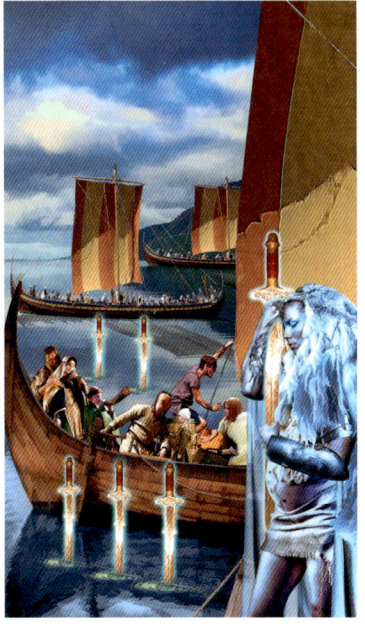

From one shore to the other the mind must travel, soul-driven and bound for new horizons. Here, in transition, the mind is free and unbound, at peace. Here might the souls settle anew in harmony. Follow the pathways of discovery, set your prow for the unknown sunrise over the edge of the horizon, and let your mind roam free. Fear not storm-tossed waters, nor think too hard on what has been left ashore, for I guard you and keep you, gently directing your course. My blessings are passed down through the ages by blood, from elder to younger, between namesakes, through memory. Know that I will always be with you, and thus you shall carry all you need for the journey: not burdensome baggage but the feather-light memories of the past and your ancestors, the timeless collection of wisdom that forms the shore from which you may launch your ship on the ocean roads. Mine is the journey of the questing mind, of the welcoming of a dawn under a new sky, of moving ever-onwards to new horizons; mine is the gentle hand leading you and the touch upon your shoulder so that you know I am following. For this is the ship leading to a new world that you create from what you have brought with you.

✎ Mystery

In the Six of Swords we have an opportunity to reconcile our warring ego with our ideas, ideals and philosophies and move to a new phase in our lives. Here we can make the transition from one way of thinking to another or test new waters. This is also the realm of the mind still growing and evolving, a fluid mind not trapped by old-fashioned ideas or boundaries. As all the Sixes of the tarot bring with them a sense of harmony and peace, so the Six in the suit of the mind brings peace of mind and mental harmony. The mind is most at peace when it is free to move forward unstifled. This is also a card of transition and movement to undiscovered areas, physically and mentally.

The Vikings are well known for their raids throughout Europe. However, after initial raids there was a period during which the Vikings settled in large numbers. This settlement of the Vikings throughout the British Isles had a lasting effect on its culture, language, law and political landscape, an influence still felt today. It marked an important transition for the Viking way of life, which in turn was influenced by the culture, language and religion of the settled land.

The card image shows a community of Viking settlers readying their ships for the journey to their new life. As the ships sail off from one shore to another, the spirit of a pregnant woman watches over them. This is the *fylgjukona*, or *fylgja*, a female spirit that followed a person and would pass onto another family member upon the death of her owner, carrying their luck to the next generation. In this way, luck and fortune were seen as transitional. The word *fylgja* was often used synonymously with *hamingja*, [299] an expression of a man's thought or mind as well as fortune and luck, which was a being that could be

---

299 Bettina Sejbjerg Sommer, "**The Norse Concept of Luck**", p. 279, in **Scandinavian Studies** vol. 79, no. 3, pp. 275–294.

seen by its owner and their family. [300] When a person died, their *hamingja* could be reincarnated in one of their descendants, as seen in the *Hallfreðar Saga*, in which a dying man's *fylgjukona* is seen and accepted by his son. [301] The passing of the *hamingja* or *fylgjukona* of a person to younger family members was particularly assured if the child was given the name of the original owner. [302] In some ways, it was believed that this would ensure the rebirth of the soul of the dead person in their family line, [303] as well as ensuring the fortune of the deceased could pass on to their descendants and protect them. Thus, Ingimundr was named after his maternal uncle so that *hamingja* would pass to him "on account of the name". [304] This link with the fortune of one's ancestors reminds us that the Six of Swords is not only about transition to a new stage of life but also the passing on of memories and ideas to others. This is the reason for the pregnancy of the *fylgjukona* in the card image, for she carries with her the memories and fortune to be passed down and the opportunities that arise from transition.

The ships in the card image are particularly important, as they represented for the Vikings the opportunities of trade, exploration, raiding and settlement. They carried them to new lands and lives, creating a new age for medieval Europe; they also may have featured as part of certain funerary rites according to the account of Ahmad ibn Fadlan, who gave an eye-witness account of a 10th-century ship burial among the Rus' Vikings. [305] This

---

300 *Ibid.*, p. 281.
301 **Hallfreðar Saga 11.**
302 Hilda Roderick Ellis, **The Road to Hel: A Study of the Conception of the Dead in Old Norse Literature**, pp. 138–147. Greenwood Press, 1969.
303 *Ibid.*, p. 132.
304 **Vatnsdæla Saga VII, quoted in** Hilda Roderick Ellis, *The Road to Hel*, p. 132.
305 Ibn Fadlan, **Ibn Fadlan and the Land of Darkness: Arab Travellers in the Far North**, trans. Caroline Stone and Paul Lunde, p. 54. Penguin Classics, 2011.

account is backed up by many examples in archaeology of ship burials. The ship, therefore, not only carried the Vikings to new life while alive but during death as well: a vehicle for transitions and the opportunities of new shores.

⇜ Revelation

Transition, movement to a new phase; re-balancing of the mind and a series of ideas; a journey, whether physical or metaphorical; passing on ideas to others; transitional and liminal forces granting new ideas; the freedom of the mind from its boundaries; harmony and peace of mind; protection and guidance from an unknown source on one's journey; new discoveries.

Negatively aspected…
Difficulty moving on or making a transition; holding on to the past; being held back by old ideas; an unwanted change; return to well-known areas of one's life; going over old ground.

Seven of Swords

Not every path you walk runs before you straight and narrow; many a path is winding, taking you on circuitous routes. Conventional wisdom eschews this path, for it breeds cunning minds and tongues of honey, yet few see that it is shaped this way to find a smoother path around obstacles. I am the snake that slithers between the gaps and the winding road of deception; I am the shifter of shape and the double-speaker: my words are truth and lies in the same moment. I am the whispers behind closed doors and the secret handshakes, the lies told and the palms greased. I am called Thief and Deceiver, yet I am created by circumstance. I am the one born from weakness and disadvantage and I have learned my way through failure in the face of the superior, those who are lauded as paragons, as virtuous, as "good". Yet these are the same that would rush headlong and proud into danger, taking risks and caring not for their consequences. I say this one thing plainly to you: the flight of the arrow is often off-course.

☙ Mystery

All the Sevens of the tarot are associated with flux, movement, flow and fluidity. In the airy, intellectual suit of Swords this flux has both positive and negative connotations. It may inspire the movement and trade of ideas, but it may also encourage their theft and pursuits of duplicity and manipulation.

In the card image, the facial expression of the youth creeping into the night having stolen weaponry displays nervousness, indicating that he knows what he has done is wrong. Around the side of the building, a warrior looks down at his empty scabbard and begins to realise that his sword has been stolen. The fire casts his long shadow beyond the building, alerting the thief to the proximity of his potential discovery. The situation is a tense one for both parties, but more so for the thief – he must now navigate his way to safety, attempting to hold onto as many of his stolen goods as possible, while remaining unseen and unheard.

This is symbolic of many situations involving theft, though the swords being stolen in the image represent ideas, words and character more often than physical property. Here is a drama played out by one or more parties, in which at least one wishes to manipulate or gain advantage over the other, taking something from them without being caught doing so. The manoeuvring that occurs when this attempt is discovered by the wronged party may also become part of the duplicity, with lies leading to more lies. The juxtaposition in the card image of the muscled warrior and the wiry youth indicates that these situations often occur when somebody perceives they are disadvantaged and can therefore only progress or achieve what they want through underhanded means, rather than facing a challenge head-on.

One of the more positive aspects of this card is that it can encourage approaching a problem from a different perspective, often taking the opposite view or thinking laterally. Where a direct approach is ineffective, a creative approach that takes a more roundabout route might work. There are a number of

Norse myths that show duplicity and manipulation in a relatively positive light, with important aspects of the cosmos or the human experience being gained through theft or trickery. In the *Poetic Edda* we learn that the mead of poetry, *Suttungmjaðar*, was stolen by Odin.[306] This mead, owned by Suttungr, was said to grant to anybody who drinks from it the abilities of a skald (poet or scholar). Initially, Odin offered to work honestly in exchange for a draught of the mead; however, when his work was done, Suttungr refused to let him drink. The direct approach ineffective, Odin began to think creatively: he shifted his shape into that of a snake and slithered into the house undetected. Of course, this was not the only trick Odin had: in three draughts he emptied the three vats that supplied the mead and, his mouth filled with the mead, he transformed into an eagle and flew away, spitting the mead into containers held out by the other gods. Thus, through theft and trickery, Odin gained the mead of poetry for the gods and for men. The Seven of Swords can be used just as effectively in our lives, cutting its way around problems to reach the desired outcome, though the methods it uses may be viewed poorly by others.

≈ Revelation

Trickery, deception, manipulation; shifting one's intentions; saying one thing and meaning another; deliberately confusing speech; misleading others; theft of ideas or work; character assassination; political machinations; putting others at a disadvantage; taking credit where it is not due.

Negatively aspected…
Wrongly accusing others of blame or wrongdoing; misplaced distrust; false victimhood; safeguarding one's ideas or work; fear of being manipulated or deceived holding one back.

---

306 Skaldskaparmal 58, The Poetic Edda,.

Eight of Swords

Since your first steps on the road of your life you have been bound by a thread unseen and unknown. The Mistresses of Law wove it for you and around you, and no step is taken without it pulling you in its direction. You are a captive to your path, a prisoner of the world; as long as you have breath you shall not escape. I tell you this for it is fated for me to do so: every dawn and nightfall and all that falls between is ordained like the order of the heavens. Yet, bound one, know that I am found in other ways: on the roads set down by those who would control you and bind your will to theirs, on the pathways of duty and circumstance. The storms of life can freeze you and isolate you, keeping hidden your means of control. Know when it is your time to fight and when it is your time to acquiesce. Know when to grasp and when to let go. It is there, in the balance between straining against your bonds and allowing them to guide you, that true freedom is granted.

∽ Mystery

All the Eights of the tarot can be seen as double-Fours, with the powers of manifestation, grounding and earthiness of the Fours amplified. Unlike the positive effect this has in some of the suits, in the airy suit of Swords it serves to chain down otherwise fast-moving ideas, limiting freedom, open discussion and new thought. The grounded, manifest nature of the Eight brings external forces to bear on internal thoughts, ideas and the mind. Coupled with the fact that the further into the Swords suit we travel, the more fragmented and unfocused the mind becomes, we find ourselves in a situation where the powers of our mind are bound; we are isolated and unable to move, lacking freedom.

Here we see a man, almost-naked, bound to a *níðstang*, also called a nithing pole. His hands and legs are tied with strong rope, which also gags him so he is unable to speak. Although he is not blindfolded, his eyes are closed; he strains with every muscle against his bindings, but to no avail. Around him, swords stab into the frozen ground and atop the *níðstang* is the clean skull of a horse. Odin's ravens tug at the red strings that weave among the swords and create a web, from which hang three runes: Isa (ice), Perthro (secrets, the hidden) and Hagalaz (hailstorm and challenges). The runes work their magic to keep the man frozen in place, beaten down, his plight hidden from others.

The *níðstang* is a form of curse attested to in the sagas. It is one of many forms of magic that was used by the Germanic Norse to affect a person's thoughts, feelings and ability to act independently. It consists of a pole on which the head of a horse is placed, oriented to face the victim's location. The most famous example was erected by Egil Skallagrímson, a skaldic poet and runic magician, against king Eric and queen Gunnhilda. He fixed a horse's head on a hazel pole and turned it to look inward to the mainland, speaking a curse against the king and queen to turn the spirits of the land against them to drive them out. [307] With this curse he not only cursed his victims

---

307 **Egil's Saga** *60, trans. W. C. Greeb, 1893.*

but also the spirits of the land, whom he tormented in order to send them after Eric and Gunnhilda. Many other cultures have used this formula of tormenting spirits of the land or the dead to send them, angry, after a curse victim – the victim is usually tormented by these spirits until they relent to the magician's desire. The torment usually occurs on a mental level, such as Skirnir's spell on a woman desired by the god Freyr: his runic curse gave her "madness and howling, tearing affliction and unbearable desire" and requested "May your mind be seized!". [308]

Other examples of Germanic magic that could bind the mind can be found in texts such as the *Galdrabók*, a 16th-century Icelandic grimoire. It has examples of spells to cause fear in a person, cause a person to fall in love with the sorcerer and put someone to sleep. Other Icelandic magic includes staves to terrify somebody and give them hallucinations. Some of this magic, while controlling, is done for a good purpose, such as to force people to reconcile. [309]

The red thread that weaves around the swords and creates a web represents the Norse concepts of *wyrd* and *ørlǫg*. Both terms have been understood as "fate" and represent a kind of determinism. Every human has *ørlǫg* and all are subject to *wyrd*. The Norns are said to weave *ørlǫg*, given to all humans at birth. *Wyrd* is mentioned in both *Beowulf* ("Fate remains wholly inexorable") and *The Wanderer* from the *Exeter Book*, in which it is represented as relentless and unavoidable ("Fate is full moveless" [310]). Each person is bound by the laws of their

---

308 *Skirnismal 27–31*, **Poetic Edda**, trans. Carolyne Larrington, pp. 65–66. Oxford University Press, 1999.

309 ***Galdrabók: an Icelandic Grimoire***, trans. Stephen E. Flowers. Samuel Weiser, 1989.

310 ***The Wanderer** 5*, trans. Clifford A. Truesdell IV, 2012.

fate, set down before they had a concept of choice. However, Odin's ravens – Hugin ("thought") and Munin ("memory") – pick at these threads, suggesting the potential for unravelling and analysis.

Being bound by external circumstance can be difficult and frustrating; for the modern mind, losing control and giving it to another force external to ourselves is often terrifying. It can also be a situation thrust upon us unbidden and unwanted, which we need to fight to escape.

✎ Revelation

Being bound or beholden; limited freedom and ability to act independently; ideas and speech blocked, controlled or prevented; external influences bearing on internal processes, usually in a negative way; deterministic attitude; somebody controlling another's will; isolation from one's power of choice and will; feeling helpless.

Negatively aspected…

Voluntarily being bound to something; being in control of another person in some way; understanding an inexorable course; following a path from which one should not deviate.

Nine of Swords

The mind is a dark and terrible place; far worse than the cages it builds are the creatures it releases, let to run wild and terrifying behind the eyes. Mine is the realm of the night terror and the midnight hag, the whispers in the dark accusing and taunting; my roads are many and fractured, some dragged slow into the mud and some cut deep into stone. My name is night-walker and fear-maker, and in my black mirror I reflect your doubts, anxieties and fears, looming larger and more hideous. Yet do not think that I reside out there, in the vague notion of blackness: I am in here, within, walking the fractured pathways of your mind, feeding on all that you fear. Fear feeds fear and its chains bind tighter with every devouring. And though you feel alone, small and insignificant, know that you are not: every human on the earth has known me since the first spark of distinction grew in their mind between I and Not-I. It is these distinctions that I love: they build more walls, create more pathways and splinters upon which I can travel, and turn the sword of the questioning mind to attack itself. I am Nightmare and Doubt, Phobia and Fear, released to walk the night-roads of your waking mind.

∽ Mystery

As the Swords suit moves further away from its purest form in the Ace, the state of the mind becomes gradually more fractured and displaced. This can be seen in the considerably darker tone of the later Swords cards. Here in the Nine we are almost at the end, so the mind is in a poor state. The Nine of Swords is often an unwelcome card in any reading, depicting a scene of night-time terrors and subconscious fears. It is in this card that we find all of our nightmares, everything that makes us anxious, our neuroses, fears and everything that keeps us awake at night. Here we also find mental illnesses and anxiety disorders, such as post-traumatic stress disorder, insomnia, depression, separation anxiety disorder, schizophrenia, and phobias (this is not an exhaustive list). Disorders that affect perception of the external world and the self also prowl in the shadows of the Nine of Swords, such as body dysmorphic disorder and eating disorders.

Every culture has its monsters. Some are alien to humankind, somehow "other", while some play an intimate role in everyday life. In Norse culture there were many monsters or creatures of "otherness", two of which are shown in this card: the *draugr* (with the ninth sword in its hand) and the *dísir* (nearest the weeping woman). *Draugr* ("deceiver") were the walking corpses of the dead that often gravitated to humans out of jealousy of the things of life. They are also referred to as *aptrganga* ("again-walker") and are "generally mischievous, and greatly to be feared". [311] They are described as having a fearsome appearance, often black, blue or corpse-pale in colour. They jealously guard the treasure of their burial mounds and attack living beings, in particular those who wronged them in

---

311 N. K. Chadwick, p. 50, "*Norse Ghosts (A Study in the Draugr and the Haugbúi)*", in Folklore, vol. 57, no. 2 (Jun., 1946), pp. 50–65.

life. A *draugr* may kill its victim by crushing them or devouring them, reminiscent of reports of sleep paralysis, in which the victim feels as though something is sitting on their chest making them unable to breathe. They may also drive their victims mad, sometimes causing them to die from this madness. [312] *Draugr* are not unintelligent zombies, however; they speak and have agendas. Glamr, the *draugr* of a shepherd, demonstrates that they act maliciously towards the living: he cursed his opponent, Grettir, to not gain strength, to be abandoned by his guardian spirit, to lose fame, and that this would eventually cause his death. [313] These malevolent undead were believed to enter the dreams of the living, leaving an object for their sleeping targets to find upon waking [314] – certainly an unnerving experience! The fact that *draugr* were once living humans reminds us that the conditions of the Nine of Swords afflict us all at some time; their ability to attack their victim in so many different ways is perhaps a suitable way of describing the mind during its darkest moments, and their ability to curse the living reminds us of the effects that mental disorders and anxiety can have on our everyday lives.

Dísir were usually benevolent spirits, guardians of a home or family, seen variously as a type of valkyrie, Norn, goddess or spirit. While they had a protective function and there is considerable evidence that they were worshipped in Scandinavia, [315] they could also become malevolent in anger, causing the deaths

---

312   Gudbrandr Vigfusson and F. York Powell, "**Floamanna Saga**" *in* **Origines Islandicae**, *vol. 2, p. 646. Clarendon Press, 1905.*

313   William Morris and Eirikr Magnusson trans. **Grettir's Saga**, *p. 53. Online at the Icelandic Saga Database http://sagadb.org/ Accessed 16 October 2015.*

314   Hilda Roderick Ellis Davidson, **The Road to Hel: A Study of the Conception of the Dead in Old Norse Literature**, *p. 163. University of Michigan Press, 1943.*

315   *We have, for instance, records of a* **disablót**, *a sacrificial festival in which they were given offerings, in* **Egil's Saga**, **Viga-Glúms Saga** *and the* **Heimskringla**.

of those they previously protected. In the story of the death of Þiðrandi, told in the *Flateyjarbók*, we are told of nine dísir dressed in black who attack the family of Hallr in anger, supposedly because the family are about to convert to Christianity and would stop serving them. [316] In the *Reginsmál* they accompany a warrior to battle, "baneful at both [his] sides", willing him to be mortally wounded. [317] The ability of these guardian spirits to turn on those they protect is chilling, reminding us that even the most ubiquitous events in our lives can cause us great anxiety and worry.

Monsters of the imagination depict the threats of this card because it often signifies worrying too much over something that either isn't a problem at all or which is blown out of proportion by worry. Odin himself gave advice in the Hávamál about worry:

"The foolish man lies awake all night
And worries about things;
He's tired out when the morning comes
And everything's just as bad as it was." [318]

∽ Revelation

Anxiety; worry; mental exhaustion and stress; insomnia; nightmares; the everyday world causing worry; overthinking problems, causing them to feel worse or have a more pronounced negative effect; negative thinking; a skewed perception that is out of touch with reality; phobias and

---

316 Hilda Roderick Ellis Davidson, ***The Road to Hel: A Study of the Conception of the Dead in Old Norse Literature***, *p. 134*.

317 Henry Adams Bellows trans. ***The Poetic Edda***, *p. 368*, ***Reginsmál*** *24*. Princeton University Press, 1936.

318 Carolyne Larrington trans., ***Havamal*** *23*. ***The Poetic Edda***, *p. 17*. Oxford University Press, 1996.

fears controlling one's thoughts; something familiar and benign being perceived as threatening; mental illness and disorder; a stressed mind that is fragmented and fractured, unable to process correctly.

Negatively aspected…
External forces being a source of worry and stress; other people causing anxiety; dreams and visions; a night-owl; refusing to acknowledge one's fears or disorders.

Ten of Swords

Here, at the end of all logic and reason, in the battlefield of the mind, night has fallen. As a warrior you walk the bloody blade-road and with every cutting away and stripping down the pain increases yet becomes clearer; with every moment of breakdown, confusion sloughs away. There is no avoidance possible, for nothing that is born can remain unchanged and unchallenged, and the years of the mind cause it to take on burdens and construct secure worlds that must eventually burn. Like the sacking of a city the mind must be pillaged; like the body on the pyre it must be incinerated in fire and blood; like the sword and the warrior it must be tested until it fails. For only in failure and the identification of weakness can strength be founded. I come to you, bloody one, on the field of raven fodder, astride great beasts that will consume you, shaking a spear and thundering the loud battlecry for all to hear: here lies a god, to whom death came lovingly! Ignore not my outstretched hand, but embrace me as a lover, for on these cutting-roads you can love tenderly your destruction and welcome your end. Let me take you as my lover and we will pass the night in your burial mound, there to welcome the new dawn with loud cries, rage and a feast for the ravens.

∽ Mystery

The treacherous journey of the Swords suit is complete; here we find the breaking point of the mind. When rational thought and state of mind move so far away from a sense of oneness and focus they fragment, their sharpness turning inwards to create anguish, self-doubt and disorder. What once cut through confusion to reveal truth now betrays itself; what once opened the way towards wisdom now shreds the feet of those who walk its path. In the Ten of Swords we have reached the lowest point, with destruction and the certainty of endings; yet, much like the Tower, it presents an opportunity to begin anew. Here, in the darkest moment of breakdown, we are released from the fragmentary, harmful thought patterns that have shackled us. The Ten of Swords, while being a painful experience, is the process by which we destroy the constructs and thought patterns that hold us back, taking apart our most affectionately held beliefs and ideas and questioning everything to its core. In this stripping down of our conceptions we enter a crisis point, the moment at which our minds snap and are freed.

For many cultures, defeat on the battlefield is an unwelcome crisis point, a sign of failure. For most of us, death and destruction are the ultimate evils to be avoided. Not so for the Norse, for whom death on the battlefield was welcomed as a good death. Those who died in this way were taken to the halls of Freyja (Sessrúmnir) or Odin (Valhalla), where they feasted and prepared for the final battle of Ragnarök. Those sent to bring the fallen from the battlefield to Valhalla were the valkyries, who "allot death to men and govern victory" [319] and were depicted in the sagas and skaldic poetry as battle maidens, wearing helmets and blood-drenched chainmail tunics, light shining from their spears. [320]

---

319 **Ibid.**, *35, p. 31.*

320 **Helgakviða Hundingsbana** *1:15,* **Poetic Edda,** *trans. Carolyne Larrington, p. 116. Oxford: Oxford University Press, 1999.*

Valkyries were often depicted as terrifying beings, in keeping with the experience of utter destruction. They are called "wound-giving valkyries" and their mounts are described as "feasting on the fodder of ravens (corpses)". [321] They are not just choosers of the slain, however: they are sometimes shown as playing an active role in the final breakdown of the self at death, as they not only devour the slain but also prophesy death. In the *Darraðarljóð* from *Njáls Saga*, twelve valkyries are witnessed prophesying the death of armies in a bloody fashion: they "cross" the "web of man grey as armor… with a crimson weft"; the warp of their weaving loom is made from human entrails, with heads for heddle-weights and bloody spears as heddle rods; the valkyries state "With swords we will weave this web of battle" and they are described as "weaving with drawn swords", their typically feminine work made brutal and warlike. [322] In Anglo-Saxon glosses the term given to valkyries – *waelcyrge* – was equated with the Latin word for "Fury" (the Greek Erinyes, chthonic deities of vengeance). [323] They also lend their names and their zeal for the death of warriors to a number of kennings that describe weapons and warfare, such as "valkyries' sport" as battle. [324]

This destruction of the self, created and administered by the valkyries on the field of battle, gives way to a final aspect of the Ten of Swords: rebirth. From the darkness comes the dawn and after destruction comes liberation. Scholars have commented that "the capacity to be reborn seems to be most frequently associated with valkyries". There are tales of a valkyrie

---

321 **Ibid.**, *p. 121.*

322 ***The Story of Burnt Njal***, *trans. George Webbe Dasent 156: Brian's Battle. Edinburgh: Edmonston and Douglas, 1861.*

323 *Hilda Ellis Davidson,* ***Roles of the Northern Goddess****, p. 178. London: Routledge, 1998.*

324 *Diana Whaley, "Skaldic Poetry" in* ***A Companion to Old Norse Icelandic Literature****, ed. Rory McTurk, p. 487. Oxford: Blackwell Publishing, 2005.*

and her lover reborn three times, each time finding each other and loving one another anew; a valkyrie granting a name to a nameless man; and a valkyrie whose act of suttee is seen as an act towards rebirth. [325]

There are instances in the sagas of dying or dead heroes falling in love with a valkyrie who welcomes them into death: Helgi joins his valkyrie lover for one night in his burial mound before riding to Valhalla, where she welcomes him. [326] As such, warriors loving valkyries is not the seduction of fate in order to change it, but the welcoming, as a lover to his bride, of inevitable destruction.

~ Revelation

Crisis point, breakdown, the snapping of the mind; the breaking down of intellectual constructs, ideas and beliefs; a painful end; something taken to its logical conclusion; welcoming destruction; stripping down conceptions and perceptions; questioning everything; the fragmented mind destroyed; delusions broken down, the death of the self and ego.

Negatively aspected…
Clinging to painful ideas or self-doubt, self-sabotage; the worst point; a crisis point dealt with poorly; an opportunity for transition blocked; over-thinking causing problems.

---

*325 N. K. Chadwick, "**Norse Ghosts (A Study in the Draugr and Hagbui)**", p. 58, in **Folklore**, vol. 57, no. 2 (Jun., 1946), pp. 50–65.*

*326 Hilda Ellis Davidson, **Roles of the Northern Goddess**, p. 176.*

Ace of Cups

It is a falsehood disguised in fact that man must enter into the earth at the end of life. In truth, it is in the beginning that you must take the road into the depths and their darkness, there to be drowned in the mysteries. For you are not born just once: you have the blessing to be twice-born if you desire it, first from the womb of woman and second from the womb of initiation. For the latter, the pathway of the soul, you must drink of that veiled cup of ecstasy and bliss, abandon and softness, and not carry a light into the darkness. There will be revealed to you a vision, received at the pinnacle of initiation through heavily lidded eyes, when you are drunk on the heady fumes of divine love. I am that madness and that bliss, that fear and that love. I am the revelation of the sacred and in the darkness of the earth and the darkness of your soul I will illuminate All. From this revealed light of the universe is reborn your soul, striving upwards as the divine light strives ever downwards to touch you. I am the mystery hidden in plain sight. I am everywhere and in all things, even the most ignoble; I am Love in all its forms, and Love at its highest, at its most nascent and primal. I am the Love that cannot be contained, that flows like the rushing waterfall out of you and into the world. I am your

soul. And this is the truth: your soul and Love are one and the same, and when you give your love to another you give to them also your soul, opening yourself to them. Love is always reciprocal, and although you give your soul in its process, it is from this that you are filled with soul. The more you love, the more soul you are filled with, the greater your inner treasures, the deeper your revelations; you become a vast ocean of peace. These mysteries will endure until the end of time, for they are naught but Love, and man will always seek Love and create it. The cup that holds that secret drink may be veiled and hidden, but seek it truly and you will find it close to hand.

Mystery

As the Aces are the raw powers and unified embodiments of their suits, the Ace of Cups is all the powers of the element of Water and the suit of Cups in their purest form. Like its sibling Aces, this card is closest in nature to the source of its element. Like the Water that it embodies, the Ace of Cups flows between the gaps of other cards in a reading, filling them with love, beauty, happiness, emotion and mystery. It also shows us a key moment in life: that of theophany – revelation of the gods – during initiation. In many traditions, the cup, or grail, is a symbol of holy mystery, and here it is unveiled deep within the initiatory cave. It is also an experience of spiritual ecstasy and bliss, of being filled with divine love and overwhelmed by realisation of mystery. As our suit of Cups is found in the ancient Mediterranean, the cup is the vessel that held the *kykeon*, the sacred drink of the Eleusinian mysteries, given to new initiates before they underwent their first rites. There is some suggestion that this drink had hallucinogenic properties, and we know that it was drunk after a fast, so the *kykeon* was likely to either aid or directly induce the states of ecstasy that the initiate would achieve during the initiation rites.

In most mystery religions of the ancient Mediterranean world, the sacred drama culminated in the unveiling or revealing of an image, icon, or item that conveyed a deep mystery of the initiation or the teachings of the mysteries. In the Roman cult of Mithras an image of the tauroctony was pivoted round to face its audience within the dark *mithraeum* (see *The Sun*); in the rites of Eleusis an ear or corn was revealed (see *High Priestess*). It was through these sacred images that life-changing experiences were instigated, and mysteries conveyed. It is the ecstatic religions and spiritual experience inspired by revelation that the Ace of Cups represents: divine madness, which manifests in so many traditions in so many different ways. When the experience of the spirit overwhelms, people speak in tongues, enter trance states, experience visions, hear voices, and more. The great mystics of the ages have written of their ecstasies and the mysteries that have been revealed to them. However, just as the sacred images revealed to initiates at Eleusis would not have such a profound impact on non-initiates, often the writings of spiritual ecstasy mean little to those who have not experienced it. The Ace of Cups is also found in the realm of the subconscious and unconscious, in our inner world that is filled with our dreams, imaginings, fantasies, hopes and feelings. This inner world is complex and deep – teeming with life like the ocean – and while we may be able to navigate its waters, others may find the task more difficult. This is why other people will always retain some mystery about them, even those we know best and love most. It is this inner landscape and imaginal world that gives us the capacity to experience the sacred, to process life events and feel emotions. It is also this part of ourselves that we feed when we undergo any form of initiation, and therefore the part of the self from which we are reborn, that part which perceives mystery and to which mystery is revealed.

The Ace of Cups is intimately linked with the Princess of Cups: it is her womb. Here is the womb of Psyche, the womb of the soul in which it gestates and grows to full life. It is also Psyche's daughter, Hedone ("Pleasure"), who gave humankind the ability to feel all kinds of pleasure. As the womb of Psyche in which all forms of pleasure are ensouled, the Ace of Cups represents the source of our mystical and spiritual experiences, as well as the source of love. Fittingly, by the 5th century in Greece and Rome it was believed that all acts of pleasure were felt by the soul rather than just the body. [327] It was at this time also that the concept of being "ensouled" came into being as a way of describing somebody or something as being alive. All living things were seen as being ensouled. [328] For this reason, the cup in the card image is filled not with water but with blood, the stuff of life. It was blood that was offered in the temples of ancient Greece and Rome, and which was therefore the foundation of a link between god and man as well as between body and soul. This cup also brings with it peace, thus the flowers of the olive tree surround its base – symbols of peace in ancient Greece.

An aspect of life most often tied to concepts of the soul is beauty and all forms of art. This too is in the purview of the Ace of Cups, which represents all ways in which one's soul is expressed or the landscape of our inner world and the imaginal world is manifested. It is for this beauty that the dolphins sacred to Aphrodite are painted onto the grotto wall in the card image. Aphrodite is the Queen of Cups in the *Tarot Apokalypsis*, and she is the queen of love, sensuality, beauty and the sea. It is the Ace of Cups that the Queen of this suit holds, showing

---

327 David B. Claus, **Toward the Soul: An Inquiry into the Meaning of ψυχή before Plato**, *pp. 73–85. London: Yale University Press, 1981.*

328 Hendrik Lorenz, **Ancient Theories of the Soul**, *online at Stanford Encyclopedia of Philosophy http://plato.stanford.edu/entries/ancient-soul/ [Accessed 4 August 2015].*

us its depth. A realisation of true beauty and of soul occurs at the moment in which we fall in love, and this revelation of the depth of another being is similar in nature to the revelation of the sacred. When we fall in love we experience theophany, and it is through love that we first come to know the divine.

≈ Revelation

Pure love; bliss, ecstasy, happiness, joy; emotions in their unadulterated form; divine madness; spiritual experiences; mystical experiences; connection to the divine or the source; communion with god; revelation, initiation; revelation of the sacred; beauty; art; manifestation of the imaginal world; expression of one's inner world; depth; the subconscious and unconscious; ensoulment.

Negatively aspected...
Blocked emotions; inability to manifest one's inner world or imaginal world; lack of emotion; deep sadness; disconnection from the source; disconnection from that which makes one happy; inability to connect with the divine.

Two of Cups

Can there be any greater blessing than to share love with another? To find the same flame that burns in your heart in the heart of another? What ills cannot be healed with companionship? What evils cannot be withstood in the name of love? In a world of anger and boundaries, it is love that will be our salvation. This is the path of hearts united, of affection given freely, of the healing words that are "I love you". This path, my path, is the path of the friend, the companion and the lover, for love is love though it manifests in a multiplicity of forms. Its power is the same no matter the hearts that are united. Walk my path and know the sweetness of care and intimacy, of whispered affections and inspiring acts. I offer a road of tenderness, the journey of becoming through another, the mirror of the soul held up in the soul of a companion. Let me reveal my mystery to you with soft kisses and words of friendship, and even on the lonely roads to come you will carry warmth of feeling and understanding of union with the divine.

~ Mystery

The Twos of the tarot represent a duality or partnership; this manifests in the emotional suit of cups as the coming together of two hearts in a relationship. This relationship is often romantic, but there are many kinds of love, such as the love between friends. Thus, after the raw source of love and emotion in the Ace of Cups, we experience it in its purest possible manifest form: love for another being.

Romantic love in the ancient Greek and Roman world was not regarded favourably, being seen instead as a type of madness or sickness. [329] Marriages were usually arranged and women were often married to men much older than them. It was not expected that husbands and wives should love each other, but that their union should produce children. However, a particular kind of relationship can be seen in ancient Greece, typified by its erotic, romantic nature and the possibility that it also represented companionship. A man could engage in a relationship with a *hetaira*, "companion", whose role was closest to that of a courtesan. Hetairai were very different to *pornai* (prostitutes) and wives, straddling the boundary between domesticity and sensuality, between public and private life. According to Demosthenes, "We keep courtesans (hetairai) for pleasure; we keep concubines for the day to day needs of the body; we keep wives for the begetting of children and for the faithful guardianship of our homes." [330]

The pleasure derived from hetairai was not just sexual but intellectual and emotional also. They were beautiful and possessed intellectual training, artistic talent and the ability to entertain their companions. [331] There are a great number of images of hetairai attending symposia, drinking parties in which games

---

329 Christopher A. Faraone, **Ancient Greek Love Magic**, *pp. 43–49. Harvard University Press, 2001.*
330 Demosthenes, **Against Neaera** *122.*
331 Sarah B. Pomeroy, **Goddesses, Whores, Wives and Slaves**, *p. 89. Schocken Books, 1995.*

were played, wine was consumed, music was enjoyed and the all-male party attendants engaged in sexual intercourse with the hetairai. Vase paintings of symposia show hetairai playing musical instruments, dancing, singing and acting out plays. [332] These hetairai frequently inspired poets to write about them, and their education made philosophers particularly fond of spending time with them. [333]

The title "hetaira" was also one of Aphrodite's epithets, in which she was Aphrodite the Companion. A shrine to her in Athens is said to have existed, with Apollodorus saying that she brought friends of both sexes together and Hesychius mentioning a shrine that male and female hetairai – friends – visited. [334]

The card image shows a man and hetaira in a romantic, intimate moment. They are sharing wine and look like they have been engaging in conversation. This is clearly not only a sexual relationship, but one in which both parties can share with each other and experience love and companionship. That we have the names of several hetairai from ancient Greece, often distinguished by their lovers, shows that these women sometimes had significant influence on the public domain via their lovers, an influence that could only have been gained through mutual affection. Records also show that they often remained lovers with certain men for long periods of time, with some hetairai being monogamous. This intimacy is both the manifestation and suggestion of the Two of Cups, the message of which is always love.

---

332 Eva C. Keuls, ***The Reign of the Phallus: Sexual Politics in Ancient Athens***, pp. 164–5. University of California Press, 1993.

333 Otto Kiefer, ***Sexual Life in Ancient Rome***, pp. 83–85. Barnes and Noble, 2003.

334 Matthew Dillon, ***Girls and Women in Classical Greece***, pp. 189–90. Routledge, 2002.

∽ Revelation

Love, romance, intimacy; friendship, companionship; sharing and expressing one's emotions with another; two hearts coming together; marriage; a healing friendship; mutual affection; art and inspiration gained through love and friendship; the importance of one's relationships.

Negatively aspected…
Difficulties in one's relationship; obstacles preventing one from expressing emotions or love for another; past hurt making it difficult to show affection; lack of affection.

Three of Cups

The gods have many faces and wear many masks: some can be found in tragedy, others in comedy; to some the sombre chorus is sung and to others the ribald satire and play is dedicated. I am the god who takes offerings of joy, whose worshippers dance with abandon in their devotional rites, crushing the flowers and the grapes beneath their feet. I am the god who comes as bridegroom and reveller, who presides over the wedding rites and blesses the holy days. My name is spoken in celebration and my image is dressed with  *garlands and wreaths of the finest blooms. Before me, the cups overflow with wine, the fields burgeon with flowers, the grapes ripen on the vine and happiness increases with each passing day. But do not seek me in solace and solitude, for I know not the whispered prayers spoken in the heart or in secret – my hymns are in ecstasy with others, joined with others in a chorus of joy. For wine drunk alone is poor and bitter, but in company it is the sweetest taste to ever pass the lips.*

~ Mystery

After the private intimacy of the Two of Cups, the more group-oriented nature of the Threes manifests in this emotional suit as a communal intimacy. Here, a joyous, carefree celebration takes place among friends, which serves not only to express joy and the reasons for celebration but also to further manifest emotional ties between individuals. As the Threes of the tarot are also concerned with manifestation, the suit of Cups now manifests emotion through art, poetry, music and playfulness.

In the card image, three young women dance around a statue of Dionysus, the god of wine and ecstasy. The flowers blossoming at their feet tell us that it is the month of Anthesterion (mid-February to mid-March), and the masks they hold, as well as the lyre and ripe grapes, show us that they are celebrating the Anthesteria, one of the four major Dionysiac festivals held in classical Greece.

The three-day Anthesteria was marked by the opening of new jars of wine, the re-opening of old wine that had been left to overwinter, decorating new jars of wine with ivy wreaths, [335] drinking competitions, symposia (see *Two of Cups*) and a sacred marriage rite. On the first day of the festival, Pithogia, the half-buried jars of old wine were re-opened and libations were poured to the chthonic (underworld) gods and the ancestors. The second day, Choës, seems to have been a preparation for the sacred marriage rite, as poetry, songs and plays were performed in honour of Dionysus as bridegroom, and later a procession of female worshippers preceded an all-night ritual in which the Basilinna, a ceremonial priestess-queen, "married" Dionysus in the form of a ceremonial king, the Archon Basileus. This seems to have been a rite attended by the women of Athens, while the men spent that time attending a symposium, during which drinking wine was the main activity. The final day of the festival marked a return to normality after the "erotica-filled" events of the previous night, with offerings being made to the spirits of the dead. [336] It was

---

335 Richard Hamilton, ***Choes and Anthesteria: Athenian Iconography and Ritual***, p. 30–1, University Press, 1992.

336 Rosemarie Taylor-Perry, ***The God Who Comes: Dionysian Mysteries Revisited***, pp. 70–3, Algora, 2003.

during the Anthesteria that male children that had reached the age of three were given their first taste of wine. [337]

As this festival was dedicated to Dionysus, we can be certain that revelry was an important part of the proceedings. The poetry, songs and plays of the second day of the Anthesteria share similarities with the City Dionysia, which were celebrated with the performance of plays, contests of dancing and singing, sporting competitions and a procession in which offerings, jars of wine, bread and phalloi – carved wooden phalluses – were carried. [338] During this festival, people would "stop work, drinks lots of wine, [and] eat some meat". [339] Dionysus brought to classical Greece the opportunity for people to let their hair down, celebrate and be joyful, bridging the gap between sacred duty and play. Like him, the Three of Cups dances into our lives urging us to make merry and give into joy, sharing our happiness with others.

✎ Revelation

Celebrations, parties and festivities; communal joy; playfulness and taking time out to play and have fun; emotions expressed to others through art; family gatherings; weddings; child welcoming ceremonies; relaxing through fun; being carefree; one's social life.

Negatively aspected...
Being too serious; refusing to have fun; missing out on events with friends; finding it difficult to free oneself of care and duty; too much fun detracting from other areas of one's life.

---

337 *Ibid.*, *p. 73.*

338 *Simon Goldhill,* ***"The Great Dionysia and Civic Ideology"****, p. 59,* ***The Journal of Hellenic Studies****, vol. 107 (1987), pp. 58–76.*

339 *O. Taplin,* ***Greek Tragedy in Action****, p. 162. Oxford University Press, 1978.*

Four of Cups

The path of the heart runs through the depths of the ocean, and there it teems with life from the world's range of emotions. We all know of love, speak fondly of affection and admire devotion, but who among us has the courage to embrace emptiness? Who can see the worth in the absence of love – not the bitterness of its loss, for that is not my mystery, but the dull plateau of disappointing not-love? Here, the waters of the heart are murky and dim, the light penetrating only briefly to the depths; earth that once nourished now mires and muddies. Joy does not sing, nor does the lover dance their abandonment here. My heart is the test of commitment and of resilience; my song is that of the familiar; my promise is the final attempt to save that which is dying. These waters may no longer refresh and awaken you, but they yet have power. It is here, in the stagnant waters of the heart, when the reflection is most clearly seen in the still surface of unmoving pools, that the face of the matter becomes known. In the mud and murk truth begins to grow.

☙ Mystery

Sometimes the earthy nature of the Fours aligns well with a suit, such as in the Four of Wands, in which it provides fuel for the fires of creativity; however, in the emotional and watery suit of Cups, the Four becomes a dead weight, sinking beneath the surface. The earth becomes mud, the stillness and peace found in other Fours creating stagnant water rather than the flow and ebb more natural to this suit. Here is a recipe for disappointment, disillusionment and boredom. This is where we get stuck in a rut and where relationships turn sour through over-familiarity.

The card image shows a magical spell being cast using two objects found frequently throughout the ancient Mediterranean: a figurine pierced with needles and a *defixio* (curse tablet). Although these items were used in a wide variety of spells, they were frequently used in amatory (love) curses. Such curses were designed to bind a victim emotionally, and the objects of the curse were often deposited in bodies of water. The lead that the curse tablet was made from was not only a popular writing material (inscriptions are found on *defixiones* with the spell, desired outcome, images and name of the victim, if known) but was also heavy, dull and cold, thus symbolic of the emotional binding magic that prevented the victim from feeling any form of love or desire for anybody but the magician. Accompanying inscriptions often "gave" the victim to the chthonic (underworld) deities or the dead. The figurines and *defixiones* were also often deposited in graves with accompanying inscriptions that exhorted the spirits of the dead to enact the curse. [340] The symbolism of the grave is also believed to cause the lifelessness and

---

340 One example of this, among many, is the "Wondrous Spell for Binding a Lover" (PGM IV. 296–466) in the **Greek Magical Papyri in Translation**, *trans. Hans Dieter Betz, pp. 44–7. University of Chicago Press, 1992.*

stillness of the dead to "infect" the victim, who would thus be bound. [341] Figurines used in amatory curses were often formed in bound poses, showing them as captives to the love being inflicted upon them, or damaged by twisting, breaking or piercing. In very few cases was this damage intended to cause physical harm: instead it represented the emotional torment sent to the victim and their inability to feel love or desire for anybody else; it made them into the emotional slaves of the magician. [342]

Some surviving examples from archaeology and literature tell us that these spells were sometimes intended to break up a happy marriage by causing one of the pair to fall out of love with the other, or to cause a man to lose desire for a *hetaira* (concubine). [343] Perhaps the woman in the card image, feeling disillusioned with the possibility of her love being returned, now turns to such magic to dull the feelings of desire and love that her lover has for his wife, binding his heart to her alone, causing him to feel despondent and bored in his marriage. Perhaps this is her final attempt at saving a marriage that has grown dull and loveless due to affection being shown elsewhere.

Boredom and disillusionment are some of the first steps towards the breakdown of emotional happiness. Like the lead curse tablet sinking to the bottom of the well, they cause our hearts to sink into a mire of stagnation.

---

341 Christopher A. Faraone, *"The Agonistic Context of Early Greek Binding Spells"*, pp. 7–8, in **Magika Hiera: Ancient Greek Magic and Religion**, eds. Christopher A. Faraone and Dirk Obbink, pp. 3–32. Oxford University Press, 1991.

342 Christopher A. Faraone, **Ancient Greek Love Magic**. Harvard University Press, 1999.

343 John G. Gager, **Curse Tablets and Binding Spells from the Ancient World**, pp. 87–91. Oxford University Press, 1992.

~ Revelation

Disappointment, disillusionment, despondence; drudgery; relationships becoming boring through over-familiarity; being unwilling to try something new in relationships; becoming stuck in a rut; tradition negatively influencing matters of love; emotions being weighed down or controlled by others; feeling put down; unhealthy obsession or fixation upon a person.

Negatively aspected…
Working one's way out of emotional servitude or obsession; trying to bring a spark back to a dull area of life; somebody willing to invest one last effort into something that looks likely to fail.

Five of Cups

After love must come pain; from all attachment comes grief. Whether through choice or unfeeling death, our beloved ones fade from us and we cling in our suffering to their shades though our cries disappear on the wind. All mortals know this deep wound in the heart, the pain that is so strong that it cannot be given to words yet will not remain silent. I am that anguished lament that is torn from the widow's throat, the cry for what has been that arises from fear of the present. I am that shadow behind all who grieve, bearing witness to the private performance of loss, knowing the pain within that outward actions only begin to express. My name is unspeakable yet I am companion to all for a time along their path. I am called Tears and the Lamentation of Sorrow, the Grip of the Dead and the Invisible One. Shrouded by my mantle you may wail and tear at your cheeks, beat your fists and rage at the heavens; I will hold you like the boat that carries sailors over storm-tossed seas. Beware that my embrace becomes too familiar: I have fingers that cling. Know that this is not my choice but yours, for it is your hand that presses my fingers to shut closer on your heart.

ᴥ Mystery

The destructive nature of the Fives of the tarot does not mix well with the emotional suit of Cups. Here, feelings are attacked, attachments swept away and negative emotions reign. Confusion clouds emotional judgements, perpetuating negative feelings. Where the Three of Swords showed us abstract grief and existential suffering, the Five of Cups presents us with a stark image of personal grief. This is the loss that is felt deep within the heart; it is also the grief in which we find ourselves stuck. Here, we are unable to move out of the past and return to the present or look to the future.

The image shows a woman dressed in funerary black wailing in grief before a family tomb; in each of her hands she holds a coin. Behind her are two cups that are upright, but next to her and in front of her three other cups have fallen, spilling offerings for the dead (milk, wine and barley) onto the earth. This lamentation for the dead had a place and role to play in Greek and Roman society, but here it is out of place, continuing long after the funerary rites have ended. She is on her own in public: an improper act for a woman; even visits to the graveside would have been in the company of other women. [344] Here is grief driving self-destructive action.

Grief in the Greek and Roman worlds was regulated, at least in its public performance; funerary rites were surrounded by a series of traditions and customs over a period of time. Ritual lament for the dead was mainly the domain of women, with archaeological evidence depicting scenes of women giving funeral laments. The purpose of the funeral lament and the accompanying rites was to "honour and appease the dead [and

---

344 *Karen Stears, "Death Becomes Her: Gender and Athenian Death Ritual", p. 150, in Ann Suter (ed)* **Lament: Studies in the Ancient Mediterranean and Beyond**. *Oxford: Oxford University Press, 2008.*

to] give expression to a wide range of conflicting emotions. It seeks to mend the fabric which had been torn by loss, and to reconcile those close to the dead to their loss". [345] Thus, grief can be seen as a potentially positive force, although in the Five of Cups it has become destructive, consuming its performer rather than allowing release and acceptance. That laws in Greece from the 6th century BCE onwards restricted and regulated public funerary laments [346] suggests that such grief, overly performed and raw, brought chaos to peaceful society. Death was seen as polluting, [347] so to spend too long dwelling on it beyond the proper funerary customs would have propagated this pollution.

The abundant flora above the tomb in the card image is the anemone, a flower created by Aphrodite from the blood of her slain lover, Adonis, during her grief. [348] It is associated with loss and death, but in this myth the lamenting woman was able to transform her grief into the creation of beauty. In the card, the woman holds two coins, representative of "Charon's fare", coinage that was placed with the deceased at the time of death or burial. In this wide and varied funerary practice, money was most commonly placed in the deceased's mouth. It was usually money of low value, and symbolised the fee that was expected by one of the chthonic deities for passage to the underworld (usually Charon, the ferryman over the rivers Styx and Acheron, although the custom was also practiced by Christians and Jews). [349] The coins being held by the grieving woman in the

---

345 Ann Suter, **Lament: Studies in the Ancient Mediterranean and Beyond**, p. 4. Oxford: Oxford University Press, 2008.
346 Gail Holst-Warhaft, **Dangerous Voices: Women's Laments and Greek Literature**, p. 3. Routledge, 1992.
347 **Ibid.**, p. 142.
348 Ovid, **Metamorphoses**, 10. 652ff.
349 Susan T. Stevens, "**Charon's Obol and Other Coins in Ancient Funerary Practice**", **Phoenix**, vol. 45, no. 3 (Autumn, 1991), pp. 215–229.

image therefore show that she cannot let go of the deceased and accept their death. Most often, the literary evidence for this practice states that a single coin is the payment expected from the deceased; however, in the myth of Psyche and her descent (while alive) into the underworld, she carried two coins – one for the journey there, and one to come back. Thus, the woman holding two coins represents both her inability to let go of the deceased and her own inability to return to the present and come out of mourning. Further, she is preventing the transition of the memories of the deceased from pain to acceptance and joy in dwelling on her grief. She kneels at a river in a similar way to the restless shades that were unable to cross the river of the underworld (due to receiving incomplete funeral rites or being untimely dead), who were left lamenting their liminality.[350] Like them, she is stuck between the worlds of the living and the dead, alive but consumed by death.

~ Revelation

Grief, loss, emotional pain and suffering; funerals and funerary rites; a period of mourning for a person, phase of life, place etc.; being stuck in grief; dwelling on the past; being unable to move forward; self-destructive behaviour caused by grief.

Negatively aspected…
Grief as a healing process; making a time and place for grief; moving out of a time of mourning.

---

350 Sarah Iles Johnston, **The Restless Dead: Encounters Between the Living and the Dead in Ancient Greece**, *p. 10. University of California Press, 2013.*

Six of Cups

The most solemn of acts begins with a small moment of joy; significance grows from simplicity. Before maturity you must be innocent; before gaining wisdom you must be naïve. But these first states are not imperfect, for you return to them time and time again, retracing your own steps back down the paths you have walked, revisiting long-loved places, faces and moments, reliving youth and joy. It is these re-trodden paths – now well-travelled and worn  *– that return you to your balance, that water the flower of kindness in your heart. These are the sweet paths of fragrant flowers and the songs almost-forgotten from the cradle, yet they are also the playful paths upon which you learn your most important lessons. But do not think these contrasts are in opposition, for they are not those of discord but of peace. These are my roads, and I am Lady Concord, the Mistress of Harmony. I give and receive many offerings, and of these I gift generously to those who know me. I am easily found: my mysteries are not in the depths of the earth nor grand temples, but in the smiles and eyes of those to whom you give kindness.*

~ Mystery

The Sixes of the tarot return to their suits a sense of balance and gentleness after the destructive nature of the Fives. In the suit of Cups, the emotional upheaval and anguish created by the aggressive Five is soothed by the Six, in which we find kindness, sweetness and care. The reciprocity of the Sixes also gives to this card a generous nature, offering us a gift and promise of some of life's simplest pleasures. This simplicity also brings with it innocence and a childlike nature.

In the card image, three Roman children perform their own simple version of a rite they have seen their parents perform. This is the day of the Caristia, also called Cara Cognatio ("dear kindred"), celebrated on 22nd February. Although it was an official festival, it was not observed publicly but rather privately in the home with one's family. Families joined together in order to bring their thoughts back to the sweetness of the living following the bleak days of the Feralia and Parentalia, celebrated in the days prior to this festival:

"Sweet it is, no doubt, to recall our thoughts to the living soon as they have dwelt upon the grave and on the dear ones dead and gone; sweet, too, after so many lost, to look upon those of our blood who are left, and to count kin with them." [351]

This day was presided over by Concordia, the goddess of peace, stability, harmony and agreement. Under her benevolent gaze, families were exhorted to make offerings of incense and food to the Lares, the household gods that blessed

---

351 Ovid, ***Fasti*** *II. 617, trans Sir James George Frazer. Massachusetts: Cambridge University Press, 1959.*

and protected the household inhabitants. During the festival, bread and wine were shared and gifts were given. [352] Scholars have called this festival a "love-feast", in which the family members could renew their mutual ties and resolve any quarrels. [353]

The household spirits that were served during this feast, the Lares, were closely attached to a particular family, their home and the area directly surrounding it. Some scholars have suggested that worship of these spirits was originally the worship of the ancestral founder of the family, who had benevolence and devotion towards its descendants. [354] They were often depicted dancing and carrying cornucopia of food. In the card image we see a typical household shrine to these spirits, and it is at the foot of this shrine that the children play out their ritual. One gives to the other a bunch of flowers, and she graciously accepts. On the floor with them three vessels are filled with offerings of wine, water and milk. A brazier's fire burns down ready to accept an incense offering. Although the children may not yet understand the reasons for this annual festival, nor the importance of regularly serving their household spirits, they know the sweetness and joy that accompanies this day and happily partake in the generosity and pleasure of the family love-feast.

---

352 John F. Donahue, "Towards a Typology of Roman Public Feasting" in **Roman Dining: A Special Issue of American Journal of Philology**, p. 105. Maryland: John Hopkins University Press, 2005.

353 H. H. Scullard, **Festivals and Ceremonies of the Roman Republic**, pp. 75–6. London: Thames and Hudson, 1981.

354 Margaret C. Waites, "The Nature of the Lares and Their Representation in Roman Art" in **American Journal of Archaeology**, vol. 24, no. 3 (Jul.–Sep., 1920), pp. 241.

∽ Revelation

Innocence and naivety; doing something because it feels good but not understanding fully why; a happy time; simple pleasures; engaging in small acts of kindness; generosity and gift-giving; caring for others; childhood and children; playfulness; learning through play; soothing.

Negatively aspected…
Nostalgia and thoughts of the past detracting from the present; longing for an idealised past; lack of maturity and understanding; childishness; killing with kindness; a gift given with malicious intent.

Seven of Cups

Men speak of what is needful and what must be done, tossing aside the gentle dreams of hope and desire in the name of necessity and honour. Fantasy is spurned as a neglected lover, written as a villain that leads the good down a path of self-destruction. This is not so if it is visited at the proper time, and without its revivifying waters the vessel of the soul will dry up. Know then, dreamer, that you must tread my flowing path from time to time and give your offerings to Morpheus and Pan. At their shrines you may dream unfettered and sate yourself of your lusts. Let yourself swim in a sea of dreams; drift among the stars of your wildest fantasies and give in to your desires. Without these uncultured and wild things, man will become uncivilised and dangerous, losing himself in a mire of filth. Follow my path and I shall show you the mysteries of the soul acquiescent to its imagined desires.

∞ Mystery

The fluidity and flux of the Sevens of the tarot manifests in the emotional suit of Cups in a distinctly unstable way. In a suit already changeable and flowing, the Seven amplifies the uncertainty and unpredictability of emotions and draws feelings away from reality into the realm of fantasy. At its most benevolent, this gives the Seven of Cups a dreamlike quality, in which the imagination may be allowed to run free; at its worst, unattainable fantasy desires to be made real and is held in higher esteem than reality.

The card image is set in a *caladarium* (hot room) inspired by the Suburban Baths of Pompeii, built in the 1st century BCE. Although public, the bathhouse had times set for men and women to bathe separately in order to maintain the code of sexual morality for respectable Roman citizens. Nevertheless, according to graffiti and frescoes that survived the centuries, preserved by the volcanic ash of Mount Vesuvius in 79 CE, a great number of sexual activities went on in these baths. These activities were not those of married men and women, so were outside the traditional sexual morality of Rome; however, their prominence in the baths tells us that they were not offensive to the general public.

A collection of frescoes depicting erotic scenes were painted in the *apodyterium* (changing room) of these baths, each above a numbered box that may have been used as s storage place for clothes. These scenes are explicit, and show acts of oral sex, a threesome, and both heterosexual and homosexual sex. [355] These images may have been memorable reminders of where bathers left their clothes; however, the graffiti preserved in a room near the entrance to the baths suggests that prostitutes could also be hired there and that these images were adverts for the services offered. Nearly all of the graffiti not only mentioned a man having sex with one or two women there, but also feasting at the same

---

355 L. Jacobelli, ***Le Pitture Erotiche delle Terme Suburbane di Pompeii***. *Rome: 'L'Erma' di Bretschneider, 1995.*

time. [356] The Suburban Baths therefore offered both a way to relax and spend time with others in a communal setting as well as a way to escape reality for a while and indulge oneself.

Pompeii abounded with erotic artwork in even the most common of places, including private homes. As with those in the Suburban Baths, some of these images were explicit in content, including several scenes of the god Pan – and mortal men and women – engaging in sexual acts with animals. [357] It seems the city may have been more libertine than other parts of Rome.

The card image shows an all-male bathing session with suggestions of homoeroticism. The Greeks and Romans accepted homosexual acts as normative in society, though adoration of young, physically attractive men was a pastime of leisure often given to the higher classes. [358] Despite this acceptance, stigma was attached to sexual passivity on the part of free male citizens, such men being called *cinaedus*. This term, which signified effeminacy, lack of manliness and un-Romanness, was also applied to anybody perceived as sexually excessive or deviant. This passivity was, despite its prevalence, often the subject of satire. Pederasty, the adoration of young men by older men, while being relatively acceptable as a means to social and political growth of the youth, was similarly ridiculed in comedy and singled out as a sign of luxury and self-indulgence. [359] Men wishing

---

356 Alison E. Cooley and M. G. L. Cooley, ***Pompeii and Herculaneum: A Sourcebook***, *p. 116. Routledge, 2014.*

357 ***Pompeii's Phallus: Eroticism in Ancient Italy***. *2013. Online at http://www.lifeinitaly.com/tourism/campania/pompeii.asp [Accessed 10 January 2016].*

358 Thomas K. Hubbard, ed. ***Homosexuality in Greece and Rome: A Sourcebook of Basic Documents***, *p. 9. University of California Press, 2003.*

359 ***Ibid.***, *pp. 6–7.*

to engage in homosexual activity were often picked up in bath houses,[360] so it is tempting to imagine that in libertine Pompeii's Suburban Baths this was done with less stigma and distaste. Here, the steamy baths of the Seven of Cups offer a place for the erotic and desired to be gently revealed and engaged with, given healthy ways into life so they do not stagnate and become poisonous.

~ Revelation

Fantasy and dreams; imagination; emotions constantly changing and in flux; being uncertain what one wants; losing oneself in fantasies at the expense of reality; wishing and hoping instead of taking action.

Negatively aspected…
Debauchery and sexual excess; indulgence of the self resulting in negative consequences; too much of a good thing; allowing one's fantasies to take control; ignoring common sense.

---

360   *Ibid.*, p. 4.

Eight of Cups

Seeker, you have arrived on the threshold of the mysteries. Here there is darkness leading down into my realm, deep rivers and torches casting shadows. To gain passage you must leave behind that which holds you back: leave at the riverside the trappings of the world and your woes; come to me naked and unashamed, with unending questions on your lips. Carry a single torch of hope into the darkness – it is all you will need. Step into the river of memory and know that the reflections are only yours, the shadows your torch-  *light creates only other faces of your self; here all is a mirror and echoes. Be brave on your quest, initiate, for you bring with you also the voices of the dead and the terrors that plague you: against these you must speak the sacred words and not be moved from your path. Your journey must not cease, so when you are unable to take another step let yourself be carried by the river; let go, give in, and it shall bring you to me. I am the Mistress of the Descent, the Key to the Mysteries and the Lightbringer, and I will show you way.*

≈ Mystery

Although the suit of Cups has shown its main concern so far to be that of the emotional and social world, these areas of life nourish our spiritual selves. Emotion, both pleasant and painful, stimulates spiritual experiences, and we often reach greater spiritual understanding through our interactions with others. In the Eight of Cups we find our spiritual world presented as a journey or quest for meaning, understanding or an initiation into mystery. The Eights of the tarot carry the earthy and manifesting energy of the Fours, but doubled; some suits they weigh down and bind, but in the Cups they create a spiritual descent into the underworld of the psyche or soul, called a *katabasis* by the ancient Greeks. [361]

A *katabasis* ("going down") could be sought in many ways. Most commonly in the ancient world this was through initiation into a mystery religion or pilgrimage. The mystery religions offered not only wisdom and spiritual understanding, but also benefits for the deceased in the afterlife. They often taught initiates secret techniques and passwords to speak after death when their souls reached the underworld, to ensure a better life there. Although we know little of what occurred in the mysteries in ancient Greece and Rome, we know that many of them took place in a cave or cave-like structure, such as that of the *mithraea* of the Roman cult of Mithras (see *The Sun*).

Pilgrimage was sought for a wide variety of reasons, including for healing, oracles and initiation. Major oracle shrines, such as those at Delphi and the oracle of Trophonios near Lebdeia, and healing shrines such as those of Asklepios, were frequent pilgrimage sites. [362] As with the mystery religions, a great number of these sites of pilgrimage were in caves, and sometimes required the pilgrim to make a descent into the cave to seek their answers. [363]

---

361 John Freccero, ***The Poetics of Conversion***, p. 108. Harvard University Press, 1988.

362 Jaś Elsner and Ian Rutherford, ***Pilgrimage in Gaeco-Roman and Early Christian Antiquity: Seeing the Gods***, pp. 14–18. Oxford University Press, 2005.

363 Yulia Ustinova, ***Caves and the Ancient Greek Mind***, pp. 53–54. Oxford University Press, 2009.

The ancient Greeks commonly associated caves with prophecy and the receiving of divine revelation, possibly because this association was embedded in their mythology. [364] Ancient writers tell us of the "holy fear" felt by pilgrims who descended into caves to receive answers. [365] This may have arisen from the identification of these caves with the underworld, entering them thus becoming a journey to an otherworld. [366] Some rivers at these sites were even identified with the rivers of the underworld, such as the Styx and Acheron. The physical journeys undertaken to these pilgrimage sites culminated not only in a physical *katabasis* but a spiritual one, in which the pilgrim descended into spiritual wisdom and revelation.

In the card image, a woman drops her last item of clothing by the riverside within a dark cave. It is lit only by torchlight, one torch held by her and the others by statues of chthonic deities – Persephone and Hades. She wades through a stream in the darkness, and a bright light shines forth from the depths of the cave, drawing her closer to wisdom. Perhaps she seeks an oracle; perhaps she has come to be healed; or perhaps this is her path to initiation into the mysteries: here she has gone down into the underground chamber of Hekate and will see "other things down below". [367]

---

364 *Ibid.*, pp. 2–3 and p. 54.

365 Guy G. Stroumsa, **Hidden Wisdom: Esoteric Traditions and the Roots of Christian Mysticism**, p. 176. Leiden, 2005.

366 Han Dieter Betz, **"Fragment of a Catabasis Ritual in a Greek Magical Papyrus"**, p. 293, in **History of Religions**, vol. 19, no. 4 (May, 1980); Yulia Ustinova, **Caves and the Ancient Greek Mind**, pp. 68–9.

367 "I have been initiated, and I went down into the [underground] chamber of the Dactyls, and I saw / the other things down below, virgin, bitch, and all the rest." From **The Greek Magical Papyri in translation**, trans. Hans Dieter Betz, LXX 4–25, a magical spell for Hekate Ereschigal, an underworld goddess. University of Chicago Press, 1986.

∽ Revelation

A spiritual quest or journey; pilgrimage; letting go of the past and moving forwards emotionally; a deeper sense of understanding; a quest for wisdom; a seeker; vision quest; engaging with one's spiritual needs; allowing healing to occur; seeking answers during a time of emotional upheaval.

Negatively aspected…
Refusing to let go or move on; a misguided search; being held back by one's emotions; being afraid of being alone or doing something on one's own; refusing to look within one's self for answers.

Nine of Cups

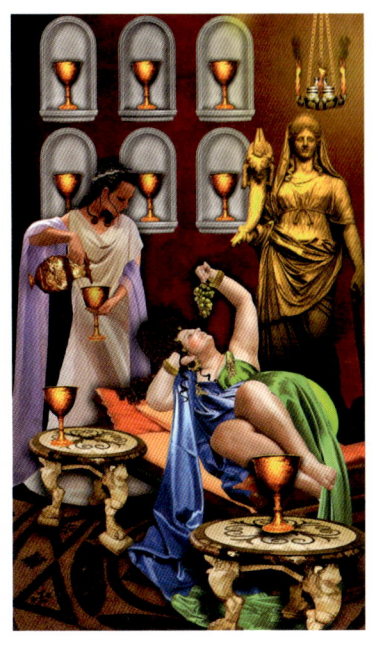

Those held aloft by chance and luck are quick to gloat their fortune; they rest content in the warm embrace of their certainty of future happiness and grow fat on its sweetness. There are some on this path who know the fluid nature of the wine they enjoy and take naught for granted. Their offerings at my feet are gratefully given and happily received, for I smile upon those that warmly greet Fortune's fickle nature. I am called Wish-giver and Abundance, the Cup Overflowing and the Fullness of Heart; my mysteries are of the horn of plenty and the rudder, of blessings and of flux. None know the direction in which I may steer their vessel, yet all celebrate beauty when it is given to them, drinking deep of the sweetness when my wheel turns them to the heavens. They think not of the fall, of the mire, of the bitter ills that may yet befall them, for that is not the nature of fulfilment. It is this I teach you: that the whims of Fortune can show you the joys of life just as readily when your wheel has descended, that true fulfilment is not in time or place but in that limitless inner sea of your heart.

❧ Mystery

Like the other cards of its suit, the Nine of Cups presents an emotional state. As it is so close to the completion of its suit, the watery energies of the Cups have gradually flowed down, closer and closer to something solid: manifestation and grounding. The later Cups cards collect all the emotional energy flowing downwards until they are full to the brim. This fullness manifests as happiness, bliss and emotional stability, though in the Nine it has not quite reached completion and is still in flux. Thus, although we find here our wishes being fulfilled and our joy being expressed in abundance, it comes with the reminder of its temporary nature: these are not long-lasting joys but fleeting ones.

In the card image a rich woman, draped in fine fabrics, her hair in an intricate style, lounges on a long seat. She revels in the moment of luxury, enjoying ripe grapes while her serving woman pours another cup of wine for her. While her serving woman's clothes are simple and plain in colour, hers are lavish and bright, a demonstration of her wealth and status. Although some of her golden goblets are being utilised in a practical fashion, the others are on prominent display.

Behind the woman is a large statue of one of the most widely worshipped deities of ancient Rome, Fortuna, whose Greek equivalent was Tyche. She was the goddess of luck and chance, bestowing abundance. [368] Her worship was supposedly founded by a mortal, Servius Tullius, in gratitude for her raising him out of slavery to riches and rulership, demonstrating her bountiful nature and her ability to turn a poor lot in life into a blessed one. [369] She was considered so important that she was celebrated in Rome as Fortuna Publica Populi Romani – "Official Good Luck of the Roman People". [370] However, like the fluid

---

368 Thomas Taylor trans. **The Hymns of Orpheus**, LXXI.12, p. 203. London, 1792.

369 H. V. Canter, "**'Fortuna' in Latin Poetry**" in **Studies in Philology**, vol. 19, no. 1 (Jan., 1922), p. 66.

370 S. Hornblower and A. Spawforth, **The Oxford Classical Dictionary**, p. 606. New York University Press, 2003.

nature of the suit of Cups, Fortuna could be fickle and inconstant, just as unexpectedly causing the bad luck and downfall of a person as their happiness:

"O Fortune, who dost bestow the throne's high boon with mocking hand, in dangerous and doubtful state thou settest the too exalted […]. Whatever Fortune has raised on high, she lifts but to bring low." [371]

Fortuna was often depicted carrying a cornucopia, symbolising her ability to bestow abundance, and a rudder, which not only signified her role in guiding the fate of individuals and populations but also her fickle nature – the rudder could be steered in either direction. [372] Thus, this card reminds us that although we may be inclined to show off our happiness, luck and the source of it to others, we should be mindful that life often delivers a swift blow to our happiness when we least expect it.

✑ Revelation

Showing your happiness, status or wealth to others; feeling lucky; good fortune; wishes being granted; a perfect set of circumstances leading to joy; emotional fulfilment; emotional abundance; almost achieving a goal in the emotional or social area of life.

Negatively aspected…
Smugness; being emotionally competitive; a stroke of poor luck; fleeting happiness; having too much of a good thing.

---

*371 Aeschylus, **Agamemnon**, trans. Frank Justus Miller. Online at: http://www.theoi.com/Text/SenecaAgamemnon.html*

*372 Darius Andre Arya, **The Goddess Fortuna in Imperial Rome: Cult, Art, Text**, p. 112. Dissertation, University of Texas at Austin, 2002.*

Ten of Cups

Life desires nourishment and fulfilment; this is reflected in the heart and soul of every creature that takes breath, for all yearn for love. A man might attain the greatest wealth and status, yet without love it is empty. What is wealth if it cannot be shared? What is status if it is not among those we love? I tell you this secret: love is the purpose of all and the origin of all; it is the goal and the driving force. Know true love, in one of its myriad forms, in acceptance and devotion, loyalty and romance, friendship and family, and you will know true happiness. I invite you to walk the path of joy, to choose it and turn aside from all else; yet know that this is no easy path: it is long and courageous, for love demands nothing though you will give everything for it. Step forward – this will be your first and last step – and take my hand, for I offer a sacred vow and protected heart, a welcome hearth and the cups of many overflowing with joy for you. Be not afraid to love and laugh, to share your happiness with the world – it is not a guilty pleasure nor a sin. It is perfect and vital, the very essence of the journey. Fall in love with the world in all its beauty and sadness, its exquisite joys and pains – all is perfect and existence is pure joy.

❧ Mystery

At the culmination of the suit of Cups we find a blissful scene of family happiness. As the emotional energy of the suit has undergone the process of fruition, it has become more profound, manifest and positive. From the undifferentiated source, the water of the suit of Cups has flowed downwards towards the earth and is now collected in cups full to the brim with emotional contentment. The many cups (symbolic of hearts and souls) in this card represent a loving community. This is the happy ending in which everything we have hoped for has come to fruition. Yet the nature of the suits is cyclical: while it is a happy ending it also engenders a new beginning.

The foreground of the card image shows a blissful family scene: a husband kisses his wife on the cheek as she stares at her newborn child in delight, falling in love with the new life she has brought into the family. Their first child gazes at her new sibling lovingly, bearing an olive branch – a symbol of peace and an indicator in ancient Greek child-welcoming ceremonies that the new child is a boy. The family is seated at the steps of a shrine in an idyllic pastoral landscape; within the shrine a midwife and priestess perform the ritual actions of the Amphidromia, an Athenian rite welcoming a new child to the family. This rite was performed five, seven or ten days after birth, and may have included a naming ceremony.[373] This was the first rite in which a person would be involved, marking the family's acceptance of the new member. It also marked the creation of a legal social identity [374] and was a "critical confirmation of the child's social identity as an accepted member of its natal family". [375]

---

373 Richard Hamilton, "**Sources for the Athenian Amphidromia**", p. 246. **GRBS** 25 (1984), pp. 243–51.

374 Maria A. Liston and Susan I. Rotroff "Babies in the Well: Archeological Evidence for Newborn Disposal in Hellenistic Greece" in **The Oxford Handbook of Education in the Classical World**, p. 77, eds. Judith Evans Grubbs and Tim Parkin. Oxford University Press, 2013.

375 Lesley A. Beaumont, **Childhood in Ancient Athens: Iconography and Social History**, p. 68. Routledge, 2012.

Ancient literature disagrees on what took place during the Amphidromia ceremony, though it seems that somebody – probably the midwife – carried the child around, or presented it to, the hearth. The house (or perhaps just the door of the house) was decorated for the festivities with olive branches if the child was a boy and garlands of wool if the child was a girl. [376] It appears that the religious formality was performed during the day by only close relatives and those who attended the birth, and the festivities continued throughout the night with feasting and gift-giving, to which other relatives and friends were invited. [377] That there was a private and public dimension to this rite reminds us that happiness manifests both inwardly and outwardly, and that our private joys often allow us to make those around us joyful also. Joy is contagious, love is for sharing.

◈ Revelation

Happiness, joy and bliss; a happy ending; a more than satisfactory conclusion to a project of love; a happy home, family and social life; acceptance by a social group or community; sharing joy with others; freely expressing one's happiness; favourable outcomes in love and friendship; spiritual and emotional fulfilment; a realisation of the joy of the world following spiritual revelation or quest.

Negatively aspected…
Delayed happiness; a home that appears happy externally but may be struggling internally; a minor dissatisfaction marring otherwise perfect happiness; feeling unable to share one's joy with others.

---

376 Daniel Ogden, **Greek Bastardy in the Classical and Hellenistic Periods**, p. 91. Clarendon Press, 1996.

377 Richard Hamilton, "**Sources for the Athenian Amphidromia**", pp. 248–250.

Ace of Pentacles

Nothing comes from nothing, and everything comes from one thing: a seed. It is this seed that contains within it all the knowledge, power and energy it needs to grow over the aeons into the most sacred of flowers, whose roots will delve deep into the mud of the world and whose petals will open to the beauty of the heavens. Here, in the simplicity of its growing and opening, in this unremarkable bloom, is contained the blueprint of all creation. That which is above is as that which is below, and this earth – which so many have disregarded and spat upon – is a mirror of the divine heavens. Beneath your feet is the stable foundation of everything that has gone before, and it is within this mire of mundanity that you might perceive the sacred. I am that power to experience and grow, the nurturing and generative force that pushes you upwards from the mud towards the sunlight; I am the first stirring of all that is, and I am the final creation from which all things are born again. Growth is slow, it does not hurry forth, and every step along my road is careful and patient. For I am every road that you have travelled and will travel; I orient you in time and space; I am the organising principle of creation and the navel of the world. It

is within my mandala that you might see the entirety of the universe churning, available to your touch. I am your place of birth, and if you accept my mysteries you may come to know the joys of the temple of Man.

∽ Mystery

The Aces of each suit are the raw power and unified embodiments of the elements with which they are associated; thus, the Ace of Pentacles contains all the powers of Earth and the suit of Pentacles in their purest form. It is the power of foundation, growth, fertility and the planting of seeds. From the Ace of Pentacles everything else may grow, and it is this Ace that is nurtured in the pregnant womb of the Princess of Pentacles, Prthvī. As the first card in its suit, it represents the first stirrings of the elemental powers of Earth, but it also contains the blueprints for completion, just as a seed contains the blueprints for a great tree. The Ace of Pentacles is the slowest and most dependable of all the Aces due to its earthy nature. The beginnings that are represented by this Ace are based on firm foundations that will stand the test of time.

The pentacle in this card is borne aloft from the waters in the centre of a sacred lotus. Behind can be seen part of the Angkor Wat, a great temple built in the Khmer Empire. Seated Buddha statues and a pair of storks flank the pentacle, and the faces of the Bodhisattva Avalokiteshvara overlook the scene. Although the temple was originally dedicated to the Hindu gods, it later featured additions during Buddhist periods of Cambodian history.

The waters that surround the base of the lotus represent the cosmic waters from which the earth originally arose in Hindu creation myths. It is important to note that the Ace of Pentacles is not the element of Earth itself, but the beginnings of those things associated with Earth: stability, foundation, the material world and resources. It was upon a lotus that the first patch of earth arose, and it is upon this sacred flower that Hindu deities are often seated in depictions. The leaf of this plant also played an important role in some cosmogony narratives: the *Taittinyasamhitā* relates how Prajapati, in the form of wind, swayed on a lotus leaf on the Primordial Ocean. On this leaf he piled up a fire, and thereby created the earth. [378] In another version, Prajapati took on the shape of a wild boar to dive into the ocean in order to find the base of the lotus leaf. He brought back some of the soil from the bottom of the ocean and spread it out on the leaf, creating the earth. [379] It can thus be seen not only as the emergence of creation but also as the material foundation for the spiritual world. The Ace of Pentacles, while bringing us firmly down to earth, reminds us that it is by virtue of the mundane experience that we are able to conceive of a spiritual reality.

The lotus is a symbol synonymous with the sacred mountain Meru in Hindu, Buddhist and Jain cosmology. It was Mount Meru that inspired the architecture and layout of many temples and stupas across India, some of the most famous being Borobodur in Java and Angkor Wat. The five towers of Angkor Wat symbolise the four mountains that surrounded the central peak of Meru, and the moat that surrounded it represented the cosmic waters around the holy mountain. Meru is considered the centre of both the inner and outer world, and it is the abode of Brahma and oth-

---

378 *Taittinyasamhitā* 5.6.4 2–3:7. Quoted in Thomas Kintaert, p. 86, "On the Role of the Lotus Leaf in South Asian Cosmography" in *Vienna Journal of South Asian Studies*, vol. 54 (2011–2012), pp. 85–120.

379 *Ibid.* p. 89.

er gods. In many earlier sources, Meru was surrounded by four continents at each of the cardinal directions like the petals of a lotus. [380] It was first mentioned in the *Taittiriya Aranyaka*, and was seen as the "cosmic equivalent of the lotus root". [381]

"Meru as a cosmic lotus provides the main organizing principle of Hindu religious symbolism. It has many layers of symbolism that exchange Meru for the cosmic man, for the temple at the centre of the universe, for the office of kingship, for the stüpa, for the mandala, and for the internal ascent undertaken by the tantric mystic. Meru is not simply a point at the center of a circle; it is a vertical shaft which links macrocosm with microcosm, gods with men, timelessness with time." [382]

Mount Meru's centrality establishes order from chaos; it is the navel that spreads the nurturing force of Earth across the entirety of creation, and it is the point at which the sacred comes into being: it is a place of birth. [383] It is also called the "seed cup of the lotus of the earth", pointing to its generative role in the universe: from the centre all things are born. [384]

---

380 Jai Pal Singh and Mumtaz Khan, p. 270, "**Saptadvīpā Vasumatī: the mythical geography of the Hindus**" in **GeoJournal**, vol. 48, no. 4 (1999), pp. 269–78.

381 F. D. F Bosch, p. 96, **The Golden Germ: An Introduction to Indian Symbolism**. Humanities Press, 1960.

382 Jai Pal Singh and Mumtaz Khan, p. 274.

383 Rommel Varma, p. 139, "**Meru and Kailasa: Exploring a Paradigm and its Model**" in **India International Centre Quarterly**, vol. 20, no. 4 (Winter, 1993), pp. 139–158.

384 Jai Pal Singh and Mumtaz Khan, p. 273.

≈ Revelation

Generation and the process of creation; new beginnings, new projects, new family members, a new home, new job or new path; the seeds of something being planted; the foundations for stability, dependability and certainty; a small, slow start to something that has grand designs; the blueprints of future success; resources and the source of one's wealth; the source of one's nurturing, generative energy; the first stirrings of a care-giving role.

Negatively aspected…
A blockage in the material world; difficulties in the beginning; obstacles in the way of projects in the early stages; lack of nurturing leading to withering; resources being wasted or misused; plans that are too ambitious for the current stage or available resources.

Two of Pentacles

The universe changes on a grand scale as befitting its cosmic design: change is its mother, flux its father; you are its child. As a product of the ebb and flow of the tidal heavens, it is your charge to enact change upon the earth and to know the careful dance of balance in order to maintain your centre. Though you may be buffeted by life's tempestuous waves, know that beneath your feet is the very foundation of the world. I teach you the mystery of managing change in the realm of earth, the gift by which you may make the best of this abode of beauty and ugliness. I speak to you in polarities and opposites, in duality and complement, for in the journey between each you come to know the balance of the scales. Yet listen well: balance is not equality; rather, it is found in the gentle shifting of weight from one side to the other, continually, and it is in the unevenness of balance that the world is recreated.

∽ Mystery

Dancing on the foundations of change is necessary once we've begun manifesting our desires. We've met change before, writ large in the world in the Wheel, but here we find it on an everyday level. Here are the ups and downs of daily life, the balance that must be found and maintained in order to manage our mundane world and the fine line between failure and success. Here also is the intricate relationship between our higher self and lower needs, between the divine and mundane in our lives and between our duties and our hopes.

The card image shows a dancer performing a classical Cambodian dance. She wears the traditional headdress of the *Robam Preah Reach Trop* ("Apsara Dance") and balances carefully on a yoni-lingam carving. The waters of one of ancient Khmer's man-made lakes are rough, the small boats riding the waves. Around her flit silver dragonflies, emblems of change. There are many aspects of the card image that symbolise the interaction between polarities and the process of change that is created through this interaction. The focus, however, is on the dancer, as the card's focus is on the human place within this continual fluctuation and landscape of change. The golden pentacles balanced in the dancer's hands are facing point-upwards (her right hand) and point-downwards (her left hand), indicating the exchange between the divine and the mundane that takes place on a daily basis. Around these pentacles, in white light, the shape of a lemniscate (figure of eight) is formed. This is a symbol of infinite flux, suggesting that the polarities of divine and mundane, up and down, can be swapped. Indeed, the dancer's headdress indicates that she, a human, is standing in for a divine being. During the *Robam Preah Reach Trop*, female dancers become Apsaras, beautiful, nymph-like divine female figures that can be found frequently on carvings from ancient Cambodian temples. [385]

---

385 *"Cambodian Dance and the Angkor Dance Troup"*, *online at http://www.hattales.com/view/hat-gallery/cambodian-dance-and-the-angkor-dance-troupe/ Accessed 12 February 2016.*

The man-made lake – or reservoir – is representative of the polarity between man and nature, here united in an attempt to harness and tame the forces of nature. Archaeologists found a copper pipe on an artificial island in the centre of the Yasodharatataka reservoir, built in the 9th century. It is surmised that the king would regularly visit and use the pipe to measure water levels to ascertain whether rice planting could begin. [386] The Two of Pentacles represents the ways in which we try to make the best of all the changes that happen around us, seeking ways to not be negatively affected by them. Like the boats in the card image, we must ride the waves of life and allow ourselves to be carried by change: if we make ourselves rigid and unmoving, we will be drowned.

The yoni-lingam upon which the dancer balances is a sacred representation of Shiva – masculine creative energy – and Shakti – feminine creative energy. These cosmic forces create and perpetuate the cycles of change and generation in the world. The union of lingam and yoni represents the "indivisible two-in-oneness of male and female, the passive space and active time from which all life originates". [387] In Taoist philosophy, this force is expressed as the yin-yang, which emphasises that the seed of one polarity is present in its opposite polarity. Thus, the dancer who balances carefully on the yoni-lingam is balancing on the fundamental force of change in the world, on that which contains the seeds of flux. In the same way, we carefully balance our everyday lives in a sea of change, making sense and order in the best way we can of an otherwise chaotic, unpredictable world.

---

*386 John Tully, **A Short History of Cambodia**, p. 44. Allen & Unwin, 2005.*

*387 Eva Rudy Jansen, **The Book of Hindu Imagery: Gods, Manifestations and Their Meaning**, p. 46. Binkey Kok Publications, 2003.*

❧ Revelation

Constant shifting and flux; small changes in everyday life; maintaining order in a chaotic situation; balance; juggling many aspects of daily life; the requirements of the everyday world all seeking attention; budgeting; time-keeping.

Negatively aspected…
Failing to keep up with changes in one's life; finding it difficult to manage in everyday tasks; feeling pulled too much in one direction; stress; feeling drained of energy by events; poor budgeting; lack of management and balance.

Three of Pentacles

The road of the craftsman is a long one, for he carves his works into the hardest parts of the world and creates the greatest of structures on the earth. Aeons after his name has been lost to the winds and memory, his work lives on, attesting to his skill and showing his heart. His legacy is long-lived and virtuous, for into his work he bleeds his mind, body and soul; he gives his entire self to the process of endeavouring. A craftsman is nothing without a craft, little without a goal to accomplish. By his work he is defined, by his accomplishments he is known. If you seek to learn the mysteries of the Great Work, you must devote your self to the strictures by which you wish to work, take on the yoke of structure and tread upon the foundations of wisdom borne from the fruit of others' labours. It is only through this that you might accomplish the greatest of endeavours. Know my name as Master, as Skilled One, as Work; tread my pathways and you shall come to the road that shall lead you to your destiny.

~ Mystery

Like the early cards of the other suits, the Pentacles suit shows us a process of manifestation. In the Ace we saw the seed of the world from which all else might grow, the raw material ready for shaping; in the Two we saw the cosmic dance of balance, the interplay of forces influencing our work; now in the Three we see manifestation from our work. As this takes place in the earthy suit of the everyday world, this creative process occurs in our daily life: our work, homes, family, finances and health. Here our labours have borne fruit, we have reached a peak of skill and ability, and have produced what some might call our *magnum opus*, our "great work". Here is the master craftsman, putting the finishing touches to his creation.

In the card image we see a man using his skills as a stonemason to carve the symbol of the Three Jewels of Buddhism onto a rock. This rock will become part of a larger building in the great temple complexes of ancient Angkor, reminding us that there is always more – and greater – work to do once we have reached completion on current projects. It is tempting to imagine that this is a foundational stone upon which these wonders will be built: in 1186 the temple of Ta Prohm had a foundational inscription that invoked the Three Jewels, [388] reminding us that the Three of Pentacles, while a manifestation of our labours, is also a foundation that supports greater endeavours.

The Three Jewels, also called the Three Refuges, are a vital aspect of Buddhism. These jewels are the Buddha, Dharma and the Sangha. The Buddha represents both the historical Buddha and the Buddha nature of each person, one's highest spiritual potential; Dharma is the teachings of the Buddha; the Sangha is the monastic community and sometimes the wider community of practicing Buddhists (see *Six of Pentacles*). Traditionally, the three pentacles of this card are associated with the three aspects of the self: mind, body and spirit, and these can be associated with the Dharma, Sangha and the Buddha respectively. Together, these three aspects of the self interact and create something truly great.

---

[388] Ian Harris, ***Cambodian Buddhism: History and Practice***, *p. 19, University of Hawai'i Press, 2005.*

Buddhists look to the Three Jewels for guidance in life and "take refuge" in them in order to indicate their dedication to the Buddhist tradition. In the *Kosalasamyatta*, for instance, King Pasenadi said, "I go for refuge to the Blessed One [Buddha], and to the Dhamma, and to the Bhikkhu Sangha. From today let the Blessed One remember me as a lay follower who has gone for refuge for life". [389] They are called Jewels because they are unchanging and indestructible, reminding us that in the Three of Pentacles we are creating long-lasting results rather than fleeting ones. Together, the Three Jewels represent the great work of the tradition accomplished: it is these Jewels that allow followers to reach enlightenment.

Structure is vitally important for the Three of Pentacles. Like the scaffolding that upholds the rock and the rope that keeps it in place in the card image, some amount of structure is necessary for us to live creative and fulfilling lives. Similarly, the Three Jewels are the fundamental supporting precepts of the Buddhist tradition, and to take refuge in them is to take on the structure they offer, allowing for the follower to learn and grow under their firm guidance.

☙ Revelation

Skills and abilities being used; great works; providing structure and support for a project; work as the basis for further endeavours; becoming a master of a skill; manifestation in the everyday world; all parts of the self working together towards a goal; building; the completion of a project.

Negatively aspected...
Lack of structure or support; lack of effort put towards a goal; failure in an endeavour; much more work still required before completion; rebellion against structure; poor quality of work.

---

389 Bhikkhu Bodhi, *The Connected Discourses of the Buddha: A New Translation of the Saṃyutta Nikāya*, p. 166. Wisdom Publications, 2000.

Four of Pentacles

When you have increased your wealth and built for yourself safe storehouses and foundations, when you can look upon the work you have wrought and see the growth of your comfort, you must become a defender, prepared to protect what is yours. Build strong fortifications, remain firm and unmoving, gamble nothing and take no risks: your security and the very foundations upon which you rely are at stake. I am the fort and the tower; I am the storehouse and the home; I offer you the comforts of the familiar and the safe and urge you to remain within the bounds of what you know. Wealth attracts wealth. Gather great stores of riches and hold them close. Yet seek not to grasp and take from others; let not greed take your heart. You must be the master of your resources, not they of you. Then you shall know my mysteries of manifestation and control and your legacy shall live forever.

~ Mystery

The stability of the Fours finds a natural home in the earthy suit of Pentacles, and the activity and manifestation of the previous cards of this suit now finds full expression in a solid, stable and tangible form. This makes the Four of Pentacles a card of strong foundations and slow but sustainable increase; it gathers to itself more material wealth and fortifies its position. This can, however, make it a slow and stubborn card: once we have secured our position and comfort, why would we risk it by moving out of it? At its best, the Four of Pentacles represents strong defences and protecting oneself, as well as building an empire and manifesting sustainable results; at its worst it shows greed and all its consequences, as well as shutting oneself away from the rest of the world in a form of misguided self-defence.

The card depicts the last of the great kings of Angkor, Jayavarman VII. He rides an elephant, a symbol of great power and wealth, and behind him three flags bearing stylised icons of the imperial umbrella (used to provide shade for rulers) and an image of Garuda, the half-human half-bird figure that can be found in so many carvings throughout the buildings from Jayavarman's reign. The king holds the four pentacles of this card close to him, maintaining his comfort and security in doing so. His empire (and legacy) rises in the distance.

The reign of Jayavarman VII from 1182–1218 CE is widely seen as the height of the Khmer Empire. [390] Much of what we see today in Angkor is a result of his rule, during which he undertook a program of building unrivalled by any other king of Angkor. Angkor Thom ("Great City"), the last and most enduring capital city of the empire, was his creation. It was surrounded by a moat on all sides across which bridges were placed; inner walls around 3 kilometres long on each side were beyond this, with entrance gateways in each wall that were looked over by large carvings of heads facing the four directions. [391] This design evokes the defensive nature of the Four of Pentacles, as well as highlighting the link between this card and the four walls of a home, or the four directions: the fundamental aspects of a feeling of security and certainty.

---

390 John Tully, *A Short History of Cambodia*, p. 27. Allen & Unwin, 2005.
391 Charles Higham, *The Civilization of Angkor*, p. 121. University of California Press, 2001.

Jayavarman VII also built the temple complexes of Ta Prohm, Preah Khan, Banteay Kdei, Bayon and Banteay Chhmar. With the architecture of his buildings he created a new style, Bayon style, named after the Buddhist state temple at the heart of Angkor Thom. [392] These buildings were at once a statement of power and the wealth of the Khmer Empire and an act of devotion. During this building program, an extensive network of roads was laid to connect every town, and rest-houses and 102 hospitals were built, showing Jayavarman VII's dedication to the overall prosperity of his empire. Scholars have noted that the "financing of construction sites was a genuine preoccupation of Khmer kings", [393] a statement most true of Jayavarman VII, whose triumphant reign was made more prosperous and more influential by his extensive building and development of the region. His legacy lives on even today, a testament to the firm foundations upon which he built his temples and palaces.

◈ Revelation

Fortification and defence; laying strong foundations; a secure and comfortable environment; wealth and luxury; gathering material wealth; slowly building a career, business, investment, home or family, a safe investment; saving money.

Negatively aspected…
Greed; grasping at wealth; hurting others to gain wealth; stubbornness; refusal to move forwards out of fear of material loss; being held back by material concerns; shutting oneself off from others or new experiences; being too defensive.

---

392 Swati Chemburkar, **"Dancing Architecture at Angkor: 'Halls with Dancers' in Jayavarman VII's Temples"** in **Journal of Southeast Asian Studies**, vol. 46, no. 3 (Oct., 2015), pp. 514–536.

393 Jacques Dumarçay and Pascal Royère, trans. Michael Smithies, **Cambodian Architecture: Eighth to Thirteenth Centuries**, p. 8. Brill, 2001.

Five of Pentacles

All is suffering and loss. This is the way of the world and the human condition. What you have in your hands will crumble to dust, but what you hold in your heart will give you comfort and shelter. You, like all others, will know the difficulties of isolation, of being cast out into the cold, of asking for aid and being refused; you will know the sound of the empty purse and the door being shut; you will know the cold of the wind on bare skin and the taste of hunger on your lips. I am that bitter fruit, the result of grasping and greed. I am the cry for help in the darkness and the reply of silence. I am the plea for compassion towards your fellow creatures and the force that ensures that you know what it is to lose and to suffer, to be excluded and ignored. What will it take to make you listen to the downtrodden, to extend your hand to those reaching out to you?

∼ Mystery

The first four cards of the suit of Pentacles gave us a positive outlook, with our labours paying off and the results being gathered. However, the aggressive, destructive energy of the Fives of the tarot does its damage even here, attacking our fundamental support structures and destroying all we have stored up from our hard work. In the Five of Pentacles we are laid low and bare, devoid of riches, unsheltered and unprotected, isolated from all forms of aid and kindness. This is the card of the homeless, of those failed by society, of those ostracised by their communities.

The card image shows two old men huddled together in a small boat, trying to take shelter beneath the branches of a tree on the lake side. One is wearing simple peasant clothing, the other wears only a loin cloth. They are thin, cold and in need of aid. Around them monsoon rains fall; behind them five golden pentacles float away on the lake, symbolic of all they have lost, and a beautiful temple rises high above the water, rich and majestic. The contrast between the condition of the men and the opulence of what is behind them is stark: it is clear they have been ignored and ostracised by a society that is capable of great art and beauty, rich in material wealth. Yet still these men go cold, hungry and unsheltered. What small action would it take to bring them out of their suffering? What kind words?

All human societies have some sort of exclusion of those who are most in need. In the Khmer Empire, the Hindu caste system was present though less rigid; however, there was little social mobility and those belonging to the lower orders of society largely accepted their status and did not seek to move outside of it. It was exacerbated by religious beliefs that suffering was the result of wrongdoing in past lives. [394] In the Hindu caste system, the lowest group of people in society were called "untouchables" and their presence was considered polluting. [395] They often performed occupations that were considered dirty or debased and were given no option for upward movement in society, maintaining their poverty and low social status. In

---

394 John Tully, **A Short History of Cambodia**, pp. 35–36. Allen & Unwin, 2005.
395 James Lochtefeld, ed. **The Illustrated Encyclopedia of Hinduism**, p. 720. The Rosen Publishing Group, 2002.

the Five of Pentacles, it is the viewing of another human being as somehow lower than ourselves that is the root of suffering, perpetuating unkindness and preventing us from extending the hand of aid out of fear of some sort of pollution.

It was an experience of this sort of suffering that caused Siddharta Gautama to become an ascetic and eventually found Buddhism, which was the state religion of the Khmer Empire for several periods. Many versions of the legend state that prince Siddhartha had been kept protected from the reality of the world's sufferings within his palace, until one day he went out on a chariot ride through the streets. There he witnessed the Four Sights: a sick man, an old man, a dying man and an ascetic. The first three sights showed Siddhartha the truth of the world: that suffering came to all beings. The sight of the ascetic showed him the means by which this suffering could be destroyed. In the same way, the sight of the Five of Pentacles reminds us of the reality of a situation that is suffering or people that need help and asks us to find a way to overcome it. Only when we break through our self-constructed limitations will we be able to break down the barriers between "us" and "them" that prevent us from helping those in need.

☙ Revelation

Financial loss and difficulty; resources suddenly being destroyed, lost or becoming inaccessible; frozen assets; isolation from avenues of help or improvement; being in need but receiving no help or support; social exclusion; being out in the cold.

Negatively aspected…
Offering a helping hand to those in need; withdrawal from the material world in order to find oneself; a retreat; charitable action; being in need and receiving help.

Six of Pentacles

In all things there must be balance; on all the paths of life you must walk hand in hand with reciprocity. Nobody is an island, and the jewel that is your community welcomes you, sustains you, and asks for sustenance in return. When you give your offerings to the gods, burn incense to your ancestors and spirits, breathe your prayers to the winds and the bodhisattvas, you give of yourself yet receive a thousandfold. Each gift of alms to those that seek them increases your joy and security in your community;  *each kind word spoken engenders a hundred more that you will receive in turn. Know that to give is to receive, but do not tread this road in order to gain: my mysteries are not of greed nor thought of self. Mine is the act of charity and the flow of wealth towards necessity; mine is the prayer of need and of gratitude in one breath; mine is the recognition of community. Do not be afraid to ask: you shall receive; give and you shall strengthen the world; offer of yourself and you shall be as the greatest sacrifice at the beginning of creation.*

∞ Mystery

In the Five of Pentacles we saw how imbalance and destruction manifested in this suit so concerned with money, home, family and everyday success. We saw people excluded from a community, pushed out and isolated, their pleas for aid refused or ignored. Happily, the Six of Pentacles returns balance to the suit, bringing with it the harmony and reciprocity of the Sixes. Like the Major Arcana numbered VI – The Lovers –, there is a sense of balance and exchange, of two different things interacting with each other, inherent in this card. This manifests as community and the flow and exchange of resources.

The card image shows a Buddhist monk, wearing the orange robes of Cambodian Buddhism, seated in meditation at the feet of a statue of the Buddha. The statue holds its right hand in the gift-giving mudra. The monk holds in his lap his begging bowl, in which he receives alms of food. In the foreground an exchange takes place: a lay person of the community offers rice to the begging bowl of another pair of outstretched hands. Another form of offering is also made in this card: incense burns in the temple in which the scene takes place, a traditional offering in many Eastern and Indian religions.

A Buddhist monk is often called a *bhikku* and a nun *bhikkuni*, meaning "beggar". [396] Traditionally, they beg for their food and accept whatever is given to them in their alms bowl, which is one of their few possessions. In this way, those that serve the wider community through teaching and religious service are in turn sustained by that community. It is common to believe that one will create good karma for one's future lives by giving food to *bhikku* and *bhikkuni*.

Despite the designation of "beggar", Buddhist monks and nuns are not homeless: the community in which they live provides everything they need. In turn, they offer their own resources back

---

396 Melford Spiro, **Buddhism and Society: A Great Tradition and its Burmese Vicissitudes**, p. 279. *University of California Press, 1982.*

to the community: their time, energy, labour and wisdom. The monastic community to which they belong works in symbiosis with the lay community of the surrounding area, each relying on the other for an aspect of life. The *Dhammapada* calls the monastic community "Sangha", one of the three jewels of Buddhism, and refers to it as "a secure refuge" in which one is released from suffering. [397] This does not mean, however, that we should rely on the community to give us refuge: all the Sixes of the tarot have a sense of reciprocity to them. As such, we should also provide refuge for those in our community, exchanging our resources with each other and creating a comfortable place in which to live. The Six of Pentacles reminds us that our resources stored in one place or hoarded are wasted: their true power lies in being offered generously, being allowed to flow to the areas of one's community where they are needed. In doing so, we often find that we, in turn, are sustained and become recipients of another's generosity. It is a card of charity, aid, philanthropy and the sharing of material wealth.

≈ Revelation

Generosity; charity; philanthropy; giving aid to those requesting it; succour; exchange of resources; flow of resources; adaptability with respect to material concerns; giving away one's wealth; bequeathments; offerings; supporting others in the everyday world; rebalance of one's material resources; community.

Negatively aspected…
Receiving help, succour or charity; needing to ask for aid; a blockage preventing the flow of resources or the direction to where they are needed; charity refused; lack of community; lack of adaptability with regard to one's resources.

---

397 Dhammapada 15.

Seven of Pentacles

With steady pace and gentle hand your course may be guided; with certainty of success there is no need to rush forth loudly, to fight for power or to compete for prestige. These do not matter to the buffalo or the rice, to the falling rains or the waiting earth: only the great cycles and time decide the progress of this slow harvest. For there are many more gratifying things on this earth than those that are gained instantly: what worth are they? Pause to listen to the seeds pushing through the earth and the leaves opening; listen to the sound of the march of time and know that what has been set in motion is inevitable. Haste will only serve to weaken it. I am the Patient One and the Slow Treader, the calming word that seeks to give you peace in a hurried world; the breath of gentleness that calls you back to the ways your kind once knew: the ways of the harvest and the rains, when there was a time for everything and all was done at the right moment. Walk by my side, and know the mysteries of measured success.

☙ Mystery

The watery fluidity of the Sevens of the tarot mixes well with the suit of Pentacles' earthy nature. Where other suits find that their sevens suffer, the Seven of Pentacles manifests this energy as weakness that can be harnessed to good results. Here, in the everyday world of the suit of Pentacles, weakness becomes slow progress; this slow progress is to be expected in certain areas of life and encouraged in some instances. Slow and steady wins the race in this card: rushing headlong or trying to move forward too hastily will risk all progress. The Seven of Pentacles also shows us the natural pace of events unfolding in their own time. There is no pretention or competition here, with patience and careful attention to the task required. A desire for instant gratification is the bane of this card, which cannot provide it. Some things take time to grow to fruition, like the crops in a field: they cannot be rushed, for they would not grow properly. Nature has its course and in the case of the Seven of Pentacles we are advised to follow it, regardless of how slow and onerous that course may seem.

In the card image a water buffalo carries the first of the season's rice harvest slowly through the water-logged rice paddies of Cambodia. On his back a small boy sits, maintaining the balance of the yoke on which the precious crops are carefully balanced. His diligent attention to them, and the slow movement of the buffalo, will ensure that they reach their destination safely. An old man walks beside the buffalo; his affection for this creature is obvious, as he rests a gentle hand on its cheek and lays his head upon it. He may be speaking to the buffalo, encouraging it, praising it, guiding it onwards. With such care and gentleness, the buffalo will surely make steady progress; if the man spurred it to be quicker by pushing, pulling, or beating it then it would undoubtedly risk the precious cargo.

Rice was one of the staple foods of the Khmer Empire.[398] It was relied upon so heavily that it is likely that forests were removed to make way for more rice paddies.[399] The cycles of nature dictated the speed at which farmers could grow and harvest their crops: for six months of the year monsoon conditions produced a great deal of water, while the other six months brought drought. Farmers worked with these conditions, using dykes, irrigation and flood retreat farming.[400] Zhou Dagan, a Chinese man who spent a year in Cambodia in the 13th century, stated that there were three or four crops a year. He emphasised that Khmer farmers needed to time the important stages of the agricultural cycle carefully to coincide with flooding and receding waters, sowing according to the height of water.[401] As with the Seven of Pentacles, such an undertaking could not be rushed: the monsoon rains would fall when they fell, the flood waters would recede when they receded, crops would grow when they grew. To try to rush the sowing or the reaping would devastate the crop. The metaphor of agriculture also reminds us that some things are not a competition with others and that to make them so will lead to eventual loss or poor quality results. Although a slow, gentle pace may be frustrating, we must try to remove our need for instant gratification and attend to our task with diligence and patience.

---

398 John Tully, *A Short History of Cambodia*, p. 42. Allen & Unwin, 2005.

399 Toshiyuki Fujuki, "Vegetation Changes in the Area of Angkor Thom Based on Pollen Analysis of Moat Deposits" p. 376 in *Water Civilization: From Yangtze to Khmer Civilizations*, p. 363–381, ed. Yoshinori Yasuda. Springer, 2013.

400 John Tully, *A Short History of Cambodia*, p. 47.

401 Chou Ta-Kuan, *The Customs of Cambodia*, trans. Paul Pelliot, p. 36. The Siam Society, 1992.

❧ Revelation

Slow progress; results assured but not for some time; patience; diligence; hard work beginning to pay off; completion yet to come; a gentle and careful approach is required; a period of waiting; a period of gestating and growing, good quality as a result of careful checking.

Negatively aspected…
Failing to achieve desired results; weakness of progress; delay; failing at the first hurdle; hasty action risking investments or results; impatience; lack of care and diligence causing problems; poor quality caused by haste.

Eight of Pentacles

The sacred thread runs through the ages, binding every student and master that has gone before you; take the path of learning and you shall be treading in the footsteps of countless sages. This is the foundation of all knowledge, of every skill and art: the enduring wisdom attained through application throughout time. This sacred thread is your right, as your ancestors carved teachings from the unhewn rocks so that those that came after might continue the quest. Yet do not take it upon your self lightly: the thread is a heavy burden, serving to remind you of your duty and the dedication and work that you must offer to that lineage of sages in order to grow and add to the repository of learning. It is the foundation and the goad, the calling of your ancestors and your blood to the work. I am the guru and the application of learning, the test and the obstacle to be overcome, the foundation of wisdom and memory, the craftsman who never stops learning and the student who drinks in the words of the ages. Sit at my feet with open ears and willing heart, and you will come to know the blessings of wisdom.

~ Mystery

As we move closer to the culmination of the suit of Pentacles, the bounty of these earthy cards increases. In their own way, each card of this suit shows different aspects and types of wealth (or lack of it); the Eight of Pentacles depicts the wealth of knowledge and skill passed down from master to apprentice. As an Eight in the tarot, this card brings with it the foundational, stable energy of the Fours and doubles it, emphasising it even further; in the earthy suit of Pentacles it therefore finds a natural home, thus showing the firmest foundation of all: wisdom. This wisdom is not necessarily intellectual in nature, however, as that would be better suited to the Swords, but practical wisdom and the search for it.

The card image shows the *upanayana*, one of the sixteen *samskāras* (rites of passage) undertaken in the Hindu community. [402] This rite marks the start of formal education, as well as the acceptance of a student by a guru. It is also used to mark the beginning of studies and apprenticeships in a wide variety of arts and skills. In many non-Vedic Hindu texts, the education that begins with a ceremony similar to the *upanayana* extended to trades and crafts that would have had guilds: pottery, architecture and weaving, for instance. [403] The practical nature of the wisdom to be acquired is demonstrated in the *Śatapatha Brāmaṇa*, the earliest detailed description of the ceremony. Following the rite, the guru gives his first instructions to the student: to sip water, to do work, and to put fuel on the fire. [404]

---

402 R. C. Prasad, ***The Upanayana: The Hindu Ceremonies of the Sacred Thread***, *p. 113. Motilal Banarsidass, 2014.*

403 *Stella Kramrisch,* **"Traditions of the Indian Craftsman"** *in* ***The Journal of American Folklore***, *vol. 71, no. 281, pp.224–230.*

404 *Brian Black,* ***The Character of the Self in Ancient India: Priests, Kings, and Women in the Early Upaniṣads***, *p. 38. State University of New York Press, 2007.*

As part of the ceremony, a sacred thread is given to the new apprentice/student, called *yajñopavītam*. This thread signifies the act of entering into the period of learning or apprenticeship. The card image shows this thread – worn already by the guru in the traditional style over the left shoulder and under the right – presenting the thread to the new apprentice. From the moment the apprentice dons the thread, he will be a part of the tradition and begin learning the wisdom of the ages as well as the practical skills for adult life.

Behind the ceremony stands a large statue of Gaṇeṣa, who was worshipped in Cambodia from the sixth century, [405] widely revered as the remover of obstacles and a patron of those undertaking study. He is said to have two consorts, Buddhi and Siddhi, "wisdom" and "success", [406] two expected outcomes from any form of study or apprenticeship. In traditional symbolism he rests in the base chakra, Muladhara, the foundation, reminding us of the stabilising nature of the Eight of Pentacles.

~ Revelation

Apprenticeship; undertaking a period of learning from somebody else's experience and wisdom; studying a craft, art or skill; practice makes perfect; applying what one has learned; hard work and dedication required.

Negatively aspected…
Neglecting to study or work hard; lack of dedication; lack of stability in one's learning environment; lacking a suitable teacher of a skill; lacking the skills required for a situation.

---

405 Robert L. Brown ed., **Ganesh: Studies of an Asian God**, p. 9. State University of New York Press, 1991.

406 Satguru Sivaya Subramuniyaswami, **Loving Gaṇeśa: Hinduism's Endearing Elephant-faced God**, p. 57. Himalayan Academy, 2000.

Nine of Pentacles

One of the sweetest things in life is to luxuriate in what you have earned, to surround yourself in the joys of your success, to taste the fruits of your labours. Even sweeter is the knowledge that your wealth is born from independent endeavours, owing nothing to others, kindled and sustained by your will alone. This is my road: the road of individual success, of the one who works on their own terms, of the generation of one's own wealth. My name is Independence and Self-Reliance and my rituals are the enjoyment of that which brings delight to the days and joy to the nights. Bejewel yourself in your glorious works; array yourself in your achievements! Rely not on others for your stability and wealth but trust that your steps along this road are holy and perfect. Understand the source of your wisdom and the foundation of your resources; seek not stasis but growth; know your greatest riches and their worth. Yet remember that these are not the source of your self-worth, for this lies in your own courage and dedication.

ᴥ Mystery

The Nine of this earthy suit, like that of the watery suit of Cups, can be seen as having almost reached fulfilment and culmination of the suit of Pentacles; however, it has not yet reached the pinnacle of what can be achieved, which comes in the Ten. The Nines of the tarot are a triple Three, bringing the influence of manifestation and productivity to the already fruitful number. In the suit of Pentacles this is expressed as wishes being fulfilled in the material realm, everyday success, comfort and luxury. Since this card appears near the end of the suit, it also reminds us of the hard work and effort that comes before success. The reason that the Nine of Pentacles does not quite reach the highest potential of this suit is that its success is focused on the individual rather than a group, community, team or family. This is the self-made business person, the successful entrepreneur, the independent individual who has carved a fulfilling life for themselves through hard work and effort.

In the card image a young woman relaxes on the low walls of her garden; behind her is her elegant and rich home, signifying the comfort and wealth in which she lives. Another indicator of her high status is her clothing: silk was imported from Siam and Champa, and patterned cloth was not affordable to those of lower ranks. [407] In the Khmer Empire women appear to have enjoyed a relative amount of independence and respect. Zhou Dagan remarked that it was women who took charge of trade, and "[f]or this reason a Chinese, arriving in the country, loses no time in getting himself a mate, for he will find her commercial instincts a great asset". [408] This is supported by the Bayon bas-reliefs that depict market scenes in which many of the traders are women. [409] This reminds us of the independent nature of the Nine of Pentacles, which often represents somebody who is independently wealthy, who does not rely on others for comfort or security.

---

407   Chou Ta-Kuan, trans. Paul Pelliot, **The Customs of Cambodia**, p. 7. The Siam Society, Bangkok, 1992.
408   *Ibid.*, p. 43.
409   John Tully, A **Short History of Cambodia**, p. 37. Allen & Unwin, 2005.

The great wealth of the woman is shown by the pentacles scattered about her, as well as the creatures that keep her company: the ivory from elephant tusks and the feathers of kingfishers were both highly sought after products from the Khmer Empire. [410] Kingfisher feathers were supposedly such an important product for the economy that there was a legend that Angkor fell into decline when kingfisher feathers became unavailable. [411] This reminds us that the Nine of Pentacles represents the ways in which others rely on us for comfort, wealth and stability. Here, we have our own territory that we have built and sustain independently. We are able to grant benefits to others from here, like the independent business person who takes on employees. Thus, from the wealth of the Nine of Pentacles we are in a position to further expand our success, also reminding us that we often need to invest resources in order to grow them.

~ Revelation

A self-made individual; a successful entrepreneur or business person; success in business and the everyday world; being one's own boss; financial independence; being solely responsible for one's everyday fulfilment; the further growth of resources through investment.

Negatively aspected…
Start-up companies and the initial stages of entrepreneurship or a business opportunity; being reliant on others for financial support and stability; delayed success in business; lack of growth in an opportunity; wealth and resources in a static state.

---

410   Chou Ta-Kuan, trans. Paul Pelliot, **The Customs of Cambodia**, p. 41.
411   John Tully, A **Short History of Cambodia**, p. 52.

Ten of Pentacles

Many people measure success in coin and personal status; they look to themselves and the journey they have taken, the path they have walked, to reach great heights of achievement. Yet the success of one dies and fades with the passing of time; it is weak and its song will not linger for long. These are my mysteries: that true success lies in all, elevating everybody rather than one; that it is found in the lineage you create; that it can be granted and inherited. This is the greatest gift you can give: to ensure that those who come after you are better than you, have greater stores of wisdom. Just as your bones will one day be the foundation upon which your descendants will rest, so let your words and wisdom, your skill and wealth, be the basis of their continued success. This is my road; my name is Long Life and Sweet Health, Memory and Lineage; I am the Lord of Long-Lasting Success and the Ties That Bind. Mine is the sweetness of knowing your memory will live on, your line will continue, and that the small difference you have made in the world in your span of years may be greater with each passing generation's success.

~ Mystery

At the culmination of the suit of Pentacles we have a happy family scene. As with the other cards of its number, the Ten of Pentacles has collected all the energy of its suit, in this case becoming increasingly wealthy and fulfilling, gathering the blessings of the everyday world into itself. It shares some similarities with the Ten of Cups, in that both show a family; however, the Ten of Cups represents emotional bliss whereas the Ten of Pentacles shows material security, lineage and family support. Here is the happiness created from the certainty of a strong family line and being able to support and protect one's descendants. The Ten of Cups also shows the family of one's choosing, which may not necessarily be linked by blood, whereas the Ten of Pentacles strongly emphasises the blood ties of the family unit.

In the card image a multigenerational family spends time in one of the many waterways of ancient Angkor. The Chinese scholar, Zhou Dagan, who wrote of his visit to Cambodia in the medieval period, reported that it is an excessively hot country, requiring bathing several times a day, and that this was often a communal activity with families having access to a pond or sharing access with nearby families. [412] Other scholars maintain the importance of waterways such as these for the everyday lives of the Cambodian people, presenting them as inseparable from Khmer religion and as a centre of daily and family activity. [413]

A number of important skills that contributed to daily life focused on waterways, such as fishing, irrigation and rice farming. The card shows some of these skills being used by members of the family: two young men use spears to catch fish, a skill they may have been taught by their father who stands nearby, petting a docile elephant.

---

412 *Chou Ta-Kuan, trans. Paul Pelliot,* **The Customs of Cambodia**, *p. 69. The Siam Society of Bangkok, 1992.*

413 *John Tully,* **A Short History of Cambodia**, *p. 46. Allen & Unwin, 2005.*

This animal symbolises long life and memory, as it lives for many decades. In the mid-ground a younger woman bathes while another washes the hair of a small boy, reminding us of the focus of the Ten of Pentacles on caring for our family and our health. In the foreground, a grandmother teaches her young grandson how to catch fish by hand, though instead of fish in their full baskets it is golden pentacles, representing the overflowing abundance of resources that they enjoy.

The scene is one of caring for one's family by providing for them, nurturing them, and ensuring that they may live long and happy lives even once you are gone. It highlights the inheritance of everyday wealth in resources as well as in wisdom, teaching and skill. It also shows the act of enabling a sustainable way of life in the family unit, of teaching others how to look after themselves, of passing on one's wisdom and skills to make the future better for one's descendants. In this way, the Ten of Pentacles reminds us that we can continually make the generation that comes after us better than our own, which can be continued by that generation in turn. The culmination of everyday success is not individual success – such as in the Nine of Pentacles – but in communal, collective success.

~ Revelation

The family unit and blood ties; ensuring the sustainability of one's family's way of life; success on a material and everyday level; long-lasting success; passing down one's skills and wisdom; lineage; long life; hereditary wealth and inheritances; communal wealth and success.

Negatively aspected…
A dysfunctional family unit; blood ties causing problems; not feeling protected, nurtured or cared for by one's family; disconnection from family wisdom; nothing being passed on or inherited; elitism leading to exclusion.

Court Cards

The Court cards of each suit depict a deity worshipped in the culture represented in that suit. The divine presence in these cards of personality allow us to see a link between the many aspects of the self and the many faces of the sacred. For millennia humankind has worshipped deities to whom they ascribed not only sacred and mythical functions but also unfailingly human personality traits, desires and experiences. Where humans underwent birth and death, so did their gods; where humans warred with one another so their gods raised weapons against demons; where humans fell in love, lust and produced art to express it, so the gods became the divine originators of those purviews.

The Court cards not only represent types of personality and traits, but also areas of human concern that are influenced by our actions and characters. They can also relate to situations and different approaches that might be required for them. Commonly they are seen as representing people.

Just as the Minor Arcana have elemental associations, so do the Court cards. As well as each suit being associated with an element (see p. 172), each rank in the Court is given an element:

Princess	Earth
Prince	Air
Queen	Water
King	Fire

Therefore, each of the sixteen Court cards is assigned a pair of elements that interact with each other to create a phenomenon [414] that relates to the card meaning:

Court card	Elemental pair	Phenomenon
Princess of Pentacles	Earthy part of Earth	The foundation, the waiting earth
Prince of Pentacles	Airy part of Earth	Fructification
Queen of Pentacles	Watery part of Earth	Mother Earth, earth as nurturer
King of Pentacles	Fiery part of Earth	Mountains, earthquakes, earth as preserver
Princess of Swords	Earthy part of Air	Fixation of the volatile, materialisation of idea
Prince of Swords	Airy part of Air	Pure air, flexible and rushing
Queen of Swords	Watery part of Air	Air's power of transmission
King of Swords	Fiery part of Air	The storm
Princess of Cups	Earthy part of Water	Crystallisation
Prince of Cups	Airy part of Water	Water's elasticity, volatility and catalytic nature
Queen of Cups	Watery part of Water	Water's power of reception and reflection

---

414 *From Aleister Crowley, The Book of Thoth, pp. 151–171. Samuel Weiser, Inc., 1998.*

King of Cups	Fiery part of Water	Rain and springs, water's power of solution
Princess of Wands	Earthy part of Fire	Fuel of fire, containment of fire
Prince of Wands	Airy part of Fire	Expanding and volatilising of fire
Queen of Wands	Watery part of Fire	Fluidity and colour of fire
King of Wands	Fiery part of Fire	Lightning flash

Each rank of the Court cards can also be seen as a level of maturity of that element – that is, its strength, power and ease of control or approach.

Princess	Immature (unformed, growing, nascent) feminine (passive, receptive)
Prince	Immature (unformed, growing, nascent) masculine (active, giving)
Queen	Mature (formed, expressive, manifested) feminine (passive, receptive)
King	Mature (formed, expressive, manifested) masculine (active, giving)

Due to their elemental nature, each rank of the tarot Court can also be given its own powers and abilities:

Princess	Awakening Earth: beginnings, opening up, instigation
Prince	Questing Air: seeking, challenging, exploring
Queen	Nurturing Water: inspiring, channelling, encouraging
King	Masterful Fire: pinnacle, paragon, activating

The cards may appear in a reading to be read in many different ways depending on their context, the question, surrounding cards and intuition. Having different approaches to their interpretation adds another tool to your tarot tool box that might come in handy at any time.

Princess of Wands

Isis, Goddess of Power, Will and Manifestation

Think not of the beginnings of all things as a step from water to shore, but as the hardening of softness in the fiery furnace of stars, for you are nothing but ancient stars fallen and made manifest; the tails of those blazing stars of so long ago still burn in our dance of life, love, creation and destruction. See my dance and see the fire and the universe I contain within; it is from my loins that kings are born and by my word that kingship is granted. I create and hold the power that rises in the beginning and I destroy it utterly at the end. I am Isis, the throne-mother of the gods, primordial child of time, the sayings of whose mouth come to pass. I am the Queen of Heaven, and desirous of earth; I am great of magic, and my blood is power and life. I know the secret names of all things within the earth and above the earth; with this power I make manifest my Will: I drive out the serpent and know how to direct it; I draw down the power and hold its fire within. I conceive from potential and possibility and out of death and inertia I coax life, giving the smallest spark the fuel to burn brighter and more hungry. Like you, star-born flame, I want, desire and yearn; nothing will ever be enough, for I am the fire that cannot be extinguished, self-fuelling and perpetual. I can teach you the true magic of harnessing your will and power, of containing and limiting it, for in limitation there is readiness and the fire contained in the furnace burns hotter for its tomb. I will show you the manifestation of desire through will-full action, for there is nothing in the heavens, on the earth or under the earth that I have desired and not attained. My Will be done.

~ Mystery

As Earth of Fire, the Princess of Wands is the fuel for fire, the creative aspect of fire and the containment of fire. She is a dynamic and powerful force, for the element of Earth rules over manifestation. Here is will and energy becoming reality, power grounded in action, and passion fuelled. This Princess adds more wood to the fire and her containing and limiting nature – for Earth binds us in one place – makes it even hotter, just as the fire in a furnace is hotter because it is contained. Her energy never ceases: she is self-fuelling and therefore achieves anything she desires. Since Fire is the element closest to Spirit, and Earth the element furthest away, the Princess of Wands represents the link between potential and manifestation, between heaven and earth. The Princess of Wands – the Egyptian goddess Isis in the *Tarot Apokalypsis* – is the process of creating through an act of will or a direction of energy. She is the dynamism required to create and the ability to focus one's energy and will so that it can burn more brightly towards a single goal. Further, she brings to life all that may have been slowly decaying or becoming stagnant.

The Princesses are the thrones of their suits, and it is from them that the Aces of that suit are born. Manifestation is their power. It is therefore apt that Isis's name means "throne" and that she was seen as the seat of power of the gods and kings in ancient Egypt. It is this throne that is seen on her headdress in the card image. She was the mother of Horus, the god that represented the king on his throne, and the king was seen as laying in the lap of Isis: she suckled him, protected him and set him upon the throne. Just like the Princess of Wands, Isis can be seen as the source and legitimisation of power. She is frequently represented in the *Pyramid Texts* as giving her milk to the dead king so that he may achieve life among the stars after death. In her mortuary role, Isis was known as "Mistress of the

Pyramid"; [415] a pyramid was the house of certain parts of the spirit after death, just as the Princess of Wands is the container of spirit, energy and life.

Isis has been given many epithets, and is perhaps the best-known of all the Egyptian deities in the modern age. She has been called "Fierce of Radiance", "Lady of the Words of Power", "She who gives birth to heaven and earth", "Mistress of the House of Life" and "The One Who is All". [416] *Weret hekau* – "great of magic" – was a term frequently given to her and she was called "Great Magician". [417] This link with magic is mentioned in Lucian's *Lovers of Lies* (34–36), in which Pancrates of Memphis spent 23 years in a secret, subterranean chamber where he learned the magical arts from Isis herself; even Pythagoras was said to have spent time underground in Egypt where the "Mother" shared her magical knowledge with him. [418] This aspect of Isis is called upon in magical texts of the Late Antique period, where she is called "Isis the Wise, the sayings of whose mouth come to pass". [419]

Isis' greatness of magic is the basis of the three seminal myths in which she features, which also serve to convey her nature as the throne of power and a director of her own will. The first tells how Isis desired to learn the true name of Ra, the creator god, because in doing so she would also obtain his magic. She

---

415 James Henry Breasted, trans. ***Ancient Records of Egypt, vol. 1: The First through the Seventeenth Dynasties***, *pp. 84–5. University of Illinois Press, 2001.*

416 *Ellen Reeder Williams, "**Isis Pelagia and a Roman Marble Matrix from the Athenian Agora" in* ***Hesperia***, *Vol. 54, No. 2. (Apr. - Jun., 1985), pp. 109-119.*

417 *Miriam Lichtheim trans.,* ***Ancient Egyptian Literature, vol. 1: The Old and Middle Kingdom***, *p. 114. University of California Press, 2006.*

418 *Bengt Ankarloo and Stuart Clark, eds.* ***Witchcraft and Magic in Europe, vol 2: Ancient Greece and Rome***, *p. 107. University of Pennsylvania Press, 1999.*

419 *Hans Deiter Betz trans.,* ***Greek Magical Papyri in Translation***, *PDM xiv. 1–92. University of Chicago Press, 1986.*

created a venomous snake, which she laid in Ra's path; when it bit him he called out for help. She attended him and tried to cure him of the venom, but was unsuccessful – only his true name, she said, would cure him. Ra revealed his true name and Isis cured him using it; in doing so she was filled with the same magical power that Ra had. [420] Because of this story, the card image in *Tarot Apokalypsis* shows Isis with a dangerous red snake coiling around her feet: she knows how to create danger, how to control the power she wields and how to direct it.

The second of her seminal myths is that of the murder of her brother-husband, Osiris. This myth is found in a variety of ancient Egyptian texts, but none give the full account. Set, the jealous brother of Osiris and Isis, wished to rule Egypt instead of Osiris, so he murdered him and cut his body into pieces, scattering them across the lands. Isis mourned for her dead husband, but sought the pieces of his body. Finding them, she pieced them together, but there was one piece she could not find – the phallus – so she fashioned a replacement. She then used her magic to conceive a son from her husband's body, before breathing life back into him. In this way, the new king (the son, Horus) can rule in his dead father's place. Here Isis breathes life into the dead, just as she gives afterlife to the dead king in the *Pyramid Texts*, and just as the Princess of Wands reinvigorates that which has become stagnant. The golden ankh hanging at her side in the card image represents the life and energy that she breathes into the dead, as this symbol referred to life and spirit. As the fiery force of power she is also called "The-Great-Ka-of-Harakhte", or "the spirit of Horus", [421] the flame of power within the pharaoh. The Princess of Wands is not only the force of dynamism

---

420 James B. Pritchard ed., **Ancient Near Eastern Texts Relating to the Old Testament**, p. 12. Princeton University Press, 1969.

421 James Henry Breasted, trans. **Ancient Records of Egypt, vol. 4: The Twentieth through the Twenty-sixth Dynasties**, 705, p. 346. Chicago: University of Illinois Press, 2001.

and containment that enthrones power, but can also be seen as power and energy itself. She is also the force that carries energy and power upwards towards completion, just as heat rises, and in this aspect Isis is represented as helping the soul of the dead king rise up to the stars and rise out of the underworld into the afterlife like Osiris on his barque (boat): "Ascend and descend; ascend with Isis, rise with the Day-bark". [422]

The final myth in which she plays an important role is *The Contendings of Horus and Set*, [423] in which her son Horus battles against Set for the rulership of Egypt. Isis, in order to trick Set into agreeing that Horus should take rulership, uses her shapeshifting ability to turn into a woman he desires. As shapeshifter she reminds us that the Princess of Wands shows us how to transmute one thing into another, just as fire changes the state of fuel as it consumes it. In the card image Isis wears the wings with which she is often depicted: she is often described as shapeshifting into a kite or falcon. [424]

In later centuries, Isis took on a more universal nature. Lucius Apuleius, a 2nd-century CE devotee of Isis, wrote of a vision he received of the goddess in which she reveals herself as "the natural mother of all things, mistress and governess of all the elements, the initial progeny of worlds, chief of powers divine, Queen of heaven, the principal of the Gods celestial, the light of the goddesses: at my will the planets of the air, the wholesome winds of the Seas, and the silences of hell be disposed". [425] This may seem lofty for a Princess of her suit, perhaps better given

---

422 R. O Faulkner trans. **The Ancient Egyptian Pyramid Texts** 210, p. 50. Oxford University Press, 1969.

423 Found in the **Papyrus Chester Beatty I**.

424 For instance, R. O Faulkner trans. **The Ancient Egyptian Pyramid Texts** 1255–1256; 1280, pp. 199–200 and p. 203.

425 Lucius Apuleius, **Metamophoses** or **The Golden Ass**. Book 11, Chap 47.

to the Queen, but the Princesses through virtue of their Earthiness are closer to the world and therefore control of it. They also contain entire universes within them, all potential and possibilities, as they carry within them the Aces like children in their mothers' wombs, like the new king in the womb of Isis. Thus, the card image shows the same starlight descending to the staff that Isis holds as in the Ace of Wands: this is the soul descending from the heavens to earth and manifestation.

≈ Revelation

Dynamism and energy; reinvigoration of self or projects; transmutation from inertia to a state of action; breathing new life into something; encouragement; containing and directing one's energy; manifesting one's goals and ambitions; the power of the will; direction of one's passions; fuelling oneself; grounding one's passions and desires in reality; consumption; a passionate and mischievous person; intensity; being playful; boundless energy; turning one's creative tendencies into reality.

Negatively aspected...
A spoiled person; somebody who will cause trouble if they don't get their own way; somebody who will burn others without meaning to; danger through mischief; not knowing when to stop; being unable to contain a situation; something getting out of hand; something out of one's control.

Prince of Wands

Set, God of Chaos, Rivalry and Aggression

There are wild, desert places parched to bones by the gaze of the sun; there are red places and the roads that snake among them, and there are the storms of skin-flaying sand that blaze their trails along the dunes. Walk these places on the edge of the acceptable, and I shall walk beside you, pushing you onwards into the heat. If greatness is what you seek, I will answer to your call only when all else has been exhausted, for I am the last reserve of fleeting, focused energy needed to push you to the threshold. I will burn you, I will strip away your flesh and I will kill you, but you will achieve greatness. Yet some day you may face me as a rival instead of a friend, then you shall know that where your backbone is strong, mine is stronger; where your war-cry is great, mine is a roar of thunder and earthquake; where you are desirous of result, I am more so, and will stop at nothing to achieve my ends. Peace is not the way. Rage and tumultuous power will overcome. Where the way lies smooth and easy, I break up the earth and create your challenge. I offer you hard-won gains and the road to the desert, where in sterility you can find strength. I can show you how to break through oppression and limitations, and where you need a powerful force of destruction I can be guided towards your ends to protect you. I am forever seeking power and ambition, but I demand them quickly. Roar your war-cry beside me, take up arms against your enemy and do not be afraid to be fierce in battle.

❧ Mystery

The active, fast-moving elements of Air and Fire unite in the Prince of Wands to form a volatile, audacious and adventurous character. As the Airy part of Fire, he is a seeker of challenge, excitement and ways to prove himself; he is a less mature form

of the powerful and charismatic King of Wands, with those qualities presenting themselves in a more chaotic form. His airy nature gives the Prince of Wands difficulty in committing to the concerns of his suit. As the suit of Wands is fiery, associated with ambition, success, power, sense of self and energy, its Prince is drawn to power and has great ambitions but lacks the staying power to stick with anything long enough to achieve greatness. He is charismatic only inasmuch as he says he is; he is powerful in short bursts; his energy burns out so quickly that it is unsustainable. This makes him a useful resource in getting a short, focused job done: he is the burst of energy needed for the final push towards completion. Yet he cannot be relied upon often, commonly bringing chaos in his wake. At his worst he can be violent, fanning the flames of conflict. He is easily bored, yet boredom is the surest trigger for his bad behaviour.

In the *Tarot Apokalypsis*, the Prince of Wands is Set, the ancient Egyptian god of the desert that fought against Horus and killed Osiris so he might usurp his throne. To the layman he is the enemy of all that is good, but ancient sources present a dichotomous image: he was both rival and helper of the "good" gods. Whilst earlier commentators presented Set as abnormal, residing on the fringes of acceptable society, [426] there is evidence that despite his negative role in several myths he was a normative figure among the gods; in several cases was given a helpful role. [427] He had many epithets, including "Great of Magic" [428] and "Great of Strength". [429] In hi-

---

426 See H. te Velde, **Seth, God of Confusion**. *Netherlands: E J. Brill, Leiden, 1967.*

427 See Eugene Cruz-Uribe, "**Seth, God of Power and Might**" in **Journal of the American Research Center in Egypt**, *vol. 45 (2009), pp. 201-226.*

428 R. O Faulkner trans. **The Ancient Egyptian Pyramid Texts** *204, p. 50 Oxford University Press, 1969.*

429 Robert A. Oden, Jr. "**The Contendings of Horus and Seth (Chester Beatty Papyrus No. 1: A Structural Interpretation**", *p. 358, in* **History of Religions** *vol. 18, no. 4 (May, 1979) pp. 352-69.*

eroglyphs he was often referred to by the glyph of the Set-animal, a fabulous creature that was a chimera-like conflation of several different animals. The Set-animal was often determined by other glyphs that tell us Set's nature: "to be grievous", "rage, storm, disaster", "to disturb, tumult", "to boast", "storm", "to be harsh", "to be violent, to roar", "to be strong" and "war-shout", among others. [430] His name was also often replaced in the *Coffin Texts* by the glyph for "to separate". [431] The Greek writer Plutarch wrote that Set's name meant "the overmastering" and "overpowering". [432] He is often given a violent, temperamental and chaotic nature, and even at his birth he demonstrated this when he "broke forth violently" from his mother's womb. [433] He was associated with the colour red, some texts saying that he had red hair and skin and that Setian personalities were typified by such complexion and were easily angered. [434]

The most well-known myth involving Set is that of his jealousy over Osiris' rulership and his murder of him in an attempt to create dominance over him. This myth makes Set the rival of Osiris and creates a contrast between the two brothers: Osiris, a god of moisture, the Nile, and the fertilising powers of life, and Set, a god of the parched desert, drought and sterility. In the *Turin Papyrus* Set speaks of himself in this aspect, saying "I am a Man of a million cubits, whose name is Evil Day. As for the day of giving birth or of conceiving, there is no giving birth and trees bear no fruit". [435]

---

430 H. te Velde. **Seth, God of Confusion**, p. 23.
431 **Ibid.**, pp. 5–6.
432 Plutarch, **De Iside et Osiride** 49, in F. C. Babbit "**Plutarch's Moralia V**" p. 120. London: Loeb Classical Library, 1957.
433 R. O Faulkner trans. **The Ancient Egyptian Pyramid Texts** 205, p. 50.
434 Deborah Schorsch and Mark T. Wypyski, "**Seth, 'Figure of Mystery'**" p. 199, in **Journal of American Research Center in Egypt**, vol. 45 (2009), pp. 177–200.
435 Quoted in J. G. Griffiths, **The Conflict of Horus and Seth**, p. 52. Liverpool, 1960.

However, the prevalence of positive images of Set throughout ancient Egyptian history suggests that the actions of Set in murdering his brother are seen as a necessary evil that explains natural occurrences and the experience of death; they enthrone the Osirian king of the otherworld, which creates the post-death process of the deceased Pharaoh ruling like Osiris in the afterlife and ascending to the Imperishable Stars (see *King of Wands*). In these Osirian afterlife texts, Set plays a helpful role: he is one of the deities powerful enough to oppose Apophis, the beast that attacks the boat of Ra as he sails through the Duat every night:

"Hail to you, O Seth, son of Nut, the great of strength in the barque of millions, felling the enemy, the snake, at the prow of the barque of Re, great of battle-cry, may you give me a good lifetime..." [436]

The battle-cry of Set may have been an important feature of the god, who is often referred to in language of noise and loud natural occurrences. He is sometimes associated with storms and thunder, particularly desert storms. He is called "Noise-maker" in a Middle Kingdom stela in Zagreb; [437] in a passage about thunder, earthquakes and hailstorms the deceased king says "... and I roar as does Seth"; [438] Set himself says that he "causes confusion and thunders in the horizon of the sky". [439] Like the Prince of Wands, Set likes to make his presence known!

The other myth that features Set prominently is the Contendings of Horus and Set, found in a number of sources but most fully in the *Papyrus Chester Beatty I*. Here Set demonstrates his aggressive, power-seeking qualities when he and Horus

---

436 Pap. Leiden I 346 II, 12, quoted in H. te Velde, **Seth God of Confusion**, p. 99.
437 William A. Ward, **"The Hiw-Ass, the Hiw-Serpent, and the God Seth"** p. 24, in **Journal of Near Eastern Studies**, vol. 37, no. 1 (Jan., 1978), pp. 23–34.
438 R. O Faulkner trans. **The Ancient Egyptian Pyramid Texts** 1149–50, p. 187.
439 E. A. Wallis Budge trans. **Book of the Dead**, ch. 39. London, 1910.

contend over the rulership of Egypt in a trial and series of contests. In one scene, Set tried to assert dominance over Horus by claiming that he had sex with him and that Horus received Set's semen. Set then tried to rape Horus, who caught his semen in his hand and threw it into the river. Later, Horus's mother Isis (see *Princess of Wands*) advised Horus to ejaculate onto a patch of lettuce – Set's favourite food (it has been suggested that Egyptian lettuce is a phallic symbol due to its shape and the fact that it secrets a white, milky sap. It is shown in the card image on Set's lower robes). Set ate the lettuce, so when they came to trial and the semen of each god was called forth, Set's came from the river and Horus's came from Set's belly, suggesting that Horus had dominance over him.

Later dynasties of ancient Egypt reconciled Set and Horus. There are a number of extant images of Set and Horus together baptising the Pharaoh (see *Four of Wands*). [440] Set was also often paired with Horus for various functions in the afterlife transformation of the Pharaoh. In the *Pyramid Texts* Set and Horus are both described as ladders upon which Osiris (and the deceased king) might ascend to the sky. [441] Even after death, the king turns to Set for his incredible strength and potency: when the different parts of his body are deified, it is his backbone and shoulders that are deified as Set, the body parts most often associated with strength. [442] Where Horus is asked to open the way for the king, Set is asked to stand guard over him while he ascends. [443]

---

440 Eugene Cruz-Uribe, **Seth, God of Power and Might**, p. 216.
441 R. O Faulkner trans. **The Ancient Egyptian Pyramid Texts** 971 and 974, p. 165–166.
442 **Ibid.**, 1309, and E. A. Wallis Budge, **Gods of the Egyptians II**, p. 246. Dover, 1969.
443 **Ibid.**, 1465.

Set may have been a deliberate instigator of conflict, a rival, a usurper, a braggart and one who brought storms, but he was also a powerful warrior, a fierce blaze of energy that protected the king in his journey to the afterlife and destroyed the Apophis-serpent, the force of chaos.

Revelation

Attempt at dominance; being usurped or needing to usurp somebody's position; grasping at power; causing confusion and chaos; short bursts of energy; fierceness; immense and focused strength for short periods of time; the final push; turbulence; seeking a sense of self; seeking to prove oneself to others; rising to a challenge; an easily angered person; swift rage.

Negatively aspected...
Mean-spirited confusion; kicking dust in your rival's face; a braggart; sterility; a drying up of creativity; burn-out; aggression; acting out.

Queen of Wands

Hathor, Goddess of Joy, Inebriety and Enchantment

Sing my hymns, play my music and let my priestesses dance in the temple! I am the Lady of Jubilation, the Golden One, the Lady of Unending Inebriety, the One Who Fills the Sanctuary with Joy! Drink deeply of my intoxicating wine, breathe deeply of my perfumed skin and live deeply the life that is gifted to you. You desire me, and I desire your worship, your love, your devotion. Your worship feeds me, but in turn it feeds you: to be enchanted, to follow beauty, to allow yourself desire nurtures you in every way. You are a charmed being, created from stardust, clothed in sunlight and blessed by moonlight; know that your desire and yearning, your urge for beauty, comes from the most divine part of your self. This is why you prostrate yourself before me. But I too desire, and it is you I long for. The path to me appears easy, but none could be more difficult. To give completely of yourself, to allow yourself to be drunk on life, ecstatic with every new day, is my charge and challenge to you. Call to me and I will see desire well up within you; call to me and I will nurture your heart of joy and song; call to me and I will teach you the dance of intoxication and fascination. My name in your heart and on your lips is the sweetest music to me, for then I know you are mine. Enchanted, intoxicated by the movement of the dance, gazing into the colour and beauty of the flames, every step towards me brings you closer to your self. Know yourself: know your divine nature, know your well of desire, know the thrust of your passions, and you will be owned by no other but yourself.

◈ Mystery

"Gods and men acclaim her, goddesses and women play the sistrum for her... Tatenen adorns her body. She is the Mistress, the Lady of Inebriety, she of the music, she of the dance." [444]

Like her sister-Queens, the Queen of Wands has an undeniable beauty that draws people in. The watery nature of her rank bestows upon this Queen a nurturing quality, the ability to channel and carry and the tendency to take into herself all the things of her suit. Residing in the Court of Wands, she is the Queen of passion, the mistress of energy, the lady of the ego, charm and charisma. She moves in the world of desire, where the ability to affect the energy and yearning of others is paramount. Her mutable watery nature applied to this fiery energy and passion gives her the ability to nurture desire, channelling and carrying her passion and that of others, feeding the energy of people, projects and groups. Yet she takes just as much as she gives, for she loves nothing more than attention: she is most alive when others are praising her and looking at her. Her leadership is like her husband's: strong, inspiring and energetic; but where the King of Wands leads through action and loud talk, the Queen of Wands leads through gentle direction, coaxing, promise of reward and inspiration.

In the *Tarot Apokalypsis* the Queen of Wands is Hathor, the Egyptian goddess of celebration, joy, drunkenness and beauty. Her cult was one of the most popular in Egypt and assimilated the worship of many other goddesses over time. Here we have Hathor in her most common form, enthroned in her temple with her sacred animals – cats – around her, her priestesses performing their sacred dance to their lotus-blossomed goddess.

---

444 Dimitri Meeks and Christine Favard-Meeks, **Daily Life of the Egyptian Gods**, p. 199. Pimlico, 1999.

Most of the priests and priestesses of Hathor were musicians, dancers and performers. For both Hathor and the Queen of Wands (who holds the sacred *sistrum* – rattle – of Hathor), the act of dance, music and celebration is a sacred act, as it channels energy, passion and desire into the physical world, mimicking the enchanting flow of both fire and water. When we dance, we call upon a deeper, more primal part of our selves and follow its beat. The Queen of Wands urges us to find the nature and focus of our inner desires, yearnings and sensual self, and to bring it out into the open to allow it to thrive. Restriction of any kind is a sin for this Queen. She also urges us to find connection with others and to share ourselves openly with them. In this role, the Queen of Wands is a social butterfly and hostess, a facilitator of other people's enjoyment, priding herself in introducing others, making people feel welcome and instigating friendships, partnerships and relationships of all kinds. To some, her need for attention may seem selfish, but it is just another way for her to ensure she has authority when making these connections for others. An example of the way the Queen of Wands uses this attention for the good of others can be found in *The Contendings of Horus and Set*, which tells of the competition between Horus and Set for rulership of Egypt. After much contention, Ra, the god chosen to judge who should rule, became withdrawn, upset by the ploys used by the two contenders, so the contest could not continue. Hathor, seeing the importance of what was at stake, raised her skirts, exposing her private parts to Ra. Seeing this, Ra laughed and cheered up, and the contest recommenced. [445] Where the Queen of Wands is, joy and laughter will follow, even if she has to put herself in the limelight to create it.

The Queen of Wands is the most social of all the tarot Queens and can be found at all kinds of gatherings. This is where

---

445 *The Contest of Horus and Seth for Rule IV, in **Ancient Near Eastern Texts Relating to the Old Testament**, ed. James B. Pritchard, p. 15. Princeton University Press, 1969.*

she truly shines and where she performs her best work. Hathor had a yearly festival during which thousands of vessels of beer were drunk, celebrating the coming of the Nile Inundation but also preventing it from overflooding. This festival commemorated the mythological tale of Hathor and Sekhmet destroying mankind, in which Hathor was asked by the gods to destroy mankind, which had become evil and selfish. She did so, destroying only the evil ones, but soon became filled with bloodlust and transformed into Sekhmet destroying everything in her path. The only way to stop her was for the priests to stain the Nile red with ochre and pour into it 7,000 vessels of beer, which Sekhmet drank thinking it was blood. Intoxicated, she fell asleep, and returned to peace once more. [446] In this tale, Hathor, the lady of cats, became so angry that she turned into Sekhmet, lady of lions, and the beast overtook her. In the same way, the Queen of Wands in her anger is uncontrollable, vicious and destructive. The fires of her rage spread quickly and burn indiscriminately.

Over time the symbols of the Egyptian goddess of cats, Bast, were assimilated into the worship of Hathor, who was originally represented by a cow. The cow's horns can still be seen on the headdress of Hathor, along with the red sun-disk reminding us that she is the daughter of the sun god Ra. As the cow goddess, Hathor was a mother, representing the perpetual fecundity of nature. As the goddess of cats, she was a mistress of pleasure and fun, but these qualities are no less important than fertility. For the Queen of Wands, a life without joy and pleasure is a life not worth living.

Hathor had many names and epithets, just as the Queen of Wands has many faces. She was called "Lady of the House of Jubilation", "The One Who Fills the Sanctuary with Joy",

---

446   E. A. Wallis Budge, ***Legends of the Egyptian Gods***, *pp. 15–23. Dover, 1994.*

"Lady of Dance", "Golden One" and "Lady of Heaven". One hymn from the fifth crypt of the Temple of Dendera (the centre of Hathor's cult in later periods), calls upon her in terms of celebration, as "Mistress of Harp-Playing, "Mistress of Leaping", "Lady of Music" and "Lady of Unending Drunkenness". [447]

The blue lotus flowers that bloom at the feet of the Queen of Wands were sacred in ancient Egypt. They close up at night and reopen in the morning to take in the sun, so they were seen as symbolic of the sun's descent into the underworld at night and rebirth from the body of Nut in the morning. They were also the more strongly perfumed of the two types of lotuses native to ancient Egypt (the blue lotus, *Nymphaea coerulea*, is actually a water lily, but called a lotus in ancient Egypt), and songs were sung for the lotus at parties and social gatherings. This flower reminds us of the optimism of the Queen of Wands, who opens to the light but turns away from darkness; it also represents her all-pervading beauty and enchantment.

The Queen of Wands is often found in the same place as her husband, the King of Wands, because they play off each other and feed each other, thus ensuring that their inner fires are forever burning. In ancient Egypt, Hathor was the wife of Horus (see *King of Wands*) and each had a cult centre: the former at Dendera, the latter at Edfu. Once a year, at the Festival of the Beautiful Reunion, the sacred statues of these deities would be taken from their respective temples and carried on a journey of more than 100 miles to meet each other, initiating a fourteen-day festival during which the statues were kept together in the temple at Edfu, husband and wife once more, bringing joy, love, laughter and fertility to the people and the land. The

---

447 ***Dendérah. Description générale du grand temple de cette ville.*** *Francois Auguste Ferdinand Mariette, 3.60. 1875. Translated by Neferuhethert, 2002, http://www.hethert.org/hymnsprayers.htm. Accessed 30/12/2012.*

boat that the statue of Hathor was carried on was called "Great of Love", reminding us that the Queen of Wands has a heart that is always open, always willing and always in love with everybody around her.

∽ Revelation

Nurturing of passion and desires; channelling energy and desire in the right direction; carrying the drive of others; inspiring action in others; nurturing the sensual, sexual self; immersing oneself in one's passions; experiencing the fullness of life; a social butterfly; a host; welcome; charm; enchantment; centre of attention; commanding the attention and love of others; being admired for one's natural talents; allowing oneself to have fun; social gatherings; encouraging the pleasure and enjoyment of others.

Negatively aspected...
Somebody with a destructive and wide-reaching temper; a spoiled brat, somebody demanding attention that does not deserve it; a drama-queen; social manipulation; magic used for destructive purposes; seduction as a means to an end.

King of Wands

Horus, God of Magic, Rulership and Ascension

The sun does not die at midnight, nor does the power of light wane in the presence of darkness. I am the light, the source of all flashing fire and cosmic brilliance. I am the sun at its height of power, its dawning and setting; I am the sun in the netherworld, where it battles for life. How would you fight for yours? You who are as imperishable as the stars in the body of Nut, I challenge you to walk with me on the roads only the fires of the sun can take. Magic is my mother, Resurrection my father; Chaos is my brother and my enemy and from him I take the rulership of all. I offer you this sovereignty if you can bear it – power in its rawest form, living on the edge of the wild places. I am the Far-strider; I walk the flaming sands of my desire and am not burned. I stretch my wings over the land and my rule is not questioned; those that follow me love me and those that hate me admire me. I am the highest of the high, flashing fire across the sky to inspire, achieve, and destroy my enemies. All before me is tamed by my will. If you can look upon me and not be blinded you may know the roads of ascension to greatness, for you are born from the fire and power of the sun, the source of all life in the heavens, upon the earth and beneath it; you are more than flesh, more than breath, more than thought and action. So I challenge you, Imperishable Star: step forward and claim the contest. Prove to the world your worth and strength: only actions provide the foundation for success. Do your will.

~ Mystery

In his exalted position as highest ruler of the suit of Fire, the King of Wands is the pinnacle of energy, action, passion, drive, ambition and will. As Fire is the element closest to spirit and furthest away from manifestation, this King is also the furthest

removed from material concerns and the most energetic and powerful. As the sovereign of will and power, he can attain anything he desires through correct direction of his will and ambition. To some this may seem like magic, but to him it is a foregone conclusion: results are assured when you direct your will and energy single-mindedly and with force and passion. Blazing into life and vitality, the King of Wands is a light that cannot be extinguished, a source of infinite energy, a courageous inspirer of others and an imperishable soul bringing light to every path he walks.

In the *Tarot Apokalypsis* the King of Wands is Horus, the warrior-ruler god of Upper and Lower Egypt, son of Isis and Osiris, enemy of Set. As his father's successor he took over the rulership of the land and the crown of the living Pharaoh, while his father continued to rule in the afterlife, watching over the dead Pharaoh. In many texts Horus is equated with the Pharaoh and his immortal soul, helping him ascend to the stars after death, there to live eternally. Many of his epithets portray him in terms of distance and height, and some authors suggest that his name means "he who is above". [448] In the *Pyramid Texts* he is called "Far-strider" and "great one, son of a great one", [449] indicating his wide-reaching and well-established rulership. These texts frequently associate him with the horizon, the sun and stars, likening him to the sun that gives life and light and rises daily from the darkness of the underworld, victorious. He is called "living of dawnings" and "the star which illuminates the sky" [450] and was syncretised in the later Dynastic eras with Ra, the sun god, as Ra-Horakhty (Ra, who is Horus of the Two

---

448 E. A. Wallis Budge, **The Gods of the Egyptians**, *Vol. 1, p. 466. Dover Publications, 1969.*

449 R. O Faulkner trans. **The Ancient Egyptian Pyramid Texts** *853; 852, p. 152 and p. 151. Oxford University Press, 1969.*

450 **Ibid.**, *7; 8; 362, p. 2 and p. 75.*

Horizons). Horus was seen as one of the most important gods in ancient Egypt, representing life at its most vital, rulership, protection and power. Of all the Kings of the tarot, the King of Wands, as Fire of Fire, is the highest. He is "at the head of the Imperishable Stars". [451]

Through his association with Ra, Horus became seen as a solar deity and god of light. Like the sun his power did not die at night but instead travelled through the underworld – he was invincible. As Heru-khuti, Horus of the Two Horizons, "[he] represented the sun in his daily course across the skies from the time he left the Mount of Sunrise […] to the time when he entered the Mount of Sunset". [452]

As a reminder of the invincibility of Horus (and therefore the soul of the dead Pharaoh), the *Pyramid Texts* tell us that, "Hemnw, Eastern Horus, Eastern Soul, and Harakhte, treated as one god, passes the night in evening-barque and wakes in morning-barque". This is reminiscent of the all-encompassing vitality of the King of Wands. A morning hymn to the sun addresses Horus, and reminds us that he, and the King of Wands, is the highest of the high, with nobody in command of him:

"May you sleep in the Night-bark,
May you wake in the Day-bark
For you are he who oversees the gods,
There is no god who oversees you!" [453]

In his solar form Horus was often called upon to aid the dead king, particularly for purification, ascent, deification and rule. Just as the fire purifies, so its flames and heat ascend ever-upwards. Fre-

---

451 **Ibid.**, *1301, p. 206.*
452 *E. A. Wallis Budge,* **The Gods of the Egyptians**, *Vol. 1, p. 470.*
453 *R. O Faulkner trans.* **The Ancient Egyptian Pyramid Texts**, *1479, p. 228.*

quently, the soul of the dead Pharaoh was likened to the light of solar Horus: "Re causes the king to shine as Horus".[454] The King of Wands, similarly, continually rises, achieving ever greater heights.

The Eye of Horus – the symbol tattooed in fiery red on our Horus' chest – was identified with the sun.[455] This Eye of Horus, called Wadjet, was a symbol of protection and royal power given by Horus or Ra; it is often seen on images of Horus' mother Isis and deities associated with her. Wadjet is derived from "*wadj*", meaning "green", and was known to the Greeks and Romans as the uraeus, from the Egyptian "*iaret*", meaning "risen one". In the *Pyramid Texts* the Eyes of Horus is used to help the dead king ascend to Horus:

"O King, I am your son, I am Horus; I have come and I bring to you Horus' own Eyes; seize them and join them to yourself. I have joined them to you and have united them to you, for they are complete. Horus [has put] them on this King's feet that they may guide [this] King [to the firmament, to Horus, to the sky, to the] great [god, that he may protect] this King from all his foes." [456]

This ascension is repeated throughout Egyptian funerary texts, with Horus leading the dead Pharaoh to the stars. He "takes his hand and leads him to the place where Orion is".[457] Just like Horus, the King of Wands urges us ever higher, invites us to rise above what we perceive as our limitations and rise to every challenge; he reminds us that we are imperishable spirits that

---

454 *Ibid.*, 2036, p. 292.
455 Thomas George Allen, **Horus in the Pyramid Texts**, p. 13. University of Chicago: 1916.
456 *Ibid.*, 70–71, pp. 23–24.
457 *Ibid.*, 802, p. 144.

are filled with vitality, power, energy and fire. We are made from stardust, from the same stuff as the sun, the great men and women of the past, those who will come after us, the earth around us: what greatness awaits us and has gone before us! What an important part we play in this universe!

Important to the myths of Horus are his warlike nature and his victory over his enemy, Set (see *Prince of Wands*). In *The Contendings of Horus and Set* we find a story of how Horus and Set fought for rulership over Upper and Lower Egypt. They had many battles and arguments, but eventually Horus showed himself to be the dominant god and took the rulership of both lands, succeeding Osiris as the king. In a text from the walls of the temple of Edfu, he is presented as going to war against the enemies of Ra, against Set and his minions in the form of dangerous creatures. He also took the form of a winged disk to fight, and emanated a piercing light that burned his enemies to death.

The form presented in the card image is closest to Heru-Behetet, the form of Heru-Khuti that prevailed in the heavens at midday, typifying the greatest power of the heat of the sun. In this form he went to war against his enemies, Set and Typhon, and destroyed them, and he is seen as light gaining victory over darkness. He bears the ankh, the symbol of life, upon his loins, reminding us of the generative and vital power of the King of Wands, and carries the two staffs of rulership in his right hand; in his left he wields a staff of magical power, topped with the red solar disk, which he also wears as his crown. His headdress is in the form of a hawk, the bird that often represented him, and at his feet is the snake that represents his enemies and evil forces. He steps forth from the midday sun and walks a path forwards, from one horizon to the other.

~ Revelation

A leader; figure of authority; role model; charismatic leader; host; facilitator; owning one's power; will power; the ability to direct one's will and energy towards a goal; the pinnacle of one's ambition; rising above; ascension; shining one's ability and light to others; showing one's strengths; exceeding expectations; inspiring others to greatness; controlling a situation; creating change in accordance with one's will; vitality; unstoppable force; unceasing activity; grasping opportunities.

Negatively aspected...
A boast; a charlatan; somebody who manipulates others using charisma; using one's position of power for the wrong ends; a controlling boss; weak will; burning out through too much activity; failure to get one's own way; being at the mercy of another; being a victim of social manipulation.

Princess of Swords

Sága, Goddess of Knowledge, Discourse and Learning

How many words have you spoken in your years? Did they fall from your mouth accidentally, or were they chosen with care in the knowledge that every utterance from your lips creates and perpetuates the universe? Words bear the sign of the gods, for they make their mark upon the world for good or ill. Learn to discount nothing in thought and speech. There is magic in these words and in the silence between them, in the intake of breath – the inspiration – necessary to fuel them. You, like the gods, can speak the divine word, bringing it down to the earth; you need only speak to create reality. To draw down to manifestation our thoughts and ensure they cannot be changed they must be written; thereafter they may be shown to others and challenged. Writing is as sacred as the speech that precedes it; the act of putting into form your nascent ideas is holy. But what is worthy of note and record? I question continually, for without asking there can be no challenge, no freedom in thought or speech. Never be afraid to ask and question. Challenge every idea, every word. I am the container of all knowledge and wisdom and it is in my hall that runs the river of knowledge. Here I meet each day with the Wanderer, the Wise One: we share of the waters of knowledge and together we create the world anew from debate and discourse. You may not find me in your heart, for I rarely reside in your passions: find me in the mind and speech of the sages and in the pages of books. There, if you challenge and question, give form to thought and manifest ideas, I will grant you the keys to wisdom.

∞ Mystery

Like her sisters, although the Princess of Swords is the lowest of her Court she performs a vital role. Residing in the suit of Air, the suit of the mind, thoughts, words and communication, the earthy role of the Princess serves to bring ideas into manifestation, apply theories to the real world and contain wisdom and knowledge. The Princess of Swords represents all the ways in which we store knowledge, ideas and wisdom, and all the ways our ideas and thoughts impact upon the world around us. She asks us to consider how our words shape our world, for it is in her realm that we find thoughts becoming reality. Since she is the youngest of her Court she also brings youth and nascence, representing the beginnings of research, the foundational steps towards an idea being put to use, plans being made to manifest new ideas and revolutionary ideas that challenge traditionally accepted wisdom. Since she is both Earth and Air, she can correspond with the grounding and containing of the mind, thought and intellect, or she can correspond with the breaking down of constructs with the application of the mind.

In the *Tarot Apokalypsis* these processes are depicted as the ásynjur Sága, a goddess who resides in her hall Sökkvabekk, who is seldom mentioned in the Eddas. Due to the lack of reference to her in the available literature, a complete study of her is impossible; she is not given any stories or myths, nor do we know anything of her personality – not once do we read anything she has spoken. However, many later scholars have extrapolated from the few references we have and have commented upon the figure of Sága. It is clear that she is an important goddess: in a list of the ásynjur (female deities) she is mentioned second only to Frigg herself, Odin's wife. [458]

---

458 *Snorri Sturluson,* **Gylfaginning** *35,* **Prose Edda** *trans. Anthony Faulkes, Everyman, 2002.*

Listing her as second-highest of the ásynjur is interesting for a goddess spoken about so rarely, yet we should not consider it unusual given the lack of information about most of the goddesses in the literature. Where goddesses (such as Frigg and Freyja) are given stories, they usually act and speak in reference to their male counterparts and rarely act independently. Some of the most vital aspects of the universe are ascribed to female figures: Idunn, the goddess who looks after the apples of youth on which the Aesir rely to maintain their immortality and power, is mentioned little and given few words and actions. Sága is similar in that she performs what would appear to be an important role in the cosmology despite her near-absence from the literature.

The etymology of her name sheds some light on her role. There are two main theories surrounding it: first, that it is connected to the Old Norse *sjá*, "to see", and second that it is linked to the words *saga* and *segja*, "to say" or "to tell". [459] The word "saga" has become the name given to the ancient Icelandic texts from 1150–1400 CE, which were likely to have originally been oral tales. The sagas have many things in common with epics, often telling the tales of great deeds performed by men, battles, voyages and the lives of kings. This use of the term "saga" carries with it associations of history and narrative [460] and of what was once fluid in oral form being set down in accepted tradition. Her etymological associations with the verb "to see" have led to suggestions that Sága is a seeress, [461] with the ability to prophecy.

Sága, with all her associations of speech, seeing, history and narrative, is described in the *Grímnismál* as being a daily drinking

---

459 Rudolf Simek, trans. Angela Hall. ***Dictionary of Northern Mythology***, p. 274. D S Brewer, 2007.
460 John Lindow, ***Norse Mythology: A Guide to Gods, Heroes, Rituals and Beliefs***, pp. 26. Oxford University Press, 2002.
461 Andy Orchard, ***Dictionary of Norse Myth and Legend***, p. 136. Cassell, 1997.

companion of Odin in her hall Sökkvabekk, "where cool waves flow". [462] Images of Sága usually depicts her in this place, conversing with Odin, pouring him drink, or both. We can imagine them discussing events of the day or having heated debates while enjoying a drink together. That Odin is a god of wisdom makes this image even more appealing: their relationship is clearly one of equals. The etymology that links her name with the verb "to say" gives us a striking image of long discourses between Sága and the Gallows God, and her association as a seeress has led people to wonder if Odin consulted her for advice.

Sökkvabekk's name is translated as "sunken bank", "sunken bench" and "treasure bank" and it is clearly a place near a water source. In Norse myth, liquid is used as a symbol for wisdom and poetry (which is synonymous with wisdom in the literature), both in the form of water and mead. In *Skáldskaparmál* 5 we find the mead of poetry, coveted by the gods and stolen by Odin; Odin sacrifices his eye for a drink from the well of Mimir, which contains all wisdom and intelligence; it is a well of water by which the Norns who shape men's destinies dwell, located in the roots of Yggdrasil (see *Ace of Swords*). Later, the waters of Sökkvabekk were associated with those from the well of Urd beneath Yggdrasil [463] and therefore with the powers of fate and wisdom. Grimm suggests that the drink that Odin and Sága share is the drink of immortality and poetry, and states that wise women, goddesses who shape destiny, Norns, *etc*. dwell besides springs and wells. [464]

---

462 *Grímnismál 7*, **The Poetic Edda**, *trans. Henry Adams Bellows, 1936.*

463 *Britt-Mari Näsström,* "**Freyja and Frigg - two aspects of the Great Goddess**" *in* **Shamanism and Northern Ecology: Papers presented at the Regional Conference on Circumpolar and Northern Religion**, *ed. Juha Pentikäinen, pp. 88–89. Mouton de Gruyter: 1990.*

464 *Jacob Grimm, trans. James Steven Stallybrass,* **Teutonic Mythology: Translated from the Fourth Edition with Notes and Appendix,** *vol. III, pp. 910–911. George Bell and Sons, 1888.*

As the Princess of Swords is the container of wisdom and thoughts, we can imagine Sága as a keeper of knowledge, the font of history and wisdom to whom even Odin turns for advice. That her name has been given to the written form of the tales that are so important in Old Norse gives her a role as a keeper of records, a guardian of writing and the ways in which nascent thoughts become manifest. In the card image she points directly at us, challenging and contesting our accepted ideas to encourage fresh ways of thinking. She stands near her river and raises her other hand to the sky from which all thoughts come – the element of air. Her sword, unsheathed from its scabbard on her belt, has been driven into the trunk of the tree – air being contained and held in earth, ideas becoming manifest – and light from the heavens illuminates it as if Sága's raised hand has drawn it down for that purpose. Either side of her we see ravens, Odin's sacred bird, representing thought and memory and reminding us of her link with wisdom; on her belt hangs a mead horn bearing Odin's face. Her scroll case represents recorded words, ideas and all forms of writing, and the keys on her belt remind us that she is a woman of power.

Revelation

The foundation of knowledge; grounding of the intellect; manifestation of ideas; theory applied; records and writing; history and wisdom that has come to pass; speech, discourse and debate; protecting records in all forms; a container of wisdom; the source of an idea; the beginnings of an intellectual project; study and becoming a student; a practical approach to learning; the power of words to shape the world around us; revolutionary ideas; an intellectual person keen to engage with new ideas and find their foundation; architects, authors, librarians and record-keepers.

Negatively aspected…
Lack of ability to apply knowledge to the real world; untestable hypotheses; reluctance to challenge and test an idea; studies and research that have no foundation; an idea that lacks staying power; writer's block; disrespect for study; changing history to suit one's own purposes.

Prince of Swords

Loki, God of Rebellion, Cunning and Deceit

They have called me Sky-Treader and Mind-Tester, Slanderer, Originator of Deceit, Lie-smith, Most-Cunning and Adversary of the Gods. A plethora of words accompany me, yet they beguile away from the truth: I am not to be bound or set down. The very gods tried to bind me beneath the earth and still I broke free of my chains. You cannot cage an idea or an implacable spirit. They have called me Air and Sky, Thunder and Fire; great is my reputation, feared is my name. They swear oaths and make laws, casting judgement upon those that would break them, yet those very oaths bind them from action and triumph: then they ask the Serpent-Father, the one who can speak and do what is taboo. Then I trick and twist the world to my ends—to their ends—and I revel in my artifice. I am my only master and I serve no mistress except she who is called World-Breaker. The truth cannot help but rush forth from within me, tripping over my tongue and aiming, sharp, at its audience. You wish to hide your sins, cower in secrecy and paint your ugliness with niceties? I shall destroy these façades and take you up into a storm of strife. I am the necessary truth that heralds battle; I am the breaker of chains and the liberator; when I speak I change the world.

≈ Mystery

"That one is also reckoned among the Aesir whom some call the Aesir's culminator and originator of deceits and the disgrace of all gods and men. […] Loki is pleasing and handsome in appearance, evil in character, very capricious in behaviour. He possessed to a greater degree than others the kind of learning that is called cunning, and tricks for every

purpose. He was always getting the Aesir into a fix and often got them out of it by trickery." [465]

This Prince resides in the suit of Swords, ruled by the lofty and intellectual element of Air. Like his brothers, he is also associated with Air through his rank, and so he is the Airy part of Air, or the most quintessential Air Court card. He is Air at its most swift, communicative, rushing and conceptual; like the other Court cards that are quintessential of their element (Princess of Pentacles, Queen of Cups and King of Wands) this gives him great strengths but also great downfalls.

The Prince of Swords is characterised by his endless rushing about. He is unable to stay in one place for any given time, physically, emotionally, intellectually or spiritually. Unlike his younger sister, the Princess of Swords, who puts her mind to practical application, the Prince perceives and conceives quickly but fails to apply his logic or intellectual understanding. He believes he does not need study: after all, he is naturally gifted with genius. The Prince of Swords has a natural aptitude for learning the abstract and conceptual and is at his best when debating or discussing a lofty concept. Where the Princess of Swords has knowledge, the Prince of Swords has intellect; where she listens and receives wisdom, he talks endlessly of what he knows. The saying that "the pen is mightier than the sword" is especially true for the Prince of Swords, for with a single word he can destroy reputations, manipulate facts and history, twist situations to his ends, inspire others and put rulers on their thrones. However, it is also true that he is "all talk and no trousers". At his worst he is full of hot air, bragging and besting others intellectually to belittle them.

---

465 Snorri Sturluson, ***Gylfaginning*** 34, ***Prose Edda***, *trans. Anthony Faulkes, p. 26. Everyman, 2002.*

Being found in the suit of Swords also gives this Prince a war-like demeanour. He often finds causes he considers worthy of championing (though he loses interest in them quickly), but he is also a rebel without a cause, constantly finding something to question, challenge and break down. He despises authority and often speaks harsh truths that figures in authority do wish to hear. People often attempt to silence him, but he always breaks free, reminding us that truth and ideas can never be chained.

In the *Tarot Apokalypsis* the Prince of Swords is Loki, the adversary of the gods and blood-brother of Odin. [466] One of his other names is Loptr, "air/sky", giving him an airy quality that is borne out by his demeanour and actions in the myths. Although he turns against the gods later in the tales, that he is a sworn brother to Odin tells us how important he is to the gods. Where they had created laws and made oaths, they often found that they were unable to do something they wanted, so they would call upon Loki to perform the taboo deeds on their behalf. His nature as trickster allowed him to traverse the boundaries created by morality and oaths. [467]

One story tells how the Aesir made a deal with a builder to create an impenetrable citadel that could not be overcome by giants. The builder demanded as payment the sun, the moon and the goddess Freyja. The gods agreed on the condition that he built the citadel in a single winter without help from any man. The builder asked that he could have aid from his stallion, Svadilfari. Loki counselled them that this would not be a problem, so the gods agreed. However, Svadilfari was a strong horse: with his help the citadel was almost complete three days

---

466 *Lokasenna* 9, ***The Poetic Edda*** *trans. Carolyne Larrington, p. 86. Oxford University Press, 1996.*

467 *Klaus-Peter Koepping,* **"Absurdity and Hidden Truth: Cunning Intelligence and Grotesque Body Images as Manifestations of the Trickster"***, p. 203, in* ***History of Religions****, vol. 24, no. 3 (Feb., 1985), pp.191–204.*

before the season was done. The gods were worried: they had agreed to a price they could not pay. They decided that Loki, who had counselled them into agreeing to the deal, would get them out of it. That night a mare emerged from the forest and tempted Svadilfari away; the following day Svadilfari was too tired to work. The builder, in his rage at seeing that he would not finish his work, revealed himself to be a giant. The gods could go back on the deal and Thor killed him. Some months later, Loki gave birth to a foal. [468]

His ability to shapeshift and disguise himself in various myths reminds us that the Prince of Swords can be manipulative and uses his cunning and wit to outsmart others – sometimes for no other reason than to "get one over" on them. In *Prose Edda* Loki engineers the death of Baldr by disguising himself as a negligible old woman in order to gain information and by shapeshifting into a stubborn giantess in order to ensure Baldr stayed in Hel (see *Three of Swords*). [469] It is from tales like this that Loki gained the epithet *frumkveði flærðanna,* "originator of deceit".

Loki's cunning served the gods well in many instances, and one of the kennings for his name is *Lævísi*, "cunning-wise". One tale tells how Loki helped disguise Thor as a bride to gain back his stolen hammer from the giants, and how he used clever words and misdirection to cover for Thor's very unladylike habits at the wedding feast. [470] However, throughout the myths he is a thief and a rebel, deliberately flouting the gods and their laws. He stole Idunn's apples of youth and Freyja's necklace Brisingamen. He is called "Mind-tester of the warrior of battle

---

468 Snorri Sturluson, **Gylfaginning** 42, *Prose Edda, trans. Anthony Faulkes, pp. 35–36.*

469 ***Ibid.**, 49, pp. 48–51.*

470 **Thrym's Poem**, *The Poetic Edda, trans. Carolyne Larrington, pp. 97–101.*

thunder", [471] indicating he tries the patience of Thor, and puts his careful, cunning words in opposition to the explosive, angry god of war.

It is his cutting words that Loki uses when he tips his precarious balance with the gods over the edge in the most interesting of the myths in which he features, *Lokasenna* (the Quarrel of Loki). Here we see Loki at his finest, his most cruel, his most malicious and vindictive, yet with words to make poets envious and nothing but truth as their content. [472] This tale reminds us that although Loki intended to hurt the gods, he told only the truth – despite his epithet "Lie-smith". The truths that he reveals are painful, and the gods they concern had obviously tried to keep them hidden. Loki, like the Prince of Swords, cannot abide the high and mighty pretending they are better than others – he eschews authority, and seeks any way he can find to tear it down, or at the very least embarrass it.

This outburst led the gods to capture Loki and bind him beneath the earth with the entrails of his son; they placed above his head a snake that dripped venom onto his face constantly, causing him immense agony. Even this binding, however, could not hold him back from being an adversary to the gods. The Norse myths foretell a catastrophe for the gods, Ragnarök, in which they will fight against the giants and the unworthy dead, and will die. Although it is not stated how Loki gets free from his chains beneath the earth, he leads the fire giants on that dreadful battle day to fight against the gods. [473]

The Prince of Swords cannot be chained or bound; his mind is cunning and crafty, his words shrewd and clever; to tie him

---

471 *Þórsdrápa* 1:5–8.
472 *Lokasenna*, **The Poetic Edda** *trans. Carolyne Larrington, pp. 84–96.*
473 *Voluspa* 51, **The Poetic Edda**, *trans. Carolyne Larrington, p. 10.*

down to one place, one thing, or one idea is difficult if not impossible. Like a rebel without a cause he will always break free, ready to challenge and fight against the status quo.

∽ Revelation

Champion of many causes; champion of truth; speaking unwanted truth; revealing the secrets of another; a cunning and shrewd mind or approach; careful and manipulative words; inability to commit to one thing; the mind at its most intellectual; the conceptual and abstract; politics and politicians; debate and discussion; ideas in an unfocused state; moving from one idea to another; anti-authoritarian or iconoclastic ideals; rebellion; refusing to be limited; seeking intellectual challenges; somebody who gets bored easily.

Negatively aspected…
Using truth to hurt; trouble-making and causing mischief; misdirection and misleading; lack of intellectual focus; a rival or adversary; destroying something out of boredom; rebel without a cause.

Queen of Swords

The Völva, the Wisewoman who Teaches and Speaks Truth

You call me for wisdom and truth, you welcome me and set me upon the High Seat, you offer to me warmth, yet you fear me. Know you not the kindness I show you? Know you not the love I bear you when I let the vapours take me and the wyrd-song carry my spirit in-between? My Mother is the great abyssal waters and the wondrous expansive air is my Father; I am the child of seeing, the daughter of prophecy and wisdom, the mother of the knowledge of the weave of the world. Let me speak and I will tell of the unknown, the forgotten, the mysteries. Let me see, and I will know the truth that lies behind the smoke, the wisdom hidden in ignorance, the honesty covered in lies. Use my answers as you will, but know that my sister is the valkyrie and truth is as sure a weapon as the hand that wields it. Hear me now, Freyja, great mistress! See my work and hear my words! I weave and spin, I sing the songs to open the roads, I breathe in the smoke. Possessor of the fallen slain, fair-tear deity, I work the seidr in your name so that the truth of all may be shown. You who welcome me and fear me: see here the weave and weft of the web the Norns have given to you; see the wyrd that connects you to all. You desire to know your fate, your place in this world, the truth that surrounds you yet you cannot see: here it is.

⇝ Mystery

The pursuit of knowledge has united humankind for millennia. There are many ways that knowledge has been sought, with teaching being the quintessential method of gaining wisdom. The Queen of Swords is a teacher, but her teaching is not that found in the Hierophant, who teaches based on authority, received wisdom and establishments. She is the encouragement

to think for oneself, to open one's mind to wisdom and knowledge, the method of perceiving truth and of applying intellect. Where the Hierophant teaches facts, the Queen of Swords teaches method. She has an intimate understanding of the human mind and the connections that exist in the gaps between facts; she uses this to nurture wisdom in others. However, her insight is often given only to those who request it: she does not let knowledge drip from her tongue like honey, but uses it as a sword to cut directly through lies, ignorance and deceit. When she speaks, those who listen grow in desire for wisdom and truth. Where she is advocate, her precisely chosen words channel the deepest truths.

In the *Tarot Apokalypsis*, the Queen of Swords is the Norse völva, a seeress. She is seated on a richly dressed throne covered in furs. Her sacred wand – the distaff – can be seen in its place on the spinning wheel, but it is not ordinary thread that is woven here. The web of gold, with light glinting like diamonds, is gently caressed by our prophesying Queen as she sees into the web of *wyrd* – the web that unites the fates of men and women with each other and that of the universe. This web would otherwise appear tangled to us, too vast to understand and too complex to navigate, but the Queen of Swords has the ability to follow its threads and unravel the connections between all things. It is this gift that she uses to bring forth wisdom and knowledge in others: by showing the connections, others can follow them and reach their own conclusions. The depth and breadth of the knowledge of the Queen of Swords can be seen in the *Voluspa*, in which a völva tells of the beginnings of the world, the birth of humankind and the eventual end of the world. She begins by demonstrating the age of her wisdom, stating that she remembers the ancient histories of men and gods from the first. [474]

---

[474] *Voluspa 1*, **The Poetic Edda**, *trans. Carolyne Larrington, p. 4. Oxford University Press, 1999.*

As the Queen of Swords plays her fingertips over the golden web of fate, we are reminded of her link with the Norns, the three *dísir* (spirits) who ruled over fate. In the Norse worldview, every person had their own individual fate, called *ørlǫg*, which was born with them, carried throughout their lives, and intertwined with the *ørlǫg* of others; all these fates woven together created the greater web of *wyrd*, the web of the universe. In the language of the Queen of Swords we are reminded of the consequences of our every action, word and thought – no man is an island, and everything we do to our strand of the web we do to others.

The Queen of Swords has a keen eye and a naturally heightened perception, and it is these skills that she uses when she puts her mind to the details that other people might miss. The 12th-century *Saxo Grammaticus* said of the ability and power of the völva to see into the weave of the universe and the lives of people that, "[t]he power of her songs was so great that she seemed to be able to see into perplexing affairs however entangled with knots and far away". [475]

The sacred distaff held by the Queen of Swords is well attested in historical and mythological texts regarding seeresses; it is also a symbol of a woman in charge of her household, as are the keys that hang from her belt. As a sign of authority and power in her own realm, the woman of the household wears the keys of the house upon her person. As with all the Queens of the tarot, the Queen of Swords finds her home in the passive world of Water; thus, we find that even this most outspoken of Queens works in a more private realm, just as her historical counterparts did. She asks us to remember that there are often

---

475 **Saxo Grammaticus**, Gesta Danorum Liber VII, quoted in **A Sourcebook of Seið**, p. 14, trans. ed. Stephen E. Flowers and James A. Chisholm. Runa-Raven Press, 2002.

subtler ways of owning and wielding power and authority than at the point of a blade, through volume of words or rank of birth. The silence of the Queen of Swords is as powerful as her speech and she says as much in her moments of pause as she does when she is talking. In those moments her eyes examine you, seeing every part of you, extracting all the information available to her through perception. The weapon of her suit, the Sword, gives this Watery woman the keen edge of reason, the sharp cunning that she shares with the King of Swords, and the unsurpassable genius of her Court. Her sword is at rest and her hand gently holds the pommel expectantly, once again reminding us that we do not always need to brandish brashly our knowledge and intelligence to make a difference.

As a priestess of Freyja, the völva is also a sister to the valkyries, the battle-maidens who liberated the bravest slain warriors from their bodies on the battlefield and carried them to Valhalla, where they would feast in the afterlife (see *Ten of Swords*). This reminds us that the sword of truth that rests at the side of the Queen can be used in battle as well as in peace.

The Queen of Swords makes an excellent advocate, speaking on behalf of others who may not be as skilled in the arts of oratory or mental acuity; as the mother of the mind she gives of her knowledge, perception and intelligence freely, seeing it as nourishing and nurturing. In the same way, the völva is the advocate of the gods and spirits, delivering their knowledge to humankind and allowing them to make informed decisions. In particular, she is dedicated to the goddess Freyja, who brought the knowledge of *seið* to the gods of Asgard. *Seið* magic was sought after and feared, just as the Queen of Swords is, as truth can lead to both joy and pain. In the *Voluspa*, the völva Heið recalls the world's first war, during which a woman named Gullveig was killed and burned yet born again as Heið. Heið "came to houses, a seeress to prophesy well, she knew gand-magic, […] she worked *seið* playing with minds, she was always dear to evil women". [476] Here, *seið* magic is called "playing with minds", and indeed the Watery power of this Queen makes her a master of mental manipulation. She understands the malleability and mutability of the mind and can influence it. This makes her one of the most persuasive of the tarot Court, often taking on the role of persuader. It gives her an excellent mind for debate and a passion for philosophy, as she is able to change her own mind at will, dispassionately accepting the failure of her current position and strength of another. This lack of passion presents her as an ice queen, cold and emotionless, loveless and bitter. However, this Queen's ability to control her emotions allows her to keep them from interfering, so her decisions are always effective and swiftly reached.

As her inscrutable, unforgiving gaze indicates, the Queen of Swords does not suffer fools gladly, nor does she accept ignorance or excuses. In one saga we are told of a seeress who is brought to a household to prophesy; two sworn brothers refused to inquire of the seeress, saying that they did not wish to know their fate sooner that it happened, adding, "I don't think my lot in life comes from the roots of your tongue". This clear misunderstanding of cause and effect, and this refusal to seek truth, didn't sit well with the seeress, who told it all anyway. [477] Fate does not come from the Queen of Swords, but it can be seen, given and shared by her. In the same way, knowledge, wisdom and understanding are not found in her but elsewhere – yet she can show you them, offer them to you, nurture them within you and channel them in the right direction so they come more easily to you.

---

476 *Voluspa 21–23*, **The Poetic Edda**, trans. Carolyne Larrington, pp. 26–27.
477 **Vatnsdoela Saga**, ch. 10, quoted in **A Sourcebook of Seið**, p. 10, trans. ed. Stephen E. Flowers and James A. Chisholm.

∽ Revelation

A teacher, advocate, lawyer, barrister, guide; debate; a philosopher; somebody who encourages knowledge in others and nurtures thought and insight; the powers of perception; the ability to see the truth through ignorance and deceit; the growth of knowledge; sharing insight with others; group study; emotional detachment; objectivity; understanding of connections; method of enquiry.

Negatively aspected...
Bitterness; jealousy; words used to bring out the worst in people; lack of emotion causing difficulties; somebody unprepared to express themselves; difficulty in learning; somebody too shy to speak their mind; lack of confidence in one's ideas.

King of Swords
Odin, God of Wisdom, Sacrifice and Battle

Oh wanderer, brief walker of the world, what would you sacrifice for knowledge? What would you be willing to give in exchange for wisdom? What oaths would you make and what promises would you break for the knowing of truth? Do not let the weak ones lie to you that knowledge is gained by sleep-walking through the world. Knowledge is hard fought for, paid for in blood and bravery by those who dare to stand. I sacrificed my very self so that I might glimpse the wisdom of the mysteries in the deep. What would you give? What would you continue to do? Knowledge is not one thing to be held and caressed, but a thing to increase and fill; it can leave you easily should you lose grasp of it. Where are your eyes in the world? Where is the source of your wisdom? On my right hand is Memory and on my left is Thought: they are my wings covering the surface of the earth with shadow; where the shadows fall there falls also my reach of knowledge. I bear within me the knowledge of all the ages – no man can win a battle against me, no god nor monster can succeed. Knowledge has its own lineage and bloodline. What is the line of your knowledge? Is your mind as quick and active as the wolf pack that runs and hunts its prey? Are you worthy of my great Wild Hunt, swift of sword and quick-aiming of arrow? Will your shield shatter at the first strike of the battle? I am the grey-cloaked wanderer, and they have called me Grim, Flashing Eye, Gallows' Burden, Wise One, Advantage Counsel, Finder of Truth and Smith of Battle. I incite you to battle for wisdom, to not lay down your arms until the end.

~ Mystery

As the leader of the Court of the suit of Air, the King of Swords is the pinnacle of knowledge and the culmination of the quest for wisdom. As the Fiery part of Air, he is also the most active part of the quest for knowledge, representing the gaining of it as well as its use and application. The King of Swords is a wealth of insight, logic and wisdom; he is the active mind obtaining new insight and applying it to the world. He is a master tactician, viewing life as a battle or strategy game that must be fought, solved and outwitted. He reminds us that much of the knowledge we search for is not passively received through inaction but gained through striving, force and will. Sometimes we must sacrifice in order to gain wisdom; it often comes with a price. As such, the King of Swords can act as a blockage, demanding payment for knowledge before progress can be made. The truths that the King of Swords gives are harsh but they are necessary. He strives for facts and verifiable truth rather than inner wisdom and understanding. He does not suffer fools gladly. Often, the King of Swords stands in judgement over people, as he is impartial, logical and careful to make decisions. He stands witness to oaths and promises, dealing harshly and quickly with those who break them.

In the *Tarot Apokalypsis*, the King of Swords is Odin, the Norse god of language and knowledge; he was also a god of warfare. He is spoken about at great length in the Eddas and sagas and given an elevated position among the gods. In the Eddas we are told that he had a hand in organising the universe and giving humans life: the basic stuff of life already existed, but Odin, Haenir and Lodur shaped it and fixed it in place, giving order to chaos. The first man and woman, Ask and Embla, had no fate, breath, vital spark or spirit. Odin gave them breath. [478] It

---

478 Carolyne Larrington trans., ***Voluspa** 4; 17–18*, *The Poetic Edda*, p. 6.

is interesting that Odin gave order to the universe though he did not create it: the King of Swords is not creative but he is an organisational force that creates the order necessary for things to work correctly. The breath that Odin gave the first humans is symbolic of language, intelligence, the ability to give form to thoughts and put thoughts into action.

Odin's name means "The Furious One", believed to come from *óðr*. As an adjective, *óðr* means "mad, frantic, furious, violent" and as a noun "mind, wit, sense" or "song, poetry". This creates an image of a god who stirs up thought to the point of action and wages war where necessary to provoke and guard. Oaths must be made, terms agreed upon and territories stated; if any of these are broken, the ruthless nature of the King of Swords will call fury upon his enemy to enforce what was agreed. Describing a statue of Odin at the temple of Uppsala, an ancient writer says: "The other, Wotan – that is, the Furious – carries on war and imparts to man strength against his enemies." [479] Odin's fierce action is further expressed by his steed: Sleipnir, an eight-legged horse birthed by Loki (see *Prince of Swords*), the fastest horse in the world.

According to the *Voluspa*, Odin took part in the first war and hurled a spear over the enemy host. [480] From then, throwing a spear over an enemy army dedicated that army and all its dead to Odin. It also shows readiness for battle and draws a line in the sand. There are times for subtlety and there are times for clear and decisive action. The King of Swords rules both. It is upon Odin's spear – Gungnir – that unbreakable oaths were made. Contracts and oaths made before the King of Swords

---

479 **Gesta Hammaburgensis** 26. *Gesta Hammaburgensis Ecclesiae Pontificum. Translation in* **History of the Archbishops of Bremen**, *trans. Francis J. Tschan. Columbia University Press, 1959.*

480 *Carolyne Larrington trans.,* **Voluspa** 24, **The Poetic Edda**, *p. 6.*

are binding whether written or spoken; a serious reprisal meets those who break them.

As the father of battle, Odin was also the father of all the chosen glorious slain and of the valkryies, the battle maidens who rode into the aftermath of a battle and chose who of the brave dead would be taken to Odin's halls to feast in the afterlife (see *Ten of Swords*). These glorious slain become *einherjar* ("once warriors") in Valhalla, where they spend their time in sports, fighting, feasting and drinking, until Ragnarök (the end of the world) comes, when they fight alongside Odin and the other gods. In some folktales the dead who did not make it to Valhalla would join Odin in the Wild Hunt that rode across the skies during the cold months; various superstitions arose around this motif, but they all give to Odin the role of leader of the dead and leader of battle.

Odin had two other halls that he maintained as his residence: Gladsheim ("Bright Home"), where he presided over a council of twelve judges from Asgard, who regulated the affairs of Asgard and the Gods, and Valaskjalf ("The Shelf of the Slain"), where the high seat Hlidskalf was placed. From here Odin could perceive everything that happened in the worlds of gods and men. Odin's role as judge and law-keeper can be seen in Gladsheim, although like the King of Swords he stands apart and objective, giving power to others to enact what must be done. His ability to see everything in the world from his high seat at Valaskjalf reminds us of the King of Swords' immense capacity for perception, wisdom, knowledge and logic. He is a gatherer of information and a mind that immediately sees links and makes necessary conclusions.

Odin's wisdom is well attested throughout his myths. He had two ravens that he sent out into the world every morning to gather information, returning to him in the evening to tell him all they had discovered. Their names are telling – Munin ("memory") and Hugin ("thought") – indicating two of the most powerful aspects of the King of Swords. Odin fears for them, however, saying, "For Hugin I fear lest he come not home, but for Munin my care is more". [481] The King of Swords understands how precious knowledge and memory are, and how easy it is to lose them and thereby lose one's power. For Odin, the wisdom that his ravens bring are a way to consolidate his power and rulership, and he reminds us that the best actions and decisions are made with full information.

Odin often goes to extreme lengths to gain more knowledge. We are told in the *Gylfaginning* of a well in the roots of Yggdrasil that "has wisdom and intelligence contained in it, and the master of the well is called Mimir. He is full of learning because he drinks of the well from the horn Giallarhorn. All-father went there and asked for a single drink from the well, but he did not get one until he placed his eye as a pledge". [482] This is why Odin is often referred to as one-eyed. It shows what he was willing to sacrifice for knowledge, reminding us that knowledge and insight are not to be passively received but strived for, fought for, sacrificed for. Another myth tells of Odin using shapeshifting and trickery to win three draughts of the mead of poetry, which he carried in his beak as an eagle and spat out over the lands of the gods so they could drink of it and gain the gift of poetry. [483] This story reminds us of the deceptive side of the King of Swords: when angered, or when he deems it necessary, he is not above using trickery and cunning to get what he

---

481 Henry Adams Bellows trans., **Grimnismol** 20. **The Poetic Edda**, p. 92. Princeton University Press, 1936.

482 Snorri Sturluson, **Gylfaginning** 15, **Prose Edda,** p. 17, trans. Anthony Faulkes. Everyman, 2002.

483 Snorri Sturluson, **Skaldskaparmal** 58, **Prose Edda**, pp. 64–66.

wants. He delights in outwitting people and at his worst views the minds of others as inferior to his own, deserving of being tricked by their own lack of knowledge, forethought or insight. While he has no patience with those who lack intelligence or wisdom, he knows how to use this lack against them.

Perhaps the most important myth about Odin in which he gains knowledge through great sacrifice is that of his winning of the runes. In the *Havamal*, "Sayings of the High One", Odin hanged from Yggdrasil for nine days and nights with no food or drink, a sacrifice to himself (Odin's sacrifices were hanged). He finally gazed down into the roots of the cosmic tree and saw the mysteries of the runes. [484] He learned eighteen runes and their powers, and thus brought the knowledge of the runes to the world. The runes are knowledge of the universe, the workings of it, the way different parts of it interplay; by gaining the wisdom of them Odin gained wisdom of everything.

Odin is known to drink daily from the waters of Sökkvabekk with Saga (see *Princess of Swords*), the goddess of history, whose name is generally connected to the Old Norse verb for "to say" or "to see". [485] He is also said to make hanged men talk to him and raised a dead völva (seeress, see *Queen of Swords*) to question her about the future. Like the King of Swords, Odin will stop at nothing to obtain knowledge. It is unsurprising then that when the Roman historian Tacitus wrote about the chief god of the Germanic tribes (probably Odin) he named him Mercury [486] – Odin shares in common with him his swiftness of thought, his learning and knowledge, his cunning and his trickery.

---

484   Carolyne Larrington trans., **The Poetic Edda**, p. 34. Oxford University Press, 1999.
485   Henry Adams Bellows trans., **Grimnismol** 7. **The Poetic Edda**, p. 89.
486   Tacitus, **Germania**. Online at http://www.fordham.edu/halsall/source/tacitus1.html Accesed 28 July 2014.

⇜ Revelation

A judge, lawyer, lawmaker and law-keeper; protecting promises, oaths and contracts; a strategist and tactician; a great thinker; an intellectual leader; an expert in an academic field; achievement of knowledge; passion and drive feeding knowledge; active communication; reaching the culmination of research; a burning desire for knowledge; deduction; willingness to sacrifice for knowledge; ambitious ideas; excelling intellectually.

Negatively aspected...
Bad temper; clouded judgement; incorrect conclusions; oaths broken; contracts not honoured; a blockage; the full weight of the law being used negatively; a tyrant.

Princess of Cups

Psyche, Goddess of the Soul and Awakening

Humankind passes its time on earth in darkness, blind and veiled. Man shares this in kind with the greatest of the universe's mysteries, for though he is blinded he might be unveiled in revelation. To understand this teaching and descend into it you must know that until now you have been dreaming, entertained by shadows on a wall. You are the divine waiting to be born to liberty. I am the way of awakening. It is my feet that trod the first dew-dropped road down the river of stars and buried into the world the soul, fugitive from its origin. I made it one drop in the ocean of being, one flame in the darkness. I am the Breath of Life, the Soul and Spirit manifest in the cave, encased in wonder and beauty; I am the eyes that look upon the abode of earth with amazement and wonder. I carry within me all Joy, Pleasure and Vision, for like you I am a mystery enshrined in the temple of flesh and the universe does not end at my skin. I, in my wonder, found awakening, and in the darkness I held out a flame to behold the divine – there I fell in love with Love, and it answered back, falling in love with the Soul. The Soul is destined to be manifested in flesh, fallen and fragile yet sacred and eternal. This is the divine dichotomy: that you are at once the lowest and the greatest in potential. But imagine yourself not as a spirit alone, separated from the far shores of the divine; for you are an ocean teeming with life; you are a river that cannot be stepped into twice; you are the cup from which the world drinks, which is beheld at the moment of revelation; and it is your eyes that behold. Fall in love with Love, and you will wonder at the visions that are granted to you.

✑ Mystery

Like the other Princesses of the tarot, the Princess of Cups represents the element of Earth and its powers of manifestation,

containment, fertility and potential, expressed in her suit of Water. Her realm is diverse and vast, experienced frequently by all. When we fall in love, we feel the power of Water manifesting within us as something filled with potential. When we awaken to emotions we open like the flowers of the earth to receive nourishing rain and moisture; we must remember that our everyday life needs emotional input, an expression of love and a connection with other people or it will die like a plant unwatered. The Princess of Cups is therefore the awakening of the emotional self. As she is Earth of Water, this Princess often takes on the role of the beloved – the object of desire. As the element of Water pertains not only to emotion but also creativity and imagination, the Princess of Cups is the muse of the tarot, the inspirer of art and beauty; she is the moment when the artist begins to express their creative and imaginative urge. She is also the vision and the ability to read signs, dreams and oracles. She is the moment the dawning of inner understanding and the oracle or the sign given. Water can be seen as a symbol of the divine and therefore the soul, and in the Princesses the soul finds a home in Earth. Only in manifestation can the soul truly come alive.

In the *Tarot Apokalypsis*, the Princess of Cups is Psyche, the beautiful maiden from Lucius Apuleius' tale in his *Metamorphoses*. The tale is about the love between the soul and love itself (or desire). Psyche means "breath of life" or "soul" in Greek, and Cupid, her lover, is from *cupido* "desire", who is also Amor or Eros ("love", see *Prince of Cups*). Psyche is often represented in art as a butterfly, or given butterfly wings, symbolising the soul and wonder. [487] She transforms from a being

---

487 See, for instance, "The Abduction of Psyche", William Adolphe Bouguereau, 1895; "Psyche and Amor", François Gérard, 1798; "Cupid and Psyche", Jacques Louise David, 1817; and a 3rd-century Roman mosaic depicting Psyche looking upon a sleeping Eros, in which she has butterfly wings (currently in the Antakya Museum, Turkey).

exhibiting little emotion, blind to her own emotional self, to an awakened soul yearning for eternal love and reunion with the divine. It is this journey of awakening on an inner level that resonates with the Princess of Cups. Psyche is first presented as extremely beautiful, "so perfect that human speech was too poor to describe or even praise [her] satisfactorily". [488] The people of the city worshipped her as another form of Venus, so no man would marry her and her family worried. Her father prayed at the temple of the gods and was given an oracle: he must dress her for a funeral and take her to a mountain top where a monster would take her as its bride. Meanwhile, Venus herself heard of the worship that was given to this maiden and became angry; she asked her son, Cupid, to cause the maiden to fall in love with as foul a creature as he could find. When her parents left her atop the mountain, the wind carried her away to a beautiful palace in a meadow. Psyche was drawn in by amazement and wonder, learning from voices that bore no physical form that all this was hers. That night, an unseen man came to her bed, described as her husband, and made her his wife. Each night he came to her in darkness and she gradually fell in love with him. However, her sisters, jealous of her riches, convinced her – now pregnant – to kill her husband, as he was clearly some monstrous being. Psyche crept that night into her husband's bedchamber carrying a knife and a lamp. When she let the light shine upon her husband's face, she discovered that it was Cupid himself who had made her his wife; she saw Cupid's quiver of arrows and picked them up to look at them, cutting herself with one. In so doing she became "in love with Love […], ever more on fire with desire for Desire." [489] Some hot oil from the lamp spilled and burned Cupid's shoulder, waking him. Upon realising that he was discovered, he abandoned Psyche. The story continues with an account of three impossible tasks that Psyche

---

488   E. J. Kenney, *trans*. ***Cupid and Psyche***, *p. 1. Penguin Books, 2004.*
489   ***Ibid.***, *p. 23.*

had to complete to win back her husband, ending with Cupid waking her from a Stygian sleep, Jupiter blessing the marriage and Psyche being made immortal and married to Cupid eternally. After their divine marriage, Psyche gave birth to their daughter, Pleasure. [490] Of all the Court cards of the tarot, the Princess of Cups is perhaps the most playful and indulging of pleasures, particularly the simple ones. She reminds us that when we unite our souls with love we create pleasure in our lives.

At the beginning of the tale Psyche suffers by being put upon a pedestal and worshipped from afar. This points to the urge of the Princess of Cups to bring love down to earth. She does not desire to be adored nor to adore, but to simply be in love and wonder at its joys. It is this which makes her the perfect artist and muse: she allows an abstract emotional concept to be expressed in concrete form. The artist wants to make an abstract love real and attainable, drawing it down to earth. For the Princess of Cups this is an exaltation, for only in the world of experience can love, wonder, beauty and emotion thrive and increase. Psyche is both lover and beloved: she is at first desired by Cupid and later, once desire has awoken her emotional self, she falls in love with him (the soul falls in love with love). However, this is before another symbolic awakening, representative of an emotional awakening and an opening of the inner eyes that make beholding mystery possible. When Psyche disobeys her husband and takes a lamp into their bedroom, she plays out one of the essential experiences of human nature: falling in love. As both are awoken – Cupid physically and Psyche spiritually – they play out the age-old tale of the awakening of love and the soul.

The role of light and darkness in the tale plays with ideas of vision, both of the physical kind and the inner kind. One can lack

---

490   Ibid., p. 46.

one while having the former, but the Princess of Cups has both. The act of seeing or gaining vision is a metaphor for gaining wisdom or truth, giving Psyche a visionary role. [491] It has also been suggested that Psyche's use of a lamp to look at her husband's face is an allusion to divination by oil lamps, common in the ancient world, by which magicians would specifically seek contact with a god. [492] The lamp is prominent in the card image in *Tarot Apokalypsis* because it plays such an important role in giving Psyche vision; here it is also a twin-flame lamp to denote the ideas of two souls being united in love (or, the human and the divine being of the same source).

In the final task, Psyche is told to go into the underworld to retrieve some of Persephone's beauty for Venus. The symbolism of the cave (depicted in the background of the card) and the entrance to the underworld that Psyche enters is another journey that the Earthing of Water enacts. The soul being earthed and grounded in the world is the soul coming into birth; to the Platonists and Neoplatonists (many interpretations of Psyche's story suggest it is Platonic in nature) this was the soul descending from its true plane (the cosmic, solar realm) to this world (the lunar realm; the moon was a generative force for the soul, hence the card image is set at night-time), the prison of matter. The world we are in is the cave, as Plato's analogy of the cave states. [493] Psyche, the soul and breath of life, must descend into the darkest parts of the earth in order to further search for her love and attain her divinity. This divine origin for Psyche is used in many retellings, such as Martianus Capella's 5th century version in which she is the daughter of the Sun (divine

---

491   Panoyotakis, Costas, "**Vision and Light in Apuleius' Tale of Psyche and Her Mysterious Husband**", p. 577, in **The Classical Quarterly**, New Series, Vol. 51, no. 2 (2001), pp. 576–583.

492   Christopolous, Karakantza, and Levaniok eds. **Light and Darkness in Ancient Greek Myth and Religion**, p. 290. Lexington Books, 2010.

493   Plato, **The Republic**, 514a–520a.

light) and Endelechia ("the ripeness of time"). [494] This makes immortality and divine reunion for Psyche – and all souls – a birthright.

In the card image we see budding red roses on a bush near Psyche, referring to a Gnostic text in which the first rose is created from the blood of Psyche's virginity on her wedding night – another symbol of her awakening. [495] There is a decorated box behind Psyche: this is the box that she will shortly take with her into the underworld to collect Persephone's beauty. It places the Psyche of the Princess of Cups in a state of awakening and being in love, while having the final stage of divine ascension yet to come. She has fallen in love with Love, seen its true form, but is not yet reunited with it and her divine origin.

~ Revelation

Awakening of emotions or love; inner vision; a visionary, mystic, dreamer or seer; the manifestation of artistic desire; the manifestation of imagination and creativity; putting foundations beneath creative endeavours; a muse; seeking inspiration; twin flames; falling in love; an object of love; the soul being awakened; allowing one's emotions to be immersive; fertility of the heart; potential of a relationship.

Negatively aspected...
Love stuck at the first hurdle; emotions stuck in the mud; an artist unable to find inspiration; creative block; a whimsical dreamer who doesn't consider reality; unrealistic expectations of love.

---

*494 Vertova, Luisa, "**Cupid and Psyche in Renaissance Painting Before Raphael**", in **Journal of the Warburg and Courtauld Institutes**, p. 104.*

*495 Cox Miller, Patricia, "**The Little Blue Flower is Red: Relics and the Poeticizing of the Body**" in **Journal of Early Christian Studies**, vol. 8, no. 2 (2000), p. 229.*

Prince of Cups

Eros, God of New Love, Romance and Chaos

The poets painted me as a boy, for I am young and each one of my loves is new, unhindered by experience and burden; yet I am also a man yearning for the Other. My soul desires connection as my body needs air and water: without love I am lost. For I am love at its most ideal, and the instigator of love; if my golden arrows did not fly true then Chaos would rule and the universe would lose the harmony that holds it together… yet they say that I am a lord of chaos! Mischievous, they call me, and cruel: the truth is that only when you rail against love does it hold any terror. But if you live as a lover, longing for beauty, desirous of the light of another's soul, then you shall not be hurt. Join me in the tremulous love song, soar with me from bliss to bliss, let your soul be transformed through love. My breath is poetry, my words are honey and desire, my gaze is passion and my footsteps are the seeking of love. I am the Lover of the Soul, and though I cause you to feel the pangs of love, know that I feel them also. I have been placed on a pedestal and I have been demonised. Mortals in their fickle way have given me a dichotomy of perfection and flaw: this is true of love also, for love is as deep as the ocean yet as tempestuous and catalytic as the winds. This dichotomy binds the universe together, and it is upon the web of love that continued existence hangs. For this I am both the oldest and the youngest of gods: love is as old as time, yet each instant in which it is felt is born anew.

✎ Mystery

Bringing the airy nature of the Princes to the watery, emotional suit of Cups, the Prince of Cups is a swift-moving, fast-talking, deep-feeling romantic and idealist, yearning always for a "one

true love". He is the stereotype and model of a lover, falling in love and being caught up in it completely; he seeks romance deeply and offers it freely to others. He feels keenly, often painfully, and his emotions run deep, yet they can be tumultuous and unpredictable. The elements of air and water combined create phenomena such as geysers, rough waves and whirlpools: the path of love does not run smoothly, and with this Prince all emotions are on the brink of drama. This drama requires very little to set off, and as such some might even suggest that this drama is all part of what the Prince of Cups thinks love should be: volatile and deeply felt. This Prince's airy nature manifests as idealism: a study of love and emotion has led him to place love on a pedestal and define what it should be rather than experiencing it for what it is. Actual experience of love may terrify the Prince of Cups, who moves on quickly at the briefest glimmer of commitment. He cannot bear to see the reality of people or situations: he prefers everything and everyone to be beautiful and perfect and anything less either turns his heart away or breaks it. He does, however, overcome heartbreak easily, as he soon falls for the next thing just as swiftly.

However, the Prince of Cups also rules over all that makes love sacred and beautiful to humankind, and he is flexible by nature: he easily adapts to new situations, and is therefore an adventurous friend or lover, facilitating new experiences. His airy nature also makes him a catalyst, whether as a person or event, and often his breezing into one's life is required for change to begin.

In the *Tarot Apokalypsis*, the Prince of Cups is Eros, the Greek god of passionate and romantic love. There are two versions of Eros in the Greek myths – one older and associated with the generative forces of nature, and one younger and associated with love – that share similar origins and are often seen as the same god in different forms. Many later writers referred to Eros as love itself, although he was also given the power of instigating love in gods and mortals. Despite this, Eros was also prey to his own expertise: he fell in love with a daughter of Okeanos [496] and with Psyche. The Greek word *erōs* was a common noun for sexual desire, but as Eros was given to romantic love, the two concepts were seen as accompanying each other.

Several early sources describe Eros as the oldest of the gods, [497] but later works say he is the youngest, usually the son of the goddess of love and beauty, Aphrodite (see *Queen of Cups*). As the older god he is envisioned as "the uniting power of love, which brought order and harmony among the conflicting elements of which Chaos consisted". As the younger god "he is purely the god of sensual love". [498] As the son of Aphrodite he was often pictured alongside Himeros ("desire"), [499] as love and desire usually walk side by side; at other times he was depicted alongside Anteros ("love returned"), although sometimes these two were seen in conflict with each other, representing the rivalry between two lovers [500] – something not uncommon for the Prince of Cups! Eros was depicted alongside Pothos ("yearning") in the temple of Aphrodite in Megara, [501] reminding us that desire and yearning usually accompany love and they are staples of the emotional state of the Prince of Cups. Eros is also sometimes depicted alongside Hymenaeus, the god that presides over weddings, though it is telling that Eros, as a god of love and passion, is not also a god of marriage. Howev-

---

496   Nonnus, **Dionysiaca** *32: 46 ff.*

497   *Hesiod,* **Theogony** *120; Aristophanes,* **The Birds** *695; Plato,* **Symposium** *178b.*

498   *William Smith ed.* **Dictionary of Greek and Roman Biography and Mythology***, p. 50. 1870.*

499   *Hesiod, Theogony 176 ff.*

500   *Pausanius,* **Description of Greece** *30.1.*

501   **Ibid***, 1.43.6.*

er, he does have the power to halt a wedding in which there is no joy,[502] so he has rulership over the happiness of a couple.

Eros had a bow from which he shot arrows at mortals and gods to strike them with desire. These arrows were of two types: gold with dove feathers to inspire love and lead with owl feathers to cause indifference. Some texts say they are fiery arrows, referring to the heat of passion. It was these arrows with which Eros was asked to pierce the mortal Psyche so that she might fall in love with an ugly, wretched man, but Eros fell in love with her first. It is from the union of Eros and Psyche that Hedone, pleasure, was born. This story (see *Princess of Cups*) is one of love itself desiring the soul and vice versa, reminding us that the soul's natural state is yearning, whether yearning for another person or yearning for something new, an experience, illumination, or connection. Union with love also makes the soul immortal, as Psyche was made immortal so she might be the wife of Eros. On a deeper level, the Prince of Cups searches for connection, beauty, wisdom, illumination and the soul. The butterflies in the card image remind us of his connection to the Princess of this suit and the evolution of the soul.

Many writers described Eros in reference to feelings of desire and love sickness. The 6th century BCE poet Sappho said, "Once again limb-loosening Eros makes me tremble, the bitter-sweet, irresistible creature". [503] In another source he is referred to as "wild", and called "first seed and beginning of generation, quickening guide of the system of the universe", [504] making him into a catalytic force and espousing the idea that love and desire enable life and growth in the universe.

---

502 Nonnus, **Dionysiaca** *7.7ff.*

503 Sappho, *Fragment 130, trans. David A Campbell*, **Greek Lyric vol. 1: Sappho and Alcaeus**. *Loeb Classical Library, 1982.*

504 Nonnus, **Dionyisiaca** *41. 128ff.*

Sappho was not the first to write of Eros in almost fearful terms: Hesiod described him as "fairest among the deathless gods, who unnerves the limbs and overcomes the mind and wise counsels of all gods and all men within them." [505] Although in the modern world we are quite familiar with the imagery and concept of love as an all-consuming emotion that overwhelms, to the ancient Greeks and Romans it was seen as a pathological disease, and they wrote of Eros in similar terms. Eros as "limb-loosener" according to Sappho, Hesiod, and Homer has been said to relate to the injuries of wounded warriors. Faraone says that "...when Homer wishes to express the feeling of erotic infatuation, he uses epic formulae that elsewhere describe dead and wounded warriors whose limbs have been 'loosened' [...]. But *erōs* is also treated as a mental disease, which attacks the various inner faculties of thought and emotion, such as the heart (*phrenes* or *thumos*) or the mind (*nous*)". [506] Eros is also referred to with imagery of violent winds and love sickness. [507] It is no wonder that some ancient writers describe people trying to avoid being struck by the arrows of Eros. [508]

Despite his volatility and fickleness, the Prince of Cups rides into everybody's life at some point, bringing with him his catalytic faculties, or his passionate madness, or an opportunity for connection with another. He may bring turbulence and uncertainty, but he commands emotional depth and desire, and he is a seeker of love and beauty wherever he goes. He may remind us of our ideals and hopes, reminding us not to settle for anything less than world-shattering, but his lead arrows can strike as quickly as his golden arrows.

---

505 *Hesiod, Theogony 116ff.*

506 *Christopher A Faraone,* **Ancient Greek Love Magic***, pp. 43–44. Harvard University Press, 2001.*

507 **Ibid***, pp. 44-45.*

508 *Musaeus,* **Hero and Leander** *39 ff (trans. Mair).*

~ Revelation

Romance; idealised love; seeking a romantic partner or emotional connection; yearning; instigating love; an ideal partner; moving on from social and romantic involvements quickly; volatility and turbulence of emotion; rivalry in love; putting love or a person on a pedestal; flirtation.

Negatively aspected…
Fickleness in love; a commitment-phobe; inability to cope with the reality of a relationship or friendship; negative volatility of emotion; desiring somebody out of reach; refusing to move on from a relationship that has ended.

Queen of Cups

Aphrodite, Goddess of Love, Beauty and Emotion

The old poet gave me birth in the foaming waves of the ocean, rising as fully-formed woman, voluptuous and in love with the world. The seas are not mine, yet I am of them and belong to them and in the beauty of their depths I hold enticement and terror. As you look upon the waves and see the sun shining like gold upon them, you see my splendour and are drawn into me; when you immerse yourself in the deep waters and see what dwells beneath, you see my inner, terrifying glory. I am the queen of beauty and love. I have been loved and worshipped for countless aeons, called shimmering-throned, enchantress, rich-crowned, mother of loves, golden, source of persuasion. I pull your desire into the depths and surround it, immerse it and mire it therein. When you are before me you will sink into my persuasion, become lost in my laughter and lithe limbs; you will be happy to drown in me. Love and Desire are my sons, Harmony and Seduction my daughters; some say also that I mothered Fertility and Passion. Yet even as my offspring bring the beauty of life to your heart, so more bring you its terror: Fear and Panic are my children who cling just as easily to your heart. These are my acts in the world and you will know me better through them. Love me, you who behold me, and you will be surrounded with beauty, immersed and lost in your heart and all its yearnings. Let the fear of drowning pass through you: when you let go and let the waves carry you, you may come to bliss in the sweetness of my embrace.

❧ Mystery

"Goddess of marriage, charming to the sight,
Mother of Loves, whom banquetings delight;

Source of persuasion, secret, fav'ring queen,
Illustrious born, apparent and unseen." [509]

The Queen of Cups, through her royal rank, draws the affection and love of all. Like her sisters she is nurturing, inspiring in others the qualities of her court. Her Watery nature as a Queen gives her a natural tendency for caring for others, channelling what others need, nourishing others and receiving what is given to her. The suit of Cups exaggerates her Watery qualities, making her the quintessential representation of Water in all its forms and powers. She is deeply emotional and feels all things keenly, exhibiting her emotions as readily as she experiences them. Due to this, she has been cast as the Queen of Love, ruling over relationships, family and social circles. She is also the Queen of Beauty. This beauty is like a siren song calling to those who would love her, drawing them in. To many she is as fickle as the ever-changing sea; to some she reflects much – like the glassy, mirror-like surface of a deep, still lake – but has no drive and direction of her own. Indeed, one of the powers of the Queen of Cups is the ability to change to reflect others and her situation. Yet she is more than what she appears, for the ocean is our planet's final frontier, into which the knowledge of humankind has only begun to penetrate. The depths of the Queen of Cups are unfathomable, filled with dreams, hopes, fears, feelings and wisdom. Few find these depths, drowning instead in the turbulent emotions of this Queen or becoming terrified of what she offers. Like the sirens and mermaids of myth, this Queen lures us in with her sweet song and beautiful visage, and in her love for us she can unwillingly drown us in her waters. She does not realise that where she swims, others drown.

---

509 ***The Hymns of Orpheus, To Venus**, 13–20*, trans. Thomas Taylor. London, 1792.

In the *Tarot Apokalypsis*, the Queen of Cups is Aphrodite, the Greek goddess of love, beauty, marriage and all the feelings of being in love, who "stirs up sweet passion in the gods and subdues the tribes of mortal men and birds that fly in the air and all the many creatures that the dry land rears, and all the sea". [510] The story of her birth from the seafoam of the ocean is one of a number of origins given to her, yet probably the most well known. According to Hesiod, the sky god Ouranos intended to make love with Gaia, the earth goddess, only to have his son Kronos cut off his genitals and throw them into the sea; they created foam (some say the semen of Ouranos) and from this foam Aphrodite emerged, already a maiden. From the beginning she was given the domain of love, "the whisperings of girls; smiles; deceptions; sweet pleasure, intimacy, and tenderness". [511]

The names of Aphrodite's offspring tell us much about her and the Queen of Cups. Most famous of her children is Eros, the god of love and desire (see *Prince of Cups*). Other sons of Aphrodite are Himeros (desire), Anteros (reciprocated love), Pothos (passionate longing), Hedylogos (sweet-talk) and Hymenaios (the god of wedding ceremonies). Aphrodite had twin sons with Ares, the god of war, called Deimos (panic) and Phobos (fear). Just like the Queen of Cups, the complexity of emotions represented by Aphrodite includes negative emotions that often appear when we become attached to something or someone – in this case, the fear of loss and the panic induced by that fear. Other children of Aphrodite are Priapos, the phallic god of garden fertility, Harmonia (harmony) and Peitho (persuasion or seduction).

---

510 *The Homeric Hymns*, 5: 1–6, trans. H. G. Evelyn-White, 1914.
511 Hesiod, **Theogeny** trans. Hugh G. Evelyn-White, p. 9. Oxford University Press, 1999.

Aphrodite was first married to Hephaistos, the god of the forge. However, she is also portrayed as fickle, falling in love with Ares, the god of war. The discovery of this unfaithfulness appears to have led to a divorce, and Aphrodite is later described by the same writers as Ares' wife. However, her fickleness of heart continues, as she is given many other loves and infatuations, both divine and mortal. Like the Queen of Cups, although she inspires love in others, she is not exempt from its power herself.

Several myths in which Aphrodite plays a pivotal role remind us of the ability of the Queen of Cups to nurture love. One tells of Pygmalion, a sculptor who was not interested in women or love, who fell in love with the statue of a beautiful maiden he carved from ivory. On Aphrodite's feast day he made offerings to the goddess, secretly wishing that he could find a woman who matched the likeness of his ivory maiden. When he returned home, upon kissing the statue he discovered that Aphrodite had granted his wish and brought the statue to life. [512] In another tale she inspired affection and passion in a husband who could not have intercourse with his wife despite her beauty. He accused her of witchcraft, blaming her for his inability, so she prayed to Aphrodite to inspire love and desire in her husband. The wish was granted, and he loved her greatly thereafter. [513] In the card image Aphrodite holds an apple, a reminder of her role in the cause of the Trojan War. Eris, the goddess of discord, threw a golden apple into a crowd of assembled goddesses at a feast, inscribed "to the fairest". Aphrodite, Hera and Athena all claimed the apple, so Zeus asked the mortal, Paris of Troy, to decide who was most worthy. Each goddess made him

---

512 Ovid, **Metamorphoses**, 10. 243–300, trans. A. D. Melville. Oxford University Press, 1998.

513 Herodotus, **Histories** 2.181, trans. A. D. Godley. Loeb Classical Library, 1920.

offers to sway his decision, but he eventually chose Aphrodite, as she promised him the most beautiful woman, Helen of Sparta, as his wife. Paris' choice of love over all other gifts and his desire for Helen sparked the Trojan War.

Like the Queen of Cups, Aphrodite has a darker side. Just as love can be beautiful, so it can also be painful and terrifying. The poet Sappho, writing of the ability of Aphrodite to torment, said "spare me, O queen, this agony and anguish, crush not my spirit". [514] She is also said to have tormented Eos with "constant passion" as a punishment for having intercourse with Ares, [515] and her beauty is so intense that a mortal man to whom she reveals herself would happily die for a chance to sleep with her. [516]

Aphrodite is represented as a jealous goddess who demands to be the most well loved and most beautiful. It is easy to incur her wrath, as the beautiful maiden Psyche experienced. Psyche (see *Princess of Cups*) would eventually become the bride of Eros, Aphrodite's son, but first she incurred Aphrodite's wrath when the people of the town neglected worship of the goddess and instead praised Psyche's beauty. Aphrodite asked her son to cause Psyche to fall in love with a wretched man, but before he did he fell in love with her himself. The story continued with many trials set before Psyche by the wrathful Aphrodite, who eventually gave in and agreed to the marriage of Psyche and Eros.

Enticing and wrathful, sweet and jealous, the Queen of Cups holds within her all the power and opportunity of emotion. She,

---

514 Sappho, **Poems of Sappo**, 1: Hymn to Aphrodite, trans. Edwin Marion Cox. 1925.

515 Pseudo-Apollodorus, **Bibliotheca** 1.27, trans. Aldrich.

516 **The Homeric Hymns**, 5.145–154, trans. H. G. Evelyn-White. Loeb Classical Library, 1914.

like our emotional world, is fickle and changeable, yet this too can be her strength, for it allows her to be adaptable and flexible. She flows around problems, nurtures our emotional lives and inspires us to feel completely, letting go and allowing ourselves to be immersed.

~ Revelation

Beauty perceived or intended; love and relationships, whether romantic, platonic or familial; nurturing emotions and feelings; reflecting the feelings of others; changing one's emotional state; inspiring love in others; caring for others emotionally; depth of emotional experience; changeability; emotional growth; adaptability; immersion.

Negatively aspected...
Jealousy; fickleness; drowning in one's emotions; feeling overwhelmed in a relationship; overly attaching oneself to another person; obsession; preoccupation with outer appearance; being acted upon rather than acting; inability to grow emotionally; suppressing or refusing to acknowledge the feelings of others.

King of Cups

Apollo, God of Healing, Oracles and the Arts

I am the Father of Healers, Lord of Muses, Voice of Prophecy, and the words I speak are true. I have been called Physician, Healer and Aid. I have blessed the wounded and sick, aiding the soul-smitten, the ones in the dark, those whom loss has consumed. I know their pain and the call of the black waters of seething emotion. I have felt the joys of love and known loss. I carry with me my feelings, deep and unending, all my passion and yearning, and all the grief and loss a heart can bear without breaking (the heart never truly breaks. It only cracks a little, but you must not drown in the ocean that floods out of it). I tell you this: there is no emotion that is a sin, yet being controlled by it is dangerous. You must not let the sirens drag you beneath the waves, and when your little ship of a soul is tossed upon the turbulent seas, you must take control of the ship and of the ocean. You must not fear. You must not drown. Look to the fires within to guard against the storm – look to the Lighthouse of the Sun. And during times of great light, when you fly above the waves untouched, be the beacon of hope in the darkness for others; be the hand offered in aid; be the words of comfort that raise up the spirit and soothe the weary heart. Be the creator of beauty and allow it to raise up your soul and that of others to the pinnacle of the human heart. You are a creative fire leading the way to inspiration, the soul guide leading the way to healing.

∽ Mystery

In the King of Cups, the fiery aspect of all the Kings of the tarot expresses itself in the suit of water. Here, we find the active, ambitious and passionate aspects of our emotional and social selves. It also represents active emotions going out into the world to positively affect others, such as compassion, care

and healing. Further, as the King is the highest rank in the tarot Court, the King of Cups shows us the possible pinnacle of our spiritual and emotional selves. As such, this card has many facets: he is a healer, saviour, prophet, lover, guide and muse. The card image presents Apollo, the Greek god who encompassed all these roles, whose oracle at Delphi was perhaps the most influential in the ancient world. He kneels on the stone steps on the edge of the ocean, his temple at Didyma in the background. This temple had a spring from which a priestess gave oracles, just as we might turn to the spring waters of the King of Cups for a source of wisdom and inspiration.

Apollo was given many names to demonstrate his several roles. He was Thearios, "Of the Oracle", Mousêgêtes, "Leader of the Muses", Paian, "Healer", Proopsios, "Foreseeing", Epikourios, "Helper", Alexikakos, "Averter of Evil" and Boedromois, "Rescuer". Homer designated him the physician of the gods, and he healed both Ares and Hades. [517] He was also called Phoibos, "shining", a name that has led many to state that he was a god of the sun, though this is uncertain. [518] This association reminds us of the fiery, passionate personality of the emotional, spiritual King of Cups.

Strabo tells us that the Milesians and Delians invoked "Apollo Oulios, […] god of health and healing, for the verb *oulein* means 'to be healthy'". [519] Pausanias gives accounts of his other names: he was called Alexikakos when he drove away the disease that afflicted Athens during the Peloponnesian War; [520] he

---

517 Homer, **Iliad** 5. 401; 899.

518 Joseph E. Fontenrose, "**Apollo and Sol in the Latin Poets of the First Century B.C**" in **Transactions of the American Philological Association**, vol. 70 (1939), pp. 439–455.

519 Strabo, **Geography Books 13–14,** 14.1.6, trans. Horace Leonard Jones. Harvard University Press, 1929.

520 Pausanias, **Description of Greece: Books 1–2**, 1.3.4, trans. W. H. S. Jones. Harvard University Press, 1918.

was given the name Epikourios when he drove plague away in Arkadia. [521] In his role as healer, Apollo was the father of Asklepios, the god of medicine, and therefore the grandfather of Hygeia (the goddess of health and cleanliness), Iaso (goddess of recuperation) and Panacea (goddess of the universal cure). [522] It is Apollo's role as healer and saviour of humankind that shows us the King of Cups' most beneficent face. He, too, heals others, for he has lived through many emotions, relationships and life experience. His experience lies most firmly in that of the wounded soul, to which he responds with counselling, wisdom and a gentle, guiding hand. He often acts like a lighthouse on the dark sea, guiding the floundering ship to shore.

There are many ways in which Apollo comes to us as a prophet, granting wisdom and guidance through visions and far seeing. He had several oracles throughout Greece, two of the most famous being the Pythian Oracle at Delphi and the Oracle at Didyma. The *Orphic Hymn to Apollo* speaks of his oracular power and kindness:

"O Delian king, whose light-producing eye views all within, and all beneath the sky: whose locks are gold, whose oracles are sure, who, omens good reveal'st, and precepts pure: hear me entreating for the human kind, hear, and be present with benignant mind." [523]

Apollo was often said to institute oracles and create seers, just as the King of Cups, in his wisdom, inspires others in turn to be wise. He gave the gift of prophecy to gods and men, and

---

521 *Ibid.*, 8.30.3–4; 8.41.7–9.

522 Anonymous, **Greek Lyric: The New School of Poetry, Anonymous Songs and Hymns**, *Fragment 939, trans. David A. Campbell. Loeb Classical Library no. 144, vol. 4. Harvard University Press, 1993.*

523 **The Hymns of Orpheus**, *XXXIII To Apollo, trans. Thomas Taylor, pp. 161–2. B. White and Son, 1792.*

ancient seers and prophets were often said to be related to him. The seers of Olympia were called Iamidai after their ancestor, Iamos, the son of Apollo, and "received the gift of divination from him". [524] The ship in the card image, as well as being a symbol of the saviour aspect of the King of Cups, reminds us of the myth of the founding of the Oracle at Delphi, in which Apollo guided a ship full of sailors to those shores in the form of a dolphin; when they landed, he revealed himself to them and decreed they were to serve at the temple as its first priests. [525] This association with Apollo's oracles and water is further expressed when we see that many of his oracles used sacred waters to gain their visions. At Delphi, the Pythia (priestess) "descended into [a] vault, drank of the holy spring, chewed some bay leaves, and mounted on to the tripod". [526] In Hysiai in Boiotia, Pausanias reports the ruins of a temple of Apollo that had a sacred well from which story oracles were obtained after drinking its waters. [527]

The wisdom and mature self-reflection of the King of Cups can be found at the Oracle of Delphi. The Delphic maxim "Know thyself" was inscribed in the forecourt there, [528] a reminder that the King of Cups not only offers aid through imparting his wisdom but by encouraging us to discover it ourselves: his is an inner healing that can only be arrived at through self-reflection and acceptance.

Apollo had many loves, divine and mortal, male and female, so he – like the King of Cups – was no stranger to the sea of

---

524 Pausanias, **Description of Greece**, 6.2.5.
525 **Homeric Hymn to Pythian Apollo**, *389–524, trans. Hugh G. Evelyn-White. Online at http://www.perseus.tufts.edu/hopper/text?doc=Perseus%3Atext%3A1999.01.0138%3Ahymn%3D3*
526 *J. Henry Middleton, p. 305*, "**The Temple of Apollo at Delphi**", *in* **The Journal of Hellenic Studies**, *vol. 9 (1888), pp. 282–322.*
527 Pausanias, **Description of Greece**, 9.2.1.
528 **Ibid.**, *10.24.1.*

emotions that might be felt by the human heart. Some of these loves ended tragically, plunging him into despair and grief. The purple hyacinth flowers in the card image stand for Hyakinthos, the youth whom Apollo loved and accidentally killed when a discus he threw struck Hyakinthos, forced by the jealous Zephyros (West Wind). [529] The white raven upon Apollo's shoulder is the raven that informed him of his lover, Koronis', infidelity; in his anger Apollo turned the raven's snow-white feathers black. [530] It is from such grief that the King of Cups has recovered and become wiser, more able to understand the emotional pain of others.

Finally, Apollo is an inspirer of art, just as the fire of the King of Cups inflames the soul and emotions to artistic expression. He was the leader of the Muses, the goddesses of all forms of art who inspired poets throughout the ages. To this day, writers seek their muse in the form of inspiration or an idealised person. In the *Homeric Hymn to Apollo* we are given a scene in which Apollo enraptures all the gods by playing music for them:

"Thence, swift as thought, he speeds from earth to Olympus, to the house of Zeus, to join the gathering of the other gods: then straightway the undying gods think only of the lyre and song, and all the Muses together, voice sweetly answering voice, hymn the unending gifts the gods enjoy..." [531]

Reigning over all the seas of emotion and soul, the King of Cups is the mature force of inspiration, healing and wisdom that can only be gained and given when we free ourselves from being lost in our feelings. His fiery nature calls us to rise above

---

529 Ovid, **Metamorphoses** *10.162.*

530 Pseudo-Apollodorus, **Bibliotheca,** *3.118.*

*531 **Homeric Hymn to Pythian Apollo**, 185–190.*

ourselves in order to gain vision, and he heats the waters of our heart so they might be purified.

~ Revelation

A healer, counsellor, therapist, psychologist; undergoing a process of spiritual, emotional and mental healing; being in need of aid; giving aid to another; emotional wounds as a mode of learning; a guide during a difficult time; rising above emotional difficulties; purification; refreshment; maturity in relationship.

Negatively aspected…
Lack of guidance; needing aid that is not forthcoming; immaturity in love; drowning in one's emotional problems; a drunkard and letch; bitterness.

Princess of Pentacles
Prthvī, Goddess of the Earth, Fertility and Nourishment

Mortals have given me as a bride to the gods of the sky, as a daughter to the gods of the sun and rain; I have been honoured and debased, raised up and trodden down; no other holds within them the opposites that I do, for I contain the fullness of the world of experience in all its manifest glory and diversity. Yet I am not just bride, nor am I just daughter: I am the Great Mother of All, seen as the lowest of the low by some but bearing and supporting the greatest. It is only from my still silence that all else gains movement and sound. It is only that I am acted upon that others may act. I am inert, yet great dragonlines move within me; I am chaste, yet I take all inside me. In my containment of all I make myself the purest. I am the Great Mother of creation, holding all that is potential in my womb, the milk from my breasts sustaining and nourishing the world. Without me you would be a breath in the void, a being without roots, with no past and no future. With me you are given a throne for your greatness, a mountain beneath your feet, a store of great power and wealth and a promise of eternal life: for when your time upon my body is done, I will wrap you within my embrace and there you shall continue in myriad forms.

✥ Mystery

"May Earth the Goddess, she who bears her treasure stored up in many a place, gold, gems, and riches, giver of opulence, grant great possessions to us bestowing them with love and favour. Earth, bearing folk of many a varied language with divers rites as suits their dwelling-places, pour, like a constant cow that never faileth, a thousand streams of treasure to enrich me!" [532]

---

532 **Atharvaveda** *12.1.44–45, trans. Ralph T. Griffith, 1895–6.*

In most mythologies there is a concept that embodies the Earth, whether as a non-sentient resource or a being with feelings and ideas. The earth beneath our feet and all around us, that sustains and supports us and to which we all return, is vital in our mythical imagination and narrative. It is found in the tarot as the Princess of Pentacles: Earth of Earth, the "lowest" of all the Court cards, yet the one that contains within it the most energy. Earth is the element that is closest to manifestation, therefore it is the most "impure" of the four elements: it has gathered within itself so much energy so that it may become the experiential, mundane world that it is not itself a pure element like Water, Air and Fire but a mixture of all the elements. All of the Court cards of the suit of Pentacles share this quality of being close to the world of manifestation, moving in a realm of practical matters, resources, family, home, money and work. The Princess of Pentacles, as the Earthy part of Earth, is the most full of the powers of manifestation. Like the dirt beneath our feet she is often overlooked or seen as worthless, but like the earth that sustains us and gives us life she is essential for our survival. She carries within her all the energy that has come down through the other Court cards beginning with the highest of the high (Fire of Fire, the King of Wands) and it now gestates within her, ready to create the universe.

The Princess of Pentacles is Mother Earth. She births everything, nourishes it, sustains it and provides a solid foundation for it as it moves through the life she has given to it; in the end she takes it back into her body. She sees that nothing is truly destroyed: matter simply changes form. She is the womb and the tomb, for she feeds us and we in turn feed her. She represents ultimate potential: an entire world waiting to be born, opportunities waiting to be manifested; she is bursting, ready to bring that force into being. In the *Tarot Apokalypsis* the Princess of Pentacles is depicted as Prthvī, the Hindu concept of the Earth as a divine female, a goddess (*devi*). Her name is Sanskrit for "earth" and she has many epithets that tell us of the way she is conceived in Hindu thought, as well as her importance in the universe. Her names relate to her qualities as a giver and sustainer of life: Bhūmi ("soil"), Dhātrī ("nursing mother"), Janitrā ("birthplace"), Dhāritrī ("nurturer"), Prśnī ("mother of plants"), Viśvadhāyā ("all-nourishing"), Viśvasvam ("source of everything"), Viśvagabhā ("world's womb"). This shows that she is not just a human mother, but the origin of all life – everything possible comes from her. In the hymn to Prthvī in the *Atharvaveda*, we read, "May that Earth grant us breath and vital power. Prithivī give me life of long duration!" [533] As the divine womb and earth, Prthvī is also the tomb: in *Rig Veda* 10.18 she is called upon to wrap the dead in her, like a son is wrapped in his mother's skirt.

Other epithets relate the power of earth as resource: Ratnagarbhā ("repository of gems"), Ratnavatī ("abounding in jewels"), Vasundharā ("bearer of treasure"). [534] The suit of Pentacles is most concerned with matters of worldly wealth, status and resources. The fact that the resources referred to with these epithets – jewels, gems, treasure – are found beneath the earth beginning as minerals, ores and unprocessed gems, reminds us that the power contained within the Princess of Pentacles is protected, held in place, yet hidden to some. Other names are related to Prthvī's role as a foundation and support, just as the earth beneath our feet is solid and reliable, holding us up: Dharā ("upholder"), Drdhā ("steady one"), Ksamā ("patient one"), Viśvadhārinī ("all-supporting"), [535] Viśvadhā ("all-preserving"), Viśvambharā ("all-bearing"). She is patient and steady, so can seem slow at first, but like her brother, the Prince of Pentacles, she is an implacable force.

---

533 *Atharvaveda* 12.1.22.
534 *Atharvaveda* 12.1.6.
535 *Atharvaveda* 12.1.26–27.

In many depictions of Prthvī as Bhūmi she is shown with either two or four arms, seated on a square platform upheld by four elements. She sometimes holds a pomegranate. As Prthvī she is sometimes shown in the form of a cow, for she is said to have been milked for her life-giving milk by Vishnu the Preserver in his avatar as Prithu, a king who restored the fertility of his land after promising to protect the Earth mother.[536] The cow in Hinduism is often seen as sacred and its milk provides the basis for many of the most important food offerings, such as ghee. The sacred cow is given the name Kamadhenu in Hinduism and is regarded as a form of the divine mother. Kamadhenu is often depicted in art as a white cow or a cow with a woman's head, whose body is filled with images of the gods, showing her as the source of everything. She is closely related to Prthvī, who sometimes shares her form as a cow; together they represent the source of all life, the origin of both the mundane and divine worlds, and the continued sustenance of life on both a physical and spiritual level.[537] In the *Atharvaveda* we read: "May Earth [Prthvī] pour out her milk for us, a mother unto me her son".[538] We can imagine that this milk gives us bodily and spiritual sustenance.

The *Tarot Apokalypsis* shows Prthvī knelt on a yoni stone. These stones, often about a metre on each side, represent the sacred vagina and womb and are often paired with the Shiva lingam, representing the divine phallus. They have grooves where water can run and a funnel to let it flow out. There are several examples of these sculptures from the Khmer Empire. In the image, Prthvī is surrounded by the flourishing earth that she has given

---

536 *Vishnu Purana 1.13*

537 *Madeleine Biardeau, "**Kamadhenu: the Religious Cow, Symbol of Prosperity**", p. 99, in **Asian Mythologies**, ed. Yves Bonnefey, University of Chicago Press: 1993 and Antonio Rigopoulos, **Dattātreya: the immortal guru, yogin and avatāra**, p. 233. SUNY Press.*

538 *Atharvaveda 12.1.10.*

birth to and sustains, and her pregnant belly is full and ripe: she is always ready to create more. She is shown seated to indicate her stillness and receptivity, her patience and her steadiness, as well as her role as supporter of life and foundation.

It is as a firm foundation that Prthvī appears in Indian Buddhism, being the first goddess to appear in Buddhist writing around the third century CE. She was present at the moment when Shakyamuni Buddha attained enlightenment, and therefore "at the moment the tradition [of Buddhism] began". [539] Further, Prthvī was depicted as providing and supporting the seat upon which the Buddha achieved enlightenment, reminding us that the Princess of Pentacles is the throne upon which the material world sits; she therefore supports and nourishes both the mundane and spiritual worlds in which we move. In Gandaran artwork (first to third centuries CE), she is frequently portrayed as emerging from the earth at the base of the throne upon which the Buddha is seated at the moment of his enlightenment, and in some she holds her arms up to support it. [540] This throne was described in many Buddhist texts as the centre of the world, the navel of the earth (*prthvī-nibhi*) and the seat of wisdom. This concept is found throughout Hindu literature also, where it is described as the "axis of the universe, supreme sacrificial altar, and seat of planetary sovereignty. […] Like the hub of a wheel, the earth's navel is the still point in a spinning world". [541] This highlights the importance of the Princess of Pentacles in the mythic landscape of the tarot Court: from her stillness, everything else gains movement and momentum; from her passivity and receptivity, everything else is given action.

---

539 Miranda Shaw, **Buddhist Goddesses of India**, *p. 17. Princeton: Princeton University Press, 2006.*

540 **Ibid**, *p. 23.*

541 **Ibid**, *p. 20–21.*

～ Revelation

Foundation, stability, firmness; production, productivity; the act of gestating; bringing something into manifestation; supporting somebody, a project or idea; being a source of strength and power for others; the environment one moves in; fertility in life; bodily and spiritual nourishment; sustaining something or someone; a source of material wealth or power; a reliable and willingly helpful person; the centre of a project or activity; potential; the growth of new beginnings.

Negatively aspected…
Stunted growth in an area of one's life; lack of potential; inability to contain ideas; difficulty bringing something to manifestation; somebody stuck in a rut; abuse of the body or environment.

Prince of Pentacles

Karttikeya, the God of Ambition Grounded in Reality

You may have become accustomed to thinking of change as chaotic and reckless, as a rushing forth of newness and energy; this is not so. It is found in the slow growth of the fruits of the earth, the ponderous movement of the buffalo as it pulls the plough to turn over the soil, the careful control of a steady investment. The ideas that last the longest and have the most profound effect are those that take time to generate and gestate, that are cared for and nurtured to fruition. This is my mystery: to show you the youthful joy in the growth of the material world, to protect that which is still in its infancy, to ground ideas in reality and thus make the greatest ambitions achievable. I am called Friend, Trustworthy and Seeking of Legacy. Though I will give my all to that which I am devoted, I have not yet the grander designs and experience of my Father-King; until then, I can protect and guard, catalyse growth and nourishment, ensuring steady movement forward. Mistake not my slowness for dullness, nor my lack of haste for lack of care, for I care for all things in heaven and earth, from the greatest mountains to the smallest creatures. My consorts are the Daughter of Air and the Daughter of Earth, and I am the bridge by which the children of the mind might find their home in the world.

~ Mystery

The airy nature of the Princes of the tarot and the earthy concerns of the suit of Pentacles unite in the Prince of Pentacles to create a youthful seeker of material wealth, wisdom and stability. Like his brothers, this Prince can be impetuous, quick-thinking and fast-acting, yet his presence in the suit of Pentacles makes him the slowest of them all. His decisions are astute

yet carefully measured, his actions are taken with speed yet not without consideration. The Prince of Pentacles may also be of an entrepreneurial mindset, seeking success in business and career matters. This Prince is concerned with the everyday world and daily life; he is thus a pragmatist and realist. Due to his union of the elements of air and earth, he is an active force for manifestation in his life, bringing it swiftly and concisely. However, the element of air that he shares with his brothers can manifest in the suit of Pentacles as vanity and a preoccupation with material wealth and status; at his worst, the Prince of Pentacles will rush forward with his plans in order to gain respect but will find he gains the opposite. Luckily, he is also the most dependable of the Princes, so can be seen as a trustworthy friend and ally, somebody that can be relied upon to keep their word.

The Prince of Pentacles in the *Tarot Apokalypsis* is the Hindu god Karttikeya, also called Skanda and Murugan (who was originally a separate deity until the two became conflated). He is depicted with his *vahana* – sacred animal mount – the peacock and bearing his sacred weapon, the spear. In the background, rice paddies are worked by buffalo, reminding us of the focus of this Prince on hard work to achieve one's goals and his ability to create rapid, sustainable and certain growth in all endeavours. He stands in his domain – mature crop fields –, the rice crop growing high and lush. Behind him are the mountains he is often associated with, the bridges between heaven and earth, the representation of lofty ambition grounded firmly in practicality and reality.

Like many other Hindu deities, Karttikeya was given numerous names and epithets that express his nature. He is often called Kumara, "young one", emphasising his youth; he is called Svaminatha, "clever", reminding us of his keen mind; this keen mind is applied to the everyday world, however, rather than to abstract thoughts, so he is also given earthy names such as Guhan, "cave-dweller". His active nature is expressed by many of his names that focus on his warlike qualities: Mahasena ("great conquering army"), Senapati ("lord of a conquering army"), Śaktidhara ("spear holder") and Tarakjit ("vanquisher of Taraka"). [542] This last refers to his destiny to kill the buffalo demon, Taraka, a tale that was later subsumed into that of Durgā's vanquishing of Mahiṣa (see *Strength*).

Many accounts of his birth give Karttikeya six heads, each having a specific function. One illuminates the world and brings it out of darkness, one grants boons to his devotees, one guards brahmin priests during their rituals, one brings enlightenment to the minds of sages, one destroys enemies, and the last gazes lovingly upon his consort, Valli. [543] This reminds us of the many aspects of the Prince of Pentacles, who can be a boon-giver, a lover of the beauty of the material world, a protector and a man of action. Although his sixth face gazes upon Valli, she is not Karttikeya's only wife: he is also married to Devasena, the daughter of Indra. Valli, however, is a woman from a tribe of hunters. Together, they represent Karttikeya's ability to "live as much on earth as in heaven". [544] Indeed, as Murugan he presides over fertility and the productivity of the forests and the land; "[w]orship of him seems to have been an affirmation of life – an extension of a joyous humanness, rather than an endeavour to enter a new order". [545] This emphasises the joyful, youthful and productive nature of the Prince of Pentacles, whose hard work and energy

---

542 George M. Williams, **Handbook of Hindu Mythology**, *p. 271. ABC Clio, 2003.*

543 Fred W. Clothey, **The Many Faces of Murukan: The History and Meaning of a South Indian God**, *p. 66. Mouton Publishers, 1978.*

544 **Ibid.**, *p. 65.*

545 **Ibid.**, *p. 71.*

cannot fail to produce results. His ability to bring growth can be seen in his rapid growth over a six-day period, during which he was conceived, became a child, grew up, become a general of an army, performed heroic deeds, received his initiations and destroyed the hosts of demons in battle. [546] It is for this reason that he, and the Prince of Pentacles, are seen as warrior princes, unlike his brother, Gaṇeśa, who is seen as a scholar. [547]

His youthful, warrior-like nature can be seen in a popular story about Karttikeya and Gaṇeśa, in which a race around the universe between the brothers was declared. At first it seemed that Karttikeya, who flew off on his peacock, swift and sure, would win, as Gaṇeśa and his mount, the rat, were slow. However, Gaṇeśa considered the challenge and realized that his mother, Parvati, and father, Shiva, constituted the universe; he simply walked around the two and thus won the race. [548] Although the Prince of Pentacles is earthy and practical in nature, he is still prone to the same quickness of action as his brothers, and does not yet represent a mature state of his element. His decisions may not be correct all the time, though his ambitions, ideals and theory are faultless. Like all the Princes, he has his own areas of concern with which he is most preoccupied; in this case, he will be easily spurned into action through the need to protect an investment or area of daily life that he cherishes and he will be a catalyst for change in matters of family, money and career.

Despite this, the Prince of Pentacles is the slowest of all the Princes, so the change he brings is often more stable and long-lasting. Similarly, his ambitions and plans usually consid-

---

546   **Ibid.**, *p. 53.*
547   *James G. Lochtefeld,* **The Illustrated Encyclopedia of Hinduism**, *p. 655. The Rosen Publishing Group, 2002.*
548   *Constance A. Jones and James D. Ryan, Encyclopedia of Hinduism, pp. 161–2. Facts on File, Inc., 2007.*

er the long term rather than focusing on any short-term gains or experiences. It is fitting, then, that Karttikeya is said to lead his armies into battle mounted on an elephant, rather than on any faster moving creature. [549] The change that this Prince leads is steady and certain, which can sometimes cause others to think it is not change at all. The Prince of Pentacles is also a controlled force of change rather than chaotic change (such as that found in the Prince of Wands). The peacock that is his mount not only symbolises the youth and beauty of Karttikeya, but also control: it is supposedly able to control snakes, "symbolising the soulful domination of the instinctive elements – or the control of the kundalini". [550] This Prince can be a welcome ally in any material endeavours, as he brings with him the certainty of positive change, careful action and protection of resources that only a keen mind, coupled with a realistic and practical approach, can create.

~ Revelation

Lofty ambition grounded in practicality and reality; slow and steady change; a catalyst for change in the material world; seeking wealth and stability; seeking success in business and career; long-term plans; careful consideration before acting; growth in the material world; a reliable friend; a protector; theory applied to practical matters; productivity.

Negatively aspected…
Action taken too slowly; lack of willingness to take a risk in order to bring about necessary change; being unreliable; growth that is too slow to be sustainable; lack of control; vanity; over-preoccupation with status and wealth.

---

549 Fred W. Clothey, ***The Many Faces of Murukan: The History and Meaning of a South Indian God***, *p. 64.*

550 Satguru Sivaya Subramuniyaswami, ***Loving Gaṇeśa: Hinduism's Endearing Elephant-faced God***, *pp. 469–70. Himalayan Academy, 2000.*

Queen of Pentacles

Lakṣmī, Goddess of Fortune and Prosperity

Since humankind first conceived in the mind it has sought fulfilment, power and nourishment. Those who have prayed for fortune are those I have heard; those who have acted to bring auspiciousness across the threshold I have followed. I am called Jewel, Mother Earth and Mother of the World. I am in love with all things upon the earth and within the earth; I yearn for its growth and preservation. My husband is the great Preserver and I am his power. My name is the office of kings and the flow of wealth. From me come all fortunes and sources of power. Upon my bosom you will find the wealth of nourishment, victory and courage, wisdom and knowledge, wealth of resources and of a neverending line. I ask only that you remember this: power is like a river that flows ever downstream, carrying with it the richness of life. It cannot move faster than it knows; it cannot be forced into a place it does not seek. Like water, power can devastate and it can nourish; it can kill and it can heal; it can become stagnant and it can be pure. It cannot be held too tightly, for it will be lost in the grasping. You do not own power: it flows through you and from you, and true power nurtures the strength of others. I long to see you flourish and grow, to see you live in this world, and I know that you will die in it and return to the earth – to me – where you shall serve others in their nourishment. Nothing is destroyed, there is only a steady cycle of matter changing form. Therefore I am also the Queen of Gratitude: I am the bringer of the bountiful harvest and the sweetest luxuries of the earth. Turn away the requests of others and I shall be deaf to your pleas; give graciously and abundantly, and you will receive riches of great worth. You must be part of the flow of fortune to receive it.

⁌ Mystery

The material world around us is recognised for its capacity to sustain and nourish us, providing for our most basic needs. We need food, water, oxygen and shelter for our most rudimentary survival. However, the material world also provides the parts of life that allow us to grow beyond beginnings, to live well, to eat healthily, to enjoy our lives. As the Queen of the suit of the material world, the Queen of Pentacles maintains the essence and vitality of everything that creates and sustains us, from the food chains of the environment we live in to the way in which our time and energy is transmuted into wealth, in turn transmuted into wellbeing and product. The Queen of Pentacles is the ultimate nurturer and nourisher, for she is Water and Earth, fertile and fecund earth full of everything that is good. She nurtures others in all aspects of their lives, most especially in health of the body, home and environment. She is the Queen of the family, the Queen of luxury and necessity. She is the force within us that needs to be cared for and to care for others; she is the nurturing milk of the breast that is full of nutrition, and she knows what is best for those in her care. She is a healer of wounds and illnesses, an advocate of healthy living and of nurturing the body, and she encourages generosity as a means to promote one's wealth and fortune.

In the *Tarot Apokalypsis* the Queen of Pentacles is the Hindu goddess Lakṣmī, wife of Viṣṇu the preserver (the *King of Pentacles*). The early Hindu texts known as the Vedas use "shri" – one of her epithets used almost universally – to represent a quality that encompassed beauty, capability, advantage, glory and skill. Later, this term became a goddess, Shri, and was applied to the ruling office of kings, showing its association with inherited power, stability, glory and wealth. When Shri is spoken of as a goddess, she consists of ten qualities coveted by other divine beings: food, royal power, universal sovereignty, noble rank, power, holy lustre, dominion, wealth, prosperity and beauty. [551] These are the areas of life Shri Lakṣmī rules over, coveted by human and divine alike. In the later Vedic period, Shri and Lakṣmī became conflated. [552] Originally, *lakṣhmī* was a word used to indicate a mark of auspiciousness, which later became the name of the goddess. In the *Bhagavata Purana,* she emerges from the primordial Ocean of Milk, floating to land upon a lotus and choosing Viṣṇu to be her husband. [553] As Viṣṇu is the preserver god of the Hindu trinity, this gives Lakṣmī also the role of preservation. She offers us wealth and prosperity and shows us how to preserve them. She is so devoted to Viṣṇu that whenever he incarnates on the earth she incarnates as his wife. She has been Sita, Padma, Radha, Dharini and Rukmini; she is therefore also a model goddess for married women who wish to preserve marital devotion and familial happiness.

There are a number of names and forms given to Lakṣmī. These include Hira ("jewel"), Indira ("powerful one"), Jaladhija ("ocean-born") and Lokamata ("mother of the world"), indicating her wealth and power. As Chanchala ("fickle") she is associated with rivers, reminding us that wealth and fortune can easily flow into our lives but just as easily flow out; it also tells us that we should allow prosperity to flow: the Queen of Pentacles urges us to pass our wealth and security onto others, particularly our family and descendants. When a woman is wed to a husband auspiciously and according to tradition, she becomes a container of Shri Gruha Lakṣmī Devi so that she might fill her home with love, fidelity and auspiciousness which blesses her family eternally. In some traditions Lakṣmī

---

551   **Satapatha Brahmana** *11.4.3.*

552   *J. Gonda,* **Aspects of Early Visnuism***, pp. 212–25. Motilal Banarsidass, 1969.*

553   **Bhagavata Purana***, 8.6–8.*

has eight secondary manifestations, called the Ashta Lakṣmī, which embody different forms of wealth: *Ādi Lakṣmī* (first manifestation), *Dhānya Lakṣmī* (wealth in granaries), *Dhairya Lakṣmī* (wealth of courage), *Gaja Lakṣmī* (symbolic wealth), *Santāna Lakṣmī* (wealth of continuous descendants and children), *Vijaya Lakṣmī* (wealth of victory), *Vidyā Lakṣmī* (wealth of knowledge and education) and *Dhana Lakṣmī* (monetary wealth). Thus we are reminded that wealth and prosperity come in a wide variety of forms and the Queen of Pentacles not only nourishes and encourages monetary wealth but also spiritual, emotional, social and intellectual wealth. She asks us to nourish our lives holistically, not just through one-minded pursuit of money and fortune.

In many of her epithets and names Lakṣmī is associated with the lotus flower. The lotus is notable symbolically because the life cycle of the plant completes itself within the flower, not needing to send its seeds out to be pollinated. "The flower holds the new seeds, nourishes them by its own sap until they themselves develop into plants in the maternal womb of the lotus flower." [554] Within the Queen of Pentacles is the entire cycle of life; she is creating, sustaining and perpetuating, and she contains the power of nourishment and growth.

Various hymns to Lakṣmī tell us more about her, including what she bestows upon her worshippers. A Puranic hymn, *Song for Lakṣmī, Gracious Bestower of Blessings*, greets her as Lotus-dweller, All-bestowing one, Mother of the World, Ocean of Mercy, Tender One, Queen of the Universe and Support of the Three Worlds. [555] The same hymn calls her Bestower of

---

554 Stella Kramrisch, *"The Indian Great Goddess" pp. 251–2*, in **History of Religions**, *Vol. 14, no. 4 (May, 1975).*

555 Constantina Rhodes, **Invoking Lakshmi: The Goddess of Wealth in Song and Ceremony**, *p.127. State University of New York, 2011.*

Abundance and ask her to "Bless us with abundant, everlasting good fortune"; she is later called the "Lady of Fortune".[556] This hymn reveals her as a generous bestower of gifts, a caring and tender mother and the foundation of the world. The same hymn goes on to invoke the increase that she provides in beauty, community, wisdom and prosperity "in every direction."[557] We can imagine the Queen of Pentacles nourishing all aspects of our lives and watching over their increase, feeding everything that is important to us. It is clear that Lakṣmī and the Queen of Pentacles are loving mothers that cares deeply for us, their children, and they challenge us to do the same for all that we hold dear.

In the *Śrī Kamalā Stotram* she is called "goddess of the household",[558] reminding us that the main area of influence of this Queen is the home and our immediate environment, our sanctuary, our support and our protection. In tantric hymns she is also called "Mother Earth", who is the "abode of abundance" as well as the "acumen in obtaining wealth",[559] reminding us that within the Queen of Pentacles is not only the source of the material world and all its products, but also the wisdom to obtain them and to use them.

To symbolise her beneficence and the auspiciousness, Lakṣmī is usually depicted with a stream of gold coins flowing from a hand that is held in the *varada mudra* – the gesture of granting boons. Depending on her aspect, she is also shown holding a variety of items of importance to her, such as a conch shell, sword, pot of sacred drink, or a bow and arrow. In almost all aspects she is shown holding at least one lotus flower. In

---

556 *Ibid*, pp. 128– 131.
557 *Ibid*, p. 129.
558 *Ibid*, p. 134.
559 *Ibid*, p.167.

the *Tarot Apokalypsis*, two of her hands also form the *gyan mudra*, the gesture of knowledge, reminding us that this Queen is found in the suit of inherited wisdom. In her sixth hand she breastfeeds a baby – this is active nurture and nourishment, reminding us that we often contain all the resources we need within ourselves.

❧ Revelation

Nourishment, nurture, care; physical healing; watching one's health; maintaining healthy balance in life; life as a holistic cycle; feeding all areas of one's life; generosity; caring for the needs of others; parenthood; looking after a family and a home; nurturing a community; taking care of the basic needs of others as well as oneself; nurturing a project, career or job.

Negatively aspected...
Martyr complex; caring for others but forgetting to look after oneself; letting others take advantage; exhaustion through looking after too many things at once; over-caution; being over-protective; inability to find luck or fortune; a blockage in the flow of resources in one's life.

King of Pentacles

Viṣṇu, God of Preservation, Riches and Protection

The earth and all its creatures change and evolve. Their needs change and the ways in which they may fail and succeed do also. Humankind has evolved to a state of lofty height, but I love it more for the work it still has left to do. I watch, I oversee and I inspire when progress is slow. Humankind often needs saving from the evils of the universe, though it is its nature to save itself. When the perils of the world become too great – for nature is red in tooth and claw – I descend from divine fire to raise humankind up once more. I was there at the beginning and I know what is at stake. I am the wide-striding god of many incarnations; I have walked this earth among you and fought beside you in your battles, worked in your fields, enjoyed the luxuries that surround you. I have been father and son, lover and brother. I have with me stores of the riches from the earth, yet no treasure hoard do I keep. I am the Preserver, the Father of All and the life-spark in all creatures; I am the heat at the centre of the earth and in the centre of all beings that drives you to success. Know me, and know the ways in which fortune manifests. Walk with me, and enjoy the comforts and bliss that are attained when the Work is completed. I am the Lord of the lowest and the highest; I set the boundaries between earth and the heavens, and maintain that order with every step. The heavens above us protect and nourish the land with sunlight and rain for I have made it so. I have merely to open my eyes and the dawn breaks; take a step and the world is traversed; rest my head and the night falls.

≈ Mystery

As a King, this card is associated with the element of Fire, so the King of Pentacles is the fiery part of Earth: the giver of life,

the sustainer and Earth's active ability to create, feed, support and provide foundation. As Fire of Earth he may also manifest as earth's explosive energy (the power of volcanic eruption) and as the sun that warms and grows the earth. The King of Pentacles is the overseer of everything that earth represents in our lives: trade, health, wealth, family, stability, environment and work. He protects our material concerns and is a providing, protective father figure. He has established a kingdom, set the wheels of productivity in motion, and now protects his investment.

Vaisnavism (devotion to Viṣṇu) grew in the Khmer Empire during the reign of Jayavarman VI. His successor, Suryavarman II, was fully Vaisnavite. The reign of Suryavarman II (1112–50) was the golden age of Vaisnavism in Cambodia. The Angkor Wat, dedicated to Viṣṇu, the preserver, was the last great Hindu temple in Cambodia. [560] It is this god that presides as the King of Pentacles in the *Tarot Apokalypsis*. It is suggested that his name derives from the root *viś*, "to settle", though according to tradition he has a thousand names. Many of these names focus on his role as the preserver of the universe: "The fundamental sustainer", "One who is food", "Father of all", "The life spark in all creatures", "Sole support of the earth", "Protector of the universe". "Narayana" is a commonly used name of Viṣṇu, describing him as the all-pervading essence of the world, the master of past, present and future, the one who supports, sustains and governs the universe. Viṣṇu was the husband of Lakṣmī (see *Queen of Pentacles*), the goddess of wealth, fortune, prosperity and luck. They make a perfect pair: Lakṣmī gives fortune to her devotees and Viṣṇu supports and preserves them.

---

560 Lawrence Palmer Briggs, *"The Syncretism of Religions in Southeast Asia, Especially in the Khmer Empire"* in ***Journal of the American Oriental Society***, *vol. 71, no. 4, (Oct.–Dec., 1951), pp. 230–249.*

He is shown here seated on his traditional snake throne, the first snake Ananta-Shesha, whose name means "that which remains". In some images, Viṣṇu is shown reclining on a bed of snakes on the ocean of milk, with a lotus flower stemming from his navel; in the centre of the lotus is Brahma (the creator) enthroned, showing the cyclical relationship between creation and preservation. Viṣṇu carries in each of his four hands his sacred weapons: the conch shell, the blowing of which foreshadows the death of Viṣṇu's enemies; the lotus flower, symbolic of spiritual attainment; the golden mace, a fearsome weapon wielded by Viṣṇu in war; and a disk, the Sudarshana chakra, used as a weapon for the destruction of an enemy. When Viṣṇu wields it he is the keeper of the celestial bodies and heavens. Its name in Sanskrit means "vision of that which is auspicious". At Viṣṇu's feet is a peacock feather, usually worn upon Viṣṇu's crown. Its many colours show that Viṣṇu preserves and rules over the many facets of life, rather than just one.

In the *Rig Veda*, an ancient collection of hymns dated to between 1700 BCE and 1100 BCE, there are several hymns dedicated to Viṣṇu. Most of them mention his most well-known myth: that he strode across the early form of world in three strides, the first stride being the earth, the second the ocean and the final one being placed above him as the sky. He is therefore said to be the god who separated the earth from the sky. [561] With these three steps, Viṣṇu gave humankind an environment in which to live. In the same hymn Viṣṇu is described as so great that his majesty knows no bounds, and as rich in sweet food, milking cows and fertile pastures. Viṣṇu is praised in another hymn as a benefactor to those who worship him, giving to men good will, comfort and wealth (horses were seen as a sign of great wealth):

---

561 *Ralph T. H. Griffith* **trans. Rig Veda**, *7.99. 1896.*

Ne'er doth the man repent, who, seeking profit, bringeth his gift to the far-striding Viṣṇu. He who adoreth him with all his spirit winneth himself so great a benefactor. Thou, Viṣṇu, constant in thy courses, gavest good-will to all men, and a hymn that lasteth, That thou mightst move us to abundant comfort of very splendid wealth with store of horses. [562]

He is also said to be the "primeval germ of Order even from his birth". [563] This reminds us that the King of Pentacles, as well as being a benefactor, father figure, protector and preserver, has put in place the order that he now protects. As with the other Pentacles Courts, he has a sense of organisation and careful order; it is often this very order that is the means to the salvation of those he protects.

Viṣṇu had nine avatars that came down to earth to save mankind, with a tenth yet to come. The first was Matsya, a fish, who saved the first man from a flood. [564] The tortoise Kurma was the second, supporting Mount Mandara on his back to help in the churning of the ocean of milk. [565] The third was Varaha, a boar, who slew the demon Hiranyaksha and retrieved the earth from the ocean. [566] The fourth was Narasimha, a man-lion, who killed the demon Hiranyakashipu to save his devotee Prahlada. [567] The fifth was Vamana, a tiny man, who restored the gods' authority over the heavens when it was stolen by the king Bali. The sixth was Parashurama, a man, who killed corrupt rulers who had neglected their duties and taken too many of the earth's resources. [568] The seventh was

---

562 ***Ibid**, 7.100.*
563 ***Ibid**, 1.156.*
564 *This story is told in many different texts, but is at its fullest in the **Matsya Purana**, one of the oldest Puranas.*
565 *Told in the **Vishnu Purana** 1.9, and **Ramayana** 1.45.*
566 ***Bhagavatapurana**, 3.12. 1981.*
567 ***Bhagavatapurana** 7, though it is also told in several other Puranic sources.*
568 *He is mentioned frequently in the **Ramayana** and **Mahabharata**.*

the well-known Rama, who killed the demon Ravana and whose story is the epic *Ramayana*. There is some disagreement as to the eighth avatar, said to be either Balrama or the Buddha. Krishna, the main figure of the *Mahabharata*, was the ninth. The tenth avatar, Kalki, is said to come at the end of this age.

All of these incarnations performed great deeds to save mankind, restore order, battle evil, protect the gods and humans, and remove corrupt rulers. Viṣṇu could not allow evil to take place in the world, where it threatened order and mankind. Like the King of Pentacles, he took action to protect his domain. There is also some suggestion that these avatars represent a gradual evolution from humankind's origins in the ocean (Matsya) through to four-legged animals (Varaha), beasts (Narasimha) and finally to humans – first, humans that lived in the wild (Parshurama and Rama lived in forests) and then humans that lived in civilisation (Balrama and Krishna). The fiery part of the King of Pentacles urges us onwards to improve, while his earthy part places that growth firmly in the mundane world. He shows us how to achieve the pinnacle of our material goals.

Viṣṇu's incarnation as Varaha, the boar, was often referred to in inscriptions in the Khmer Empire, being depicted as a man with a boar's head, holding aloft a small earth goddess (representative of the earth he pulled out of the ocean). The myth of Varaha was used to glorify kings, the masters of the earth, giving to them the same powers of being able to support the earth.[569] The kings of the Khmer Empire were often likened to Viṣṇu in this aspect of supporting the earth, his divine power being attributed to them as the great protectors and preservers of their kingdoms.[570]

---

569 *Madeleine Giteau, "**The Boar Aspect of Viṣṇu in Khmer Art**", p. 237 in **Artibus Asiae**, vol. 19, no. 3/4 (1956), pp. 234–239.*

570 ***Ibid**, pp. 237–8.*

From his lofty heights as the ruler of the Court of Earth, watching over it as a benevolent ruler, giving good fortune to his people with the auspicious aid of his wife, the Queen of Pentacles, the King of Pentacles perhaps comes closer to a god on earth than any other Court card of the tarot pack.

≈ Revelation

Preservation and protection; taking care of one's assets and investments; protecting family; setting boundaries and order in the material world; taking action to save something; a benefactor; a father figure; a generous person willing to share resources; somebody living a comfortable and wealthy life (in both material possessions and family/friends); being ruler of one's domain; responsibility for others; reaching material goals; a successful businessperson; overseeing trade, monetary affairs or the work of others.

Negatively aspected...
A greedy person unwilling to share their resources; somebody only in it for themselves; a boss who does not have the interests of their employees at heart; acting to save oneself at the expense of others; poor investments; finding it difficult to accept responsibility or create order in one's life.

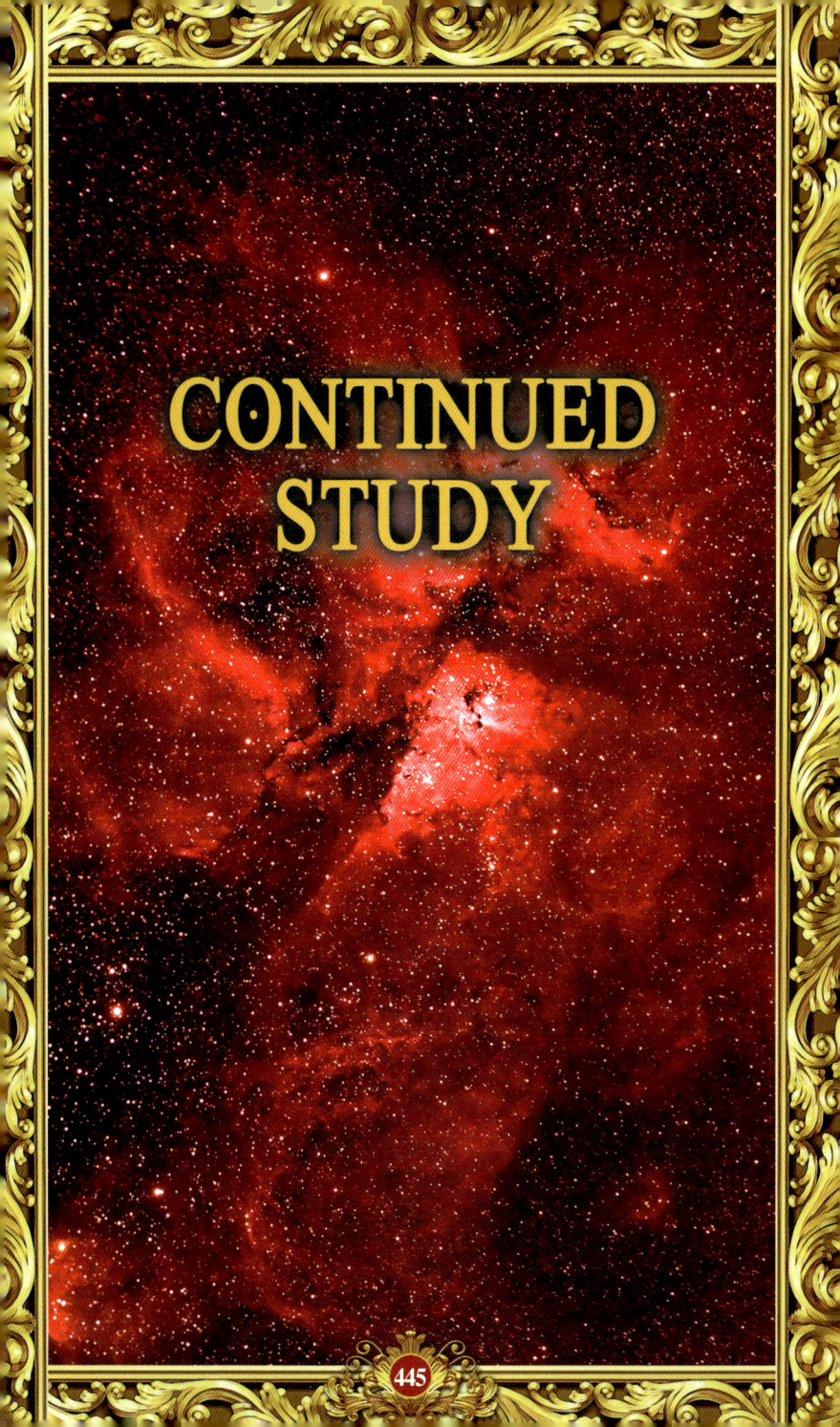

CONTINUED STUDY

Practice and exercises

Your understanding of tarot will increase as you gain experience with the cards. Over time, you will give readings in which a new idea of a card comes to you; you'll read more books and discover more decks that present other aspects or interpretations; you'll find your way around the various symbolic systems that feed the tarot – astrology, numerology, kabbalah, alchemy and more – and start to create a symbolic landscape for each card. Eventually, when a card is in front of you it will open up that landscape in your mind and you will have a wealth of wisdom and understanding of the card from which to give an interpretation. Intuition plays a vital role in knowing which parts of that landscape apply in each reading and at a precise moment. As such, your continued study of tarot should take you not only into further exploration of the cards themselves but into learning how to read more effectively, how to engage with your intuition and how to create your tarot voice. The following pages give just a few ways you can continue your tarot study to encompass these aspects of being a tarot reader.

Keeping a tarot journal

Many tarot readers enjoy keeping a tarot journal in which they can record all their thoughts, realisations, readings and more. A tarot journal will eventually become a record for your readings allowing you to go back in time and see how things turned out, as well as a way of keeping in one place all of your new knowledge about the cards. The ways in which a tarot journal are kept are as varied as the reader: one of the joys of it is making it your own. Some people enjoy hand writing their journal in a notebook, others prefer keeping a ring binder to which they can add sheets as they write them and re-order them; some like to scrapbook their journal, others prefer typing on a computer. It is important to ensure that the way you keep your journal is conducive to the way you learn best and that it encourages you to interact with your cards and have fun.

You can include anything you like in your journal, but just a few suggestions include:

Records of your readings	Exercises with the cards
Diary entries of your insights	Notes from books you are reading
Quotes from books that are helpful	Notes from tarot workshops you attend
Sketches/collages of cards	Reading lists of books you want
Spreads you find useful	List of decks you'd like to buy
Daily draw entries (see below)	Poetry or other creative writing on the cards
Things you'd like to research	Information about symbolism

The tarot journal is most useful for making the tarot journey your own. It helps you learn in the way you learn best, tailoring your tarot path to suit your needs.

~ Daily draw

Tarot most fully integrates into the psyche when it is practiced or engaged with regularly. Having a regular practice of drawing a card or performing a short reading not only deepens your understanding of the cards but also improves your reading technique and develops your tarot voice.

For a daily draw, pick one card at random from the tarot deck either in the morning or evening. If you do this in the morning, spend a few minutes examining the card and asking yourself what it might foretell for the coming day. What awaits you? What strength will you need? What challenges might you face? What will be the theme of the day? If you do it in the evening, spend some time reflecting on what has happened and how the card relates to it. What events happened? Who was particularly important today? How did you feel today? What is the lesson you can take from today's events? It is most useful to write a paragraph or two about your reflections in your tarot journal or to give yourself a reading stating these reflections aloud (some people like to record them so they can listen to them later). Doing this forces you to put into coherent form what might otherwise remain unformed and half-interpreted. Besides, when you read for other people, you'll be giving your interpretations aloud, so this is good practice!

If a daily draw is too frequent for you, you could try a weekly draw. If you do, why not draw three cards instead – after all, more has happened in a week than a day. The important aspect of this exercise is to see how the cards relate to real life and the everyday world in terms that you are familiar with. It also improves your intuition and the way that you interpret the cards, and can lead to realisations about the cards that change your way of thinking about them.

The three-symbol reading

This is a useful exercise to try when you feel your intuition is getting rusty or your ideas of card meanings are becoming stagnant. Simply draw a single card and examine it. Now pick three symbols that stand out to you from the card image: one from the foreground, one from the mid-ground and one from the background. Don't think too hard about them and try to allow the symbols you choose to be those that came to your eyes first or which really stand out. No second guessing!

Each of these symbols expresses a meaning in a specific context:

The **foreground** symbol tells you what is the most influential on you at this time, or brings out an issue that is on your mind a lot.

The **mid-ground** symbol tells you about influences, events or circumstances that are acting upon you but aren't as clear to you or as obvious.

The **background** symbol tells you what is hidden, unexpected, or what you are unaware of that has an influence upon you at the time.

You can also use this as a Past-Present-Future exercise: foreground symbol represents the past, mid-ground the present and background the future.

This exercise not only gives you a quick, simple reading: it also helps you improve your ability to draw links between symbols and to discover in-depth information in the cards. Sometimes, one card is all you need to get your answers.

Further reading

Reading widely will add further depth to your understanding of the tarot and allow you to add even more tools to your tarot toolbox. Every author and deck creator in the tarot world can bring something new to your knowledge with their works, but also remember not to stick rigidly to one book or one author – tarot is not a dogma but a personal journey towards wisdom, so it's up to you to choose the nature of your tarot approach. These are just some of the great tarot works out there.

Around the Tarot in 78 Days, by Marcus Katz and Tali Goodwin. Llewellyn, 2012.
Complete Guide to Tarot Illuminati, by Kim Huggens. Llewellyn, 2013.*
Initiation into the Tarot, by Naomi Ozaniec. Watkins, 2002.
Meditations on the Tarot, trans. Robert Powell. Penguin, 2002.
Tarot 101: Mastering the Art of Reading the Cards, by Kim Huggens. Llewellyn, 2010.
Tarosophy, by Marcus Katz. Forge Press, 2016.
Tarot and Astrology, by Corrine Kenner. Llewellyn, 2011.
Tarot Fundamentals, ed. Sasha Graham. Lo Scarabeo, 2015.
Tarot Outside the Box, by Valerie Sim. Llewellyn, 2004.
Tarot Tells the Tale, by James Ricklef. Llewellyn, 2003.
The Tarot Court Cards, by Kate Warwick-Smith. Destiny Books, 2003.
Understanding Aleister Crowley's Thoth Tarot, by Lon Milo DuQuette. Weiser Books, 2003.*

* Although these books are designed as a guide for a specific deck, the information they contain can be applied to a wide variety of decks.

ABOUT THE AUTHORS

Erik C. Dunne

Erik C. Dunne discovered the Tarot almost thirty years ago, inspiring a long journey that would result in the creation of his first deck, the award-winning *Tarot Illuminati* (awarded Tarot Professionals "Tarot Deck of the Year 2013", "Outstanding Tarot Deck 2014", "Outstanding Illustrator for a Tarot deck 2013" and "Outstanding Collaboration for a Tarot Deck 2013" in the PECTO Awards), with his High Priestess quickly becoming one of the most iconic and recognizable images in modern Tarot. Erik has travelled extensively and lived for some years in the Middle East. He has retraced the footsteps of legendary kings and queens, ridden camels across the dunes of Persia and galloped heavy steeds across fields of gold. His diverse life-experiences are matched only by his opulent imagination, both of which manifest in his artwork. Although a classically trained artist, his medium of choice is digital, where his passion for costume design and his roots in the theater are clearly expressed in his artwork. The colorful and fantastical story which began in the *Tarot Illuminati* has continued to play out in the *Tarot Apokalypsis*, with Erik's love of mythology and world cultures being brought to the forefront of his imagery. Erik currently lives in the United States on a small horse farm he shares with his best friend and mentor, his Mother, where he pursues other great passions, including animal rescue, horse training and gardening.

Kim Huggens

Kim Huggens is the author of the *Complete Guide to Tarot Illuminati* (Llewellyn, 2013), which was awarded "Best Tarot Book of the Year 2013" by Tarot Professionals and "Outstanding Cartomancy Book 2013" in the PECTO Awards, *Tarot 101: Mastering the Art of Reading the Cards* (Llewellyn, 2010), and the co-creator with Nic Phillips of *Sol Invictus: the God Tarot* (Schiffer, 2007) and *Pistis Sophia: the Goddess Tarot* (forthcoming). She also writers papers on her academic research subjects, which have been published in collections such as *The Conjure Codex* (Hadean Press, 2011), *Priestesses, Pythonesses and Sibyls* (Avalonia, 2008), *Both Sides of Heaven* (Avalonia, 2009), and *Memento Mori* (Avalonia, 2012). Kim holds an undergraduate degree in Philosophy and postgraduate degree in Ancient History; her research has focused on religion in late antiquity, malefic-erotic magic in the Graeco-Roman period, necromancy throughout history, mystery religions of the ancient world and mythology. She has been studying tarot for over 20 years and has given lectures and workshops internationally and reads professionally. Kim was initiated into Vodou in Sosyete Gade Nou Leve in 2009 and has found her spiritual home there. In her spare time, Kim is a tabletop roleplayer (D&D, etc) and LARPer; she spends most of her weekends on battlefields bearing sword and shield. She lives with her partner and cat in Cardiff, Wales.

Notes

Notes

Notes

Notes